T0323766

THE COLORS OF JEWS

The Colors of Jews

Racial Politics and Radical Diasporism

MELANIE KAYE/KANTROWITZ

Indiana University Press
Bloomington and Indianapolis

THIS BOOK IS A PUBLICATION OF

Indiana University Press
601 North Morton Street
Bloomington, IN 47404-3797 USA

http://iupress.indiana.edu

Telephone orders	800-842-6796
Fax orders	812-855-7931
Orders by e-mail	iuporder@indiana.edu

The paper used in this publication meets the minimum requirements of American National Standard for Information Sciences—Permanence of Paper for Printed Library Materials, ANSI Z39.48-1984.

Manufactured in the United States of America

LIBRARY OF CONGRESS CATALOGING-IN-PUBLICATION DATA

Kaye/Kantrowitz, Melanie.
      The colors of Jews : racial politics and radical diasporism /
Melanie Kaye/Kantrowitz.
            p.   cm.
      Includes bibliographical references and index.
      ISBN-13: 978-0-253-34902-6 (cloth : alk. paper)
      ISBN-10: 0-253-34902-8 (cloth : alk. paper)
      ISBN-13: 978-0-253-21927-5 (pbk. : alk. paper)
      ISBN-10: 0-253-21927-2 (pbk. : alk. paper)
            1. Jews—United States—Identity. 2. Ethnicity—United States. 3. Race—
Religious aspects—Judaism. 4. Jewish families—United States. 5. United
States—Ethnic relations. I. Title.
      E184.36.E84K39   2007
      305.892'4073—dc22
                                                      2006034287

      1 2 3 4 5   12 11 10 09 08 07

For the young brave diasporists
heading into this new century's heart
seeking each other

I can't go back
where I came from was
burned off the map

I'm a Jew
anywhere is someone else's land

—MELANIE KAYE/KANTROWITZ,
from "Notes from an Immigrant Daughter: Atlanta"

CONTENTS

Who, what is the Jewish people? The question dazed me when I first asked it. I thought I knew, had always known, the answer. The Jewish people lived in Brooklyn, and if your father made money, you moved to a coveted "private house" on Long Island. (Mine didn't.) Jewish grandparents had foreign accents. Jewish grandmothers made chopped liver. Only old-fashioned Jews went to shul.

I grew up in Flatbush assuming that Adlai Stevenson, the Democrat who lost two presidential elections to Eisenhower, was Jewish because my parents adored him in that familial way. Stevenson was ours. Similarly I believed that a picture of FDR on our wall was god in modern drag—Jewish, for sure. The whiteness of their skin and ours made these assumptions possible. I expected all Jews to share my parents' progressive politics, to support unions and civil rights, to oppose McCarthy and bomb-testing. Some Jews said *shvartse*. We did not. My knowledge of Jews of color was limited to Sammy Davis, Jr. (who is to Jewish multiculturalism as Anne Frank is to the Holocaust; as, for that matter, Seinfeld is to Jewish culture as a whole; that is, the one scrap of knowledge that allows the knower to imagine s/he knows enough).

I was, I see now, a lazily secular Jew in the Jewish land of Brooklyn, for whom Jewish was how you looked, talked, smelled: Jewish was something you were born to. Everything to do with Yiddish as the bass line against which your English resonated (how old was I when I learned that words like *tukhes, meshugene, mishpokhe,* and *bubbe* were not English?). Everything to do with cabbage soup and kasha varnishkes and the smells in the stairwell of your walk-up apartment. I don't remember hearing the term Ashkenazi, or when I learned that it meant Jews whose path, like my family's, once traced through Germany and so spoke Yiddish. While believing that all Jews shared my family's politics, I simultaneously longed to escape what I thought of as the "Jewish" Jews—meaning religious or bourgeois. I didn't yet understand that my attitude was a New York luxury.

I was in my thirties when Evelyn Beck, who knew my writing from lesbian and feminist venues, asked me to write something for a book she was editing, which became *Nice Jewish Girls: A Lesbian Anthology.* Though I refused at first—I was Jewish but had nothing to say about *being* Jewish—

the invitation put Jewishness in my face. I was living in New Mexico. Jews were rare, invisible, or thought to have horns. I began to encounter my own Jewishness.

A year later I wrote Evelyn to ask if it was too late. It was not and the book (my essay included) went on to gain a wide readership among feminist and lesbian Jews and to form the rudiments of Jewish feminist community. Included in the anthology were essays by an Iraqi/Egyptian Jew who'd grown up in Japan; a Syrian Jew who'd grown up in England; a Jewish daughter of an African American–Native American mother and an Ashkenazi father. A couple of years later, beginning to work on the anthology *The Tribe of Dina*, which I coedited with Irena Klepfisz,[1] we received work by women from Argentina, Greece, Palestine, Syria, Turkey, Spain; from Sephardi and Mizrahi Jews whose paths traced through the Middle East, North Africa, or the Iberian Peninsula; Jews whose ancestors spoke Ladino (Judeo-Español) or Judeo-Arabic.

I had thought Jewish identity was simple, but suddenly it was not simple at all. I remembered my mother's hospital roommate with whom she became briefly friendly explained by my mother as "Sephardic," but as she understood it, confusingly, not through geography, history or culture, but—in a way that now feels ironically, classically anti-semitic—as "Jews who are rich, dark, and stick together." I recalled my high school best friend Susan Hassan, whose grandparents came from Iraq—the beginning and end of my information. As teenagers, biographical data on grandparents was simply not interesting. Nor, as an early atheist, did I take seriously the concept of Judaism-the-religion as a binding force. To me, you either were or weren't Jewish; it was not something you could become.

As my political work became increasingly focused on Jewish community, on support for the Israeli and Palestinian women's peace movement, and on racism and economic injustice here in the United States, I began to meet more Jews like and not like myself, observant and secular, Mizrahi and Sephardi as well as Ashkenazi, born and by choice, radical and liberal (and, on the other side, right wing). As I and my comrades in Jews for Racial and Economic Justice worked in New York to educate and remind Jews of our proud radical history, we tried to create a broad inclusive tent. The issue of Jewish racial and cultural diversity surrounded us and yet was rarely articulated.

◦ ◦ ◦

This book departs from several assumptions with the explicit intent of changing them. That all Jews came from Eastern Europe and spoke

Yiddish. That Jewishness is only religion; that secular Judaism is a contradiction in terms; that real Jews are born Jewish. That calling (all) Jews "white" explains anything. That calling (all) Jews people of color explains anything. That American Jews and African Americans used to be best friends and are now enemies. That Jews and Arabs were always enemies and could never be friends. That life in the diaspora has always been a vale of tears that all Jews aspire to escape.

I write this book to overturn these assumptions, but also to strengthen the identity and practice of Jewish antiracism, including the often buried strand of economic justice. To heighten understanding among Jews of diverse backgrounds/cultures/ethnicities that we need each other in part *because of* our differences. To help Jews grasp that those Jews who are cultural minorities within a hegemonic Ashkenazi community are often best equipped to help the Jewish world reckon with our multiculturality, and to know that this multiculturality is an enormous asset when it comes to combating racism and anti-semitism and to building social justice coalitions.

I name this identity and practice of Jewish anti-racism *Diasporism*.[2]

The common Jewish practice is to name our experience differently from those with whom we might share it. Jews say *anti-semitism*, not racism against Jews; Jews say *Zionism*, not nationalism for Jews.[3] We cling to the term *Holocaust* as ours only, anxious about whether other genocides deserve the name. All this separate naming makes it harder to identify and analyze commonality and difference.

I want to contextualize Jewish experience in a common language. *Diaspora*—of Greek origin—has had a Jewish life; *galut* in Hebrew and Ladino; *goles* in Yiddish: both mean exile. But centuries of migration for many mean many live in diaspora, and not always—Jew or not—experiencing diaspora as exile. Ella Shohat, whose family migrated from Iraq to Israel, stands on its head the exilic psalm: "By the waters of Zion, we sat and wept, when we remembered Babylon."[4]

Diaspora, in the early twenty-first century, emerges in postcolonial and postmodern discourse as a dynamic concept to name the experience of many peoples. The African Diaspora; the Chinese Diaspora; the South Asian Diaspora; and of course the Palestinian Diaspora.

Diasporism, then, embraces diaspora, offers a place we might join with others who value this history of dispersion; others who stand in opposition to nationalism and the nation state; who choose instead to value border crossing as envisioned by the late Gloria Anzaldúa in her work about mestiza consciousness,[5] or by the founders of the New Association of Sephardi/Mizrahi Artists & Writers, International (Ivri/NASAWI); "*[I]vri*

. . . means border-crosser, predates the word Jew. Jew is what the Romans called the Israelites, and we thought *ivri* was actually what Hebrews called themselves."[6] Diasporism joins those who see borders as lines to cross. Who seek the memory or possibility or value of motion, fluidity, and multiple vision.

I name this ideology and practice *Diasporism* as a deliberate counter to Zionism. Zionism/Jewish nationalism is one choice Jews make, but not the only choice. It's time someone named and explored and pressed into existence the choice most Jews are making in practice.

And *radical* Diasporism? Because this is no casual invitation to perpetually wander. The Diasporism I have in mind recognizes the persecution and danger that have made many long for home and passport, yearn to leave the wandering behind. Inside this longing, Diasporism represents tension, resistance to both assimilation and nostalgia, to both corporate globalization that destroys peoples and cultures, and to nationalism, which promises to preserve people and cultures but so often distorts them through the prisms of masculinism, racism, and militarism. Radical Diasporism, *sans* army, *sans* military heroes and victories, meshes well with feminism in valuing a strength and heroism available to those without armies; and suits queerness, in rejecting the constraints of traditional gendered existence.[7]

This book is organized into six parts. I begin by examining the contradictory historical racial assumptions about Jews, recognizing that the history of Ashkenazim has often been read as all of Jewish history. Next I mine both history and popular culture to explore the mythic construction of Jewish and African Americans as inherent comrades or intrinsic enemies. The third section explores the racial and cultural diversity of the Jewish people, the question with which this preface begins: Who, what is the Jewish people? The next two sections present voices of Jewish antiracist and diversity activists, Jews who are busily working to dismantle racism and/or to promote Jewish racial and cultural diversity. And, finally, arriving back at diaspora, I posit a Jewish identity that embraces diversity and resists a closed circle. My hope is to join a debate about home, diversity, and justice.

A NOTE ON LANGUAGE

Antiracist activists learn pretty early on if you are naming the race of people of color, you should also be naming the whites. Otherwise, you are saying, implicitly, that white is so normative that only its absence warrants a mention. This kind of racial or cultural marking feels awkward because it focuses attention on something that has escaped notice, been taken for granted: white normativity.

Part of my argument in this book relies on a similar refusal to assume whiteness in Jews. But the linguistic options are even more complicated given the problematic naming of any Jews as white; and equally problematic of *not* naming any Jews as white. So if we acknowledge we can only leave Jews freestanding and unmarked if we mean, really, all Jews; then what do we say to distinguish Jews of different races?

Do we say Jews of color, thereby imposing on some Jews a term they might not use about themselves? Mizrahim and Sephardim have the virtue of specificity, but people use the terms to mean different things, with Sephardi sometimes encompassing Mizrahi, and sometimes being completely distinct. As for Jews who might be termed white, or Ashkenazi, or Euro-Jews, I have tried here to use the marker that seems most relevant to the context: *white* when race seems the leading edge (Jews seen or seeing themselves as white); Ashkenazi when origin, culture, or language is most significant; and Euro-Jews when it's neither of these, or when place of origin is the relevant concept. Yet we can trip over the large numbers of Arab Jews living in France, perhaps for several generations: are they not Euro-Jews? Do we really want to forcibly reinscribe origin, as those Spanish and Portuguese Jews who converted remained eternally *New Christians?* The solution to these dilemmas of language is not rules but heightened consciousness. Naturally, the process of arriving at language that feels comfortable will itself be awkward. My solutions in this book are provisional.

ACKNOWLEDGMENTS

A book like this rests on the generosity of many. I thank all the people who shared with me their time, perspectives, and experience: (in alphabetical order) Ammiel Alcalay, Katya Gibel Azoulay (a.k.a. Mevorach), Beejhy Barhany, Naomi Braine, Jordan Elgrably, Rabbi Capers Funnye, Rachel Goldstein, Lewis Gordon, Rabbi Lynn Gottlieb, Linda Holtzman, Esther Kaplan, Shira Katz, Joyce Maio, Yavilah McCoy, Navonah, Jane Ramsey, Vic Rosenthal, Emily Schnee, and Rabbi Susan Talve. A special thank you to Yavilah McCoy, who not only agreed to be interviewed but who created much of the discourse on the subject of Jewish diversity, and whose work has guided and deepened mine. I thank those writers and thinkers whose narratives and essays ground this book in experience, especially Ella Shohat, and Loolwa Khazzoom whose work on Jewish multiculturalism and whose anthology *The Flying Camel* have been so valuable. I am grateful for the information and connective tissue supplied by the amazing David Shasha's weekly *Sephardic Heritage Update*, an incredible resource and labor of love (to receive *Sephardic Heritage Update* for free, e-mail Davidshasha@ aol.com). I thank Aurora Levins Morales, Julie Iny, Hilary Than, Angela Buchdale Wernick, Kyla Wazana Tompkins, Miri Hunter Haruach, and Ruth Behar for their words. Thanks also to Ruth Behar for sending me— with extreme graciousness—a copy of her gorgeous and inspiring film *Adio Kerida* about Jews and Cuba. A special thanks to Diane Tobin, Gary Tobin, and Scott Rubin for their infinitely useful book *In Every Tongue*.

I thank Jenny Romaine for her immense theatrical talent and her generous appreciation of this manuscript. Hilary Gold, librarian extraordinaire in Phoenicia, New York, found everything I asked for, including some amazingly obscure texts. Temim Fruchter, activist musician and walking library, answered my peppering of e-mail questions at the last minute. Kate Crane and Tennessee Jones transcribed interviews with speed and accuracy. I thank my coworkers during the time I was writing, especially June Cumberbatch, for absorbing the slack so cheerfully, and for helping to protect my writing time. Sarah Swartz was an astute and kind editor. Yavilah McCoy, Esther Kaplan, and Leslie Cagan all read and offered useful critiques on part or all of the manuscript. Loie Hayes was incisive and helpful. I owe a special thanks to my editors at Indiana University

Press, Lee Sandweiss and Linda Oblack, for patience and competence in the face of a host of technical difficulties. I thank William Rukeyser for permission to quote his brilliant mother's brilliant poem. A posthumous thanks to Gloria Anzaldúa, much missed, for her work and for her loving support of mine. Thanks to my sister Roni Natov—that paragon of sisterhood—who has always cheered me on. Thumbs up to my nephew Jonathan Natov, who picked up the Jewish ball in Baton Rouge, Louisiana, and has been running with it ever since.

In addition, there have been three profound sources I want to acknowledge: first, the opportunity I had in 1963–1965 as a teenager to work in the Harlem Education Project, part of the Northern Student Movement, which was "the Northern arm of the Student Non-Violent Coordinating Committee" (SNCC). I got my left political values from my parents and the culture of working- and lower-middle-class Brooklyn Jews, but my political vision and sense of possibility came from the Harlem civil rights movement.

Second—it must be said—the women's liberation movement: I was a sturdy committed activist before the movement, but what women's liberation released in me and in who knows how many millions of other women, is a power I will never imagine is mine alone.

Third, in 1992 I was offered the extraordinary opportunity to come home to New York City and walk into a poorly paid, overworked dream job as the first director of Jews for Racial and Economic Justice. I want to thank everyone who worked with JFREJ in those early years: members, activists, and allies, and the founders of JFREJ who had confidence in me, especially Donna Nevel and Marilyn Kleinberg Neimark, Alisa Solomon, Marlene Provizer, and the late and sorely missed Rabbi Marshall Meyer, Henry Schwartzchild and Gary Rubin. Most especially, I want to thank my comrade and sister Esther Kaplan, who came to work with me there in 1993, and who so splendidly became JFREJ's next director. Esther's commitment, street smarts, and the immense good will she brought to JFREJ from all the New York activists who had worked with her—notably in ACT UP—contributed vastly to what JFREJ has been able to accomplish.

Finally, my greatest debt—for questioning, encouragement, editing, optimism, and indefatigable sense of humor—is to my beloved partner in defiance, Leslie Cagan, a quintessential "non-Jewish Jew" who, with inspired and unflappable leadership, has guided movements for peace and justice for the past forty years.

What weaknesses remain in this book are mine alone.

I wrote this book in the period between 2002 and 2006. But many of the parts—ideas and some of the actual writing—came earlier, as talks or as essays, including "Some Notes on Jewish Lesbian Identity," published first in the groundbreaking anthology *Nice Jewish Girls: A Lesbian Anthology*, Evelyn Torton Beck, ed. (Watertown, MA: Persephone Press, 1982); "Class, Feminism, and 'the Black-Jewish Question'," a talk from the first Tikkun conference in 1988, published in *Tikkun* (July 1989); "Jews, Class, Color and the Cost of Whiteness," a talk from the New Jewish Agenda Conference *Fighting Anti-Semitism and Racism* (1991); "To Be a Radical Jew in the Late 20th Century," published in *The Tribe of Dina: A Jewish Women's Anthology*, Melanie Kaye/Kantrowitz and Irena Klepfisz, eds. (Boston: Beacon, 1989; 1st pub., Montpelier, Vt: Sinister Wisdom Books, 1986). These four essays were all republished in my collection of essays *The Issue Is Power: Essays on Women, Jews, Violence, and Resistance* (San Francisco: Aunt Lute Books, 1992). In addition, I draw on "The Cost of Heroism: Review, Gillian Slovo, *Red Dust* and *Every Secret Thing*," in *Women's Review of Books* (July 2002); "Post 9/11: Assessing Anti-Semitism," *Sojourner* (March 2002); "Notes from the (Shifting) Middle: Some Ways of Looking at Jews," *Jewish Locations: Traversing Racialized Landscapes*, Lisa Tessman and Bat-Ami Bar On, eds. (Lanham, Md: Rowman and Littlefield, 2001); "Diasporism, Feminism, and Coalition," *Jewish Women's Voices: From Memory to Transformation*, Sarah Swartz and Margie Wolfe, eds. (Toronto: Second Story Press, 1998); and "Jews in the U.S.: The Rising Cost of Whiteness," in *Names We Call Home*, Becky Thompson and Sangeeta Tyagi, eds. (New York: Routledge, 1986).

THE COLORS OF JEWS

[1] ARE JEWS WHITE?

People have suggested that if I have experienced racism, I am of color. But what if I have experienced racism in Israel and white privilege in the United States? I read essays that describe Arab Jews as Jews of color, but still I feel confused. If I am light-skinned, am I of color? What if I am light, but others in my family are dark?

—JULIE INY (Iraqi-Indian/Russian-American Jew), "Ashkenazi Eyes"

No one was white before he/she came to America. It took generations, and a vast amount of coercion, before this became a white country. It is probable that it is the Jewish community—or more accurately, perhaps, its remnants—that in America has paid the highest and most extraordinary price for becoming white. For the Jews came here from countries where they were not white, and they came here in part because they were not white; and incontestably—in the eyes of the Black American (and not only in those eyes) American Jews have opted to become white. . . .

—JAMES BALDWIN, "On Being 'White' . . ."

If I were to snap my fingers and bring every Jewish person in this world into the room, we'd be more colorful than a rainbow, but when I walk into the average mainstream synagogue in the United States and talk about Jews of Color I often encounter the assumption that to be a Jew of Color one must be a convert or adopted.

— YAVILAH MCCOY, interview

In the early 1980s, as an experienced antiracist activist, I began thinking and writing about being a Jew, and became engaged in progressive Jewish politics. As I wrestled with racism and anti-semitism, people asked me constantly, *Are Jews white?* Are they? Are they white? The urgency and anxiety behind the question were palpable and took me a while to understand. First assumption, there was one answer for all Jews. Second, the answer was either yes or no: Jews were white or they were of color. Third, whichever category one chose to file Jews into was a political decision: Jews were either down with the people of color, innocent and victimized, or lumped in with whites, guilty and victimizing.

The more I have learned about Jews, anti-semitism, and race and racialization, the more complex the situation gets. I still get asked, but now I want to give several simultaneous answers, and they are all questions: Have you heard of Arab, African, Indian, Asian, Latin Jews? Were European Jews white in Europe? What do you mean by white? Why are you asking? What does it matter?

And when I answer tersely and correctly, *Jews are a multiracial multiethnic people,* the asker most frequently succumbs to a tempting shorthand: *Yeah, but white Jews: Are white Jews white?*

WHAT'S WHITE?

1952: I am seven, and my ex-dancer mother enrolls me in dance class. The teacher, Ronnie All, is a tall graceful young man. His most important characteristic from my point of view is: he is not mean. I am a clumsy child and he does not mock me. On parents' day, my mother comes to observe. Afterwards she gushes to me, my father, all her friends, and the gush content is this: I have not noticed or mentioned that Ronnie All is Negro. For my ever self-reflexive mother, not saying/not noticing means that she has raised an unprejudiced child.

Let me credit her aspiration, more than most Jewish housewives in Flatbush aspired to in the early fifties, "niggerlovingcommiejew" stereotypes not withstanding. The truth is I don't notice not because I am color blind—who by age seven is?—but because I come from a Jewish family and neighborhood with wide varieties of skin color in which someone like Ronnie All—a light-skinned black man—does not stand out as different (except maybe for being gay which I realize now he probably was). Had his skin been darker, would I have noticed? Probably. Would I have mentioned it? I'm not sure. Might I have already absorbed the polite hushed norm? I certainly knew that my mother's response was peculiar, that *not* noticing was a weird thing to get credit for.

In 1964, at a Freedom School organized in a Harlem Church as part of a public school boycott, I lead a discussion with half a dozen seven-year-olds. The smallest girl, hair tightly braided, sits in my lap. Lenora. I am eighteen years old, not much more than a child myself.

"Why are you here instead of at your regular school?" I ask.

"Because our schools are bad. They don't teach us anything."

"We don't learn about black people."

"We don't learn about freedom, like here."

"The schools are segagated."

"Do you know what segregated means?" I ask these seven-year-olds.

Silence. How to explain this in a way that doesn't make the presence of white people sound like salvation?

"Segregation is separating people of different races, you know. Black and white people."

"If white people come to my school, I'm going to throw them out the window," Lenora says.

"Why?"

"My father says white people are bad and mean. They do terrible things. I'd throw them out the window." She sits snuggled into my lap. I debate whether to tell her. Then I say it.

"Lenora, I'm white."

She looks at me with affectionate scorn. "No you're not."

"I'm not?"

"No way." She shakes her head emphatically.

"What am I?"

"Sort of pink." I look at my hand. She has a point.

"What's white?"

She scrambles off my lap, takes my (pink) hand and drags me around the room looking for something. The other seven-year-olds trail behind.

"This"—Lenora waves a piece of white paper triumphantly—"is white!"

Understanding dawns.

"Lenora, have you ever seen a white person?"

"No. My father told me about them from when he was in Mississippi."

Point one: the minute I ask, "What's white?" the stories that bubble up into memory are framed by blackness. Whiteness, in the words of Cornel West, exists only as "a politically constructed category parasitic on 'Blackness'."[1]

Point two: children need to be taught absolute distinctions of color. Left to their own eyes, who knows what they would see? A Jewish woman with a common Ashkenazi last name and skin tone like my sister's turns out to have a Sri Lankan mother. A labor organizer I have known for years, and never wondered if she was Jewish or African American (in other words, I wordlessly assumed she was neither) turns out to be an African American Jew.

Point three: slippage. The white in both stories is me and/or my family, i.e., Jews. But the people in Mississippi who did horrible things to Lenora's people were most probably *not* Jews. Probably did not see Jews as white. Probably would have wanted to do those things to my people too.

1998: I am teaching a class at Brooklyn College called "Anti-semitism, Racism, and Class." One of my students, Marina Stein, is a Jew from Ukraine. She tells us how *Jewish* was stamped on their papers, how children in Ukraine mocked and teased her and her sister, refused to play with them. One summer they went to camp and Marina lied about her name, "and I was the most popular there, and so was my sister." In the course of a semester she will tell us this story at least three times.

Since coming to the United States, Marina tells us, she hates Russian Jews: they're so insular, so conservative, stupid, and racist.

During the last week of classes, Marina suddenly blurts out, "I'm sick of hearing about race. I'm sick of talking about it. I just want to be a person. Can't we just be people?"

In America, in Brooklyn, she has been told that this is possible, for her.

"That's what racism costs you," I explain. "That's your cost. You don't get to just be a person." I tell the class about a bumper sticker I've imagined: "When men stop raping women I'll pick up male hitchhikers." The women are nodding; the men aren't sure, the turf has suddenly shifted.

"Until there's no more rape," I continue, "mistrust poisons the air, and that's the cost to men. It's not the same as for women, whose cost is much much higher. But I guess every woman would like to say, I just want to be a person. And I guess every person of color might say, yeah, I just want to be a person. No one gets that as long as there's sexism. As long as there's racism."

Point one: In Ukraine Marina was a Jew. Here she has perhaps the opportunity to become white.

Point two: Marina wants this opportunity. She can be tired of race, can experience racism as an annoying bundle she'd like to put down, while her classmates with dark skin don't get to be tired of it, can't stop thinking about it. That's Marina's white privilege, courtesy of the United States.

What is white that shifts from continent to continent? Mostly the question hasn't been asked. Yet suddenly by 1998, according to an article in the *New York Times Magazine,* where political, cultural, and intellectual trends get translated into popular middlebrow knowledge, investigation of whiteness had become an academic minifad.[2] The *Times* article stressed the work of those who proudly identify "white culture" with "white trash," a home kick, nouveau-chic nosethumb at a hyperrefined institution, an impassioned choice of beer and chips over sherry and biscotti; macaroni and cheese instead of pasta and arugula with *chevres.*

We might speculate that these whiteness enthusiasts are at least partly animated by the ravenous need of young academics for new topics. But while White Studies provides fresh meat for the feeding frenzy of doctoral students, upper-class white culture remains significantly unnamed and unexamined, ignoring both whiteness as privilege and the existence of economically privileged whites. This emphasis is odd, given that "Racial inequities in unemployment, family income, imprisonment, average wealth and infant mortality are actually worse than [in 1968] when Dr. King was killed."[3]

To examine and honor white working-class culture is a fine idea, if class is the leading edge, and whiteness is probed. But with class submerged and whiteness foregrounded, what gets celebrated in part is racial dominance. Like the Harvard student who flew a Confederate flag out her window to honor her southern heritage, claiming—and perhaps believing —she was not (also) celebrating slavery.[4] Right-wing racist organizing— bizarre and marginal as these groups are—is on the rise: neo-Nazi militia, Christian identity, white identity, National Alliance all distribute literature and mobilize especially among young white disenfranchised men, and, more recently, among women as well.[5] For these groups, whiteness is palpable, sacred, and endangered; they are not investigating whiteness but organizing to strengthen its power.

Unmentioned in the *Times* article is the less trendy but more significant work that follows in the tradition of social constructionists such as Theodore Allen, Michael Omi, Howard Winant, and David Roediger.[6] These scholars expose the process of racialization, the arbitrary construction of race and racial distinctions when the truth is that we are almost all mixed; and seek to develop new analyses to undergird antiracist activism. Antiracist examinations of whiteness stress two things: privilege and an apparent emptiness, an unmarked status. As the construct *a doctor/a woman doctor* reveals the unmarked status of male, the normalness—no one says *a man doctor*—so constructs such as *the writer/the black writer, my friend/my Chinese friend, the teacher/the Puerto Rican teacher* reveal the unmarked, the implied: white.

Thus Robert Terry notes succinctly, "To be white in America is not to have to think about it,"[7] and Peter McLaren states, "Being white is an entitlement . . . a raceless subjectivity."[8] Ruth Frankenberg, in *White Women, Race Matters*, defines whiteness as a location of structural advantage.[9] Whiteness carries with it a sense of normality, safety, a constant assurance of superiority. Peggy McIntosh, whose article "Unpacking the Invisible Knapsack [of white privilege]"[10] has a become a standard text in Women's Studies and Ethnic Studies classes, offers a long list of advantages not available to people of color, from irksome ("flesh colored" Band-Aids and makeup) to life-threatening. However we problematize Jewish/whiteness, when I, with my—in Lenora's words—"pink" skin, am stopped by police, they do not assume I am a criminal; they smile, wave me on, say, *We're looking for a car like this. Sorry.*

Sorry. What about all the stories I've heard from people of color, in which a quick look is *not* followed by a friendly wave and an apology?

Stories of beatings, arrests, terror. Life and death. Anthony Baez, playing football in front of his Bronx apartment, strangled by a cop in broad daylight. Amadou Diallo trying to show his wallet to four plainclothes cops who fired at him forty-one times in the lobby of his apartment building. Most recently, in Queens near where I live, a police barrage of fifty bullets killed an unarmed man—Sean Bell—on his wedding day, and seriously wounded his friends Trent Benefield and Joseph Guzman, also unarmed.

Faddist White Studies fails to acknowledge the larger context of racism against which whiteness exists. "No one was white before he/she came to America," James Baldwin observed in the mid-eighties. They were English, German, Irish, Italian, Russian, Polish. . . . In the United States, race begins to be produced by European land-theft and murder of the people who lived here, and with the enslavement of Africans and suppression of their cultures. By the time the founding fathers imagined a meritocracy, race was commonly invoked to naturalize slavery, as, later, it would simultaneously mask and naturalize class. A construct of whiteness begins to appear, conferring on indentured European labor the privilege of not being the lowest in the social order, and justifying theft, massacre, and enslavement on the ground of white supremacy and Christian morality. From there, as Toni Morrison remarks, "It is no accident and no mistake that immigrant populations (and much immigrant literature) understood their 'Americanness' as an opposition to the resident black population."[11] As American identity is born, the indigenous people of the North American continent are confined to reservations, made invisible, their religion suppressed and frequently overlaid with enforced conversion so that American easily equals white/Christian. In the nineteenth century, expansionists would invoke manifest destiny. Born to rule.

Constructing white identity took time and law. In *Black, Jewish, and Interracial,* Katya Gibel Azoulay points out that the Supreme Court 1896 decision in *Plessy v. Ferguson,* the case that legalized segregation, the doctrine of separate but equal, also set a "legal definition of what constitutes a black person":

> In this case Homer Plessy had argued that he was visibly white and therefore should be allowed to sit in the train's white section. Overriding his skin color as an indicator of *not* being a Negro, the Court instead took "judicial notice" of the fact that a Negro is *any* person known to have Black ancestry.[12]

In a later essay, Gibel Azoulay clarifies: "Homer Plessy was a white-skinned man who had to inform the railroad company that he was a Negro who intended to sit in the Whites Only car in an intrastate train. Without

7

the advance notice, his white skin would never have drawn the attention of either the conductor or his fellow passengers."[13] Black by notification. Similarly, in 1982–83 in Louisiana, Susie Phipps, "having lived her whole life thinking that she was white . . . suddenly discovers that by legal definition she is not. . . . The *state* claims she is black."[14] Phipps challenged the state to change her racial classification from black to white, but her suit was denied, reaffirming a 1970 state law which designated anyone with 1/32nd "Negro blood" as legally black.

And then there's white by notification; Gibel Azoulay talks about speaking in Indiana:

> . . . and an Ethiopian American came up to me and said, did you know Ethiopians are considered white? So that kind of shocked me. She said she had a relative in litigation over a job position because he wanted to be counted as a minority. But because he came from Northeast Africa he was officially categorized as white.[15]

Official categories notwithstanding, in 1988 Ethiopian Mulugeta Seraw was beaten to death by white skinheads in Portland, Oregon, for being a black man on the street.[16]

Visuals, law, custom, history shift from moment to moment and site to site. What does not change is a fierce attachment to racial boundaries. Wherever they are drawn, the critical point is that they be closely monitored. Evidence of race-mixing still evokes near-psychosis in racists. In 1998, for example, a baby of mixed racial parentage who died and was buried in a Georgia churchyard near her (white) mother's people, almost got dug up by the white church deacons when they realized that the baby's father was African American. Only after media exposure and public uproar did the deacons relent and let the baby rest in peace.[17] Shall we count this as progress?

The Turner Diaries, a scarily popular novel written and published in 1978 by neo-Nazi William Pierce under the pseudonym "Andrew Macdonald," depicts impending race war in service of imposing absolute segregation. The novel describes the gruesome hanging of thousands of "white women who were married to or living with Blacks, with Jews, or other non-White males."[18] Significantly it includes Jews, along with mixed race people, as "mongrels" who need to be killed first because they confuse things. White supremacists want their racial differences clear.

Love, especially sex, across racial borders is enraging and terrifying to white supremacists; perhaps merely titillating or fetishistic to white liberal racists. Racism of either sort inevitably conspires with contempt for the flesh and fear of its desires, projecting all sexual impulse onto the racial other. Such love also contradicts core racist ideology, namely that we are naturally different, naturally antagonistic, and most important, naturally unequal: no way might we be humanly connected enough to love.

Never mind that these unions and these children are increasing all the time. As people fall in love, marry, and reproduce across race lines, we note an increasingly fierce policing of racial borders. Whites, as we know, are already a minority in the world, a rapidly shrinking majority in the United States. A minority can retain privilege, perhaps not forever, as South Africa exemplifies, but for a long time. However, sooner or later racism requires a police state. Across the nation we are building more prisons than schools in which African American and Latino children disproportionately land with heavy sentences, marginalized and disenfranchised.

And Jews? Along the city streets and state highways, where black and brown people are routinely stopped, harassed, sometimes tortured and killed, it is fair to say that some Jews pass freely, however typically "Jewish" (European/Ashkenazi) they may look. In stores, no one immediately pegs them as shoplifters. Encountering these Jews in apartment building lobbies or elevators, no one assumes that they don't belong. Hate violence against these Jews is manifested, almost always, in Jewish spaces or to Jews who visibly mark themselves, usually religiously observant men.

And what about the other Jews, the ones who don't look white, those who by anyone's definition are not white: Jewish African Americans, Jews from the Middle East, Latin America, Ethiopia, the Caribbean, India, China. Jews of any race who chose Judaism. Biracial and multiracial Jews. Children of mixed marriages. Children of color adopted by Ashkenazim.

Invisible, marginalized, not even imagined.

If people act surprised to see a Black Jewish woman representing Israel, I don't understand it. I tell them to look at a map: the Middle East and Africa are closer to each other than Russia or Poland and Israel. So, I ask them, "Why are you surprised to see a Black Jew?"

—BELAYNESH ZEVADIA,
Israeli diplomat of Ethiopian origin

Are you Jewish? You don't look Jewish.

—Countless people, to Ethiopian-born EPHRAIM ISAAC

9

Ethiopia is mentioned in the Bible over 50 times, but Poland not once.

—EPHRAIM ISAAC, Director of the Institute of
Semitic Studies at Princeton University,

Being African American and Jewish isn't a dilemma. The dilemma occurs when I attempt to disconnect from one or the other and not live as my full self. The dilemma occurs when I am not seen as my complete self. Ashkenazi Jews often see me as an African American moving in a Jewish world or as an Ethiopian or Yemenite Jew. African Americans never see me as Jewish.

—MIRI HUNTER HARUACH, "Born Again Yemenite"

Yet it's still more complicated. The Jew who looks white on New York City's Upper West or Lower East Side may be responded to in Maine or Idaho as a person of color.[19] Besides, what happens when you speak your (Jewish-sounding) name, or when your (less-white-looking) parent or child or lover meets you at work? What happens to your whiteness when you enter a Jewish space: a synagogue, Judaica bookstore, Jewish cultural event? In the United States, whiteness is a badge of normality, sameness, protection; and Jewish space is exactly the opposite: a place of separateness, vulnerability. African American Jewish scholar Katya Gibel Azoulay remarks that the Jews she feels most connected to are "the very people who didn't grow up identifying as white, they grew up identifying as Jewish. They knew they were Jewish, they left Europe because they were Jewish. Being Jewish is what defines them. *Not* being white."[20]

Yet filmmaker Ruth Behar (Sephardic/Ashkenazi/Cuban/American) tells how in the 1920s the United States was closing its doors to Jews fleeing European anti-semitism, while Cuba welcomed the fleeing Jews; thus her family survived. She says, "I am Jewish because I am Cuban." Behar's gratitude was later muted as she learned "our survival was an accident of racism." The white rulers of Cuba, afraid that Afro-Cubans might take over the island, were willing to accept the (whiter more European) Jews, to maintain white dominance over the "Black Peril."[21] Context is everything, or almost.

THE PEOPLE OF CONTRADICTIONS

In Europe, class was naturalized, biologized by themes of noble blood, high born and low born, the depravity of the peasants and lower classes;

the natural intelligence and nobility of the aristocracy. Also in Europe, excluding centuries of multiethnicity in Iberia, and allowing for some overstatement, Jews *were* difference. In a bipolar racial landscape, non-Jews located Jews on a series of axes at either extreme.

Their logic is not negligible: Jews can be simultaneously communist and capitalist, for example, because they are seen as obsessed with, essentially made of, power-through-money. Similarly, whether under- or over-sexed, something is *wrong* with Jewish sexuality.

In the United States, with its submerged multiracial history, racial diversity stretched much wider than the uncertain terrain of Jews. Early in this century, immigrant Jews (along with Irish, Italians, and other so-called ethnic whites) were widely viewed as filthy, diseased, verminous, intellectually inferior, criminal, and morally deficient. Karen Brodkin's *How Jews Became White Folks*, following Stephen Steinberg's analysis in *The Ethnic Myth*, studies the upward trajectory after World War II, when Euro-Jews in the United States participated along with other white ethnics in what she calls a massive affirmative action program for Euro-origin men. She describes the benefits offered unequally to white men under the GI bill, and through the Federal Housing Authority and Veterans Administration, smoothing the three great paths of upward mobility: education; jobs; and mortgages to purchase homes which can be passed on to the next generation.[22] In Brodkin's argument, class whitens; white Jews move up and racialization drops away.

Observing Jewish history, notes Ethnic Studies scholar Nancy Ordover, offers an opportunity to break down this process of racialization, because, by leaving Europe, Ashkenazi Jews "changed" their "race," even as our skin pigment remained the same.[23] Jewish Studies scholar Daniel Itzkovitz claims:

> As opposed to Europe, where "the Jew" is constructed as an allegory for otherness, in twentieth-century America the Jews have often seemed a good metaphor for the notion of "American" itself—the "American," that is, was an identity whose imagined severed ties to the land and to tradition, and whose obsession with money, reminded many of the stereotypic Jew.[24]

Izkovitz's "Jew-qua-American" is persuasive if by *Jew* we mean *assimilated Ashkenazi*, yet the persistence of Jewishness as racial/ethnic/cultural marker suggests a limit to Jewish attempts to assimilate into mere ethnic whiteness. Instead values and qualities about which "America" is ambivalent get projected onto the marked Jew, as the Jewish marker shrinks or expands like Alice in *Through the Looking Glass;* one minute nothing more than a bagel or *mazel tov,* the next minute, Holocaust victim or Shylock's eternal pound of flesh.

Non-Jews frequently expect Jews to be absolutely identifiable by looks, or else—in true liberal fashion—they pride themselves on never thinking about it. The former never imagine they might know someone Jewish; the latter usually can't imagine what's the big deal. But in general, those Jews about whom you "can't tell" make non-Jews anxious. So Jewish and yet so invisible? The uncertainty of Jewish identification makes Jewish difference extremely flexible, darker, or lighter according to context.[25] In Crown Heights or Williamsburg, for example—Brooklyn neighborhoods with large Hasidic communities—even those least passing of all Jews, the Hasidim, are in the eyes of municipal government and police whiter than their neighbors of African descent. On Park Avenue or even on the Upper West Side, Hasidim play very differently, never mind in Boise or even San Francisco.

Cultural representations of Jews are nothing if not slippery. In *Friends,* for example—a TV sitcom with a half-life like uranium—carefully blond Rachel, despite being a Streisand look-alike-sans-nose, is only occasionally, casually Jewish, by dint of her materialism and rich father. Racial location is one of the unresolved polarities circling the Jewish people. Are Jews white, of color, or race mongrels?[26] European or "Asiatic"? Western or Middle Eastern? Where does "Semitic" fit in? Are Jews and Arabs bound together racially as well as linguistically?

But the list extends beyond the color line. Are Jews mainstream or marginal? Model Americans or Eternal Foreigners? Oversexed or impotent/frigid? Jack the Ripper or Woody Allen? Monica Lewinsky or Marjorie Morningstar? Holocaust victim or Israeli paratrooper? Capitalist or communist? Henry Kissinger or Noam Chomsky?[27]

Slippery, uncertain: the direction in which Jews deviate from the norm. Are Jews above or below, more or less, too much or too little?

Stable, predictable: the slipperiness itself and the fact of deviation, too much *and* too little. Also stable: the sites of contestation: the charged arenas of sex, money, power, intelligence, culture, and belief system.

Itzkovitz's research reveals that the most salient characteristic, historically, of the "are Jews white?" debate *is* this indeterminacy and the anxiety it provokes.[28] In Europe, when Jews were systematically murdered for pernicious racial inferiority, part of the perniciousness, Itzkovitz demonstrates, was, exactly, that you couldn't always tell. So dangerous and yet so passing.

In Europe, the normative concept was not white but Christian. Christianity equated *Christian* and *decent* (as in, *Act like a Christian*), and identified Jews and other non-Christians with Satan, the original infidel. Distinguishing Christian from infidel meant, in practice, distinguishing Christian from inhuman. As secularization proceeded, the categories shifted from Christian to ethnic or national identities, German, Polish, Russian, French, and so on, against which Jews, even as newly emancipated citizens, were measured and, often but not always, found foreign and dangerous. As German merged into Aryan, racial categories may have served to lure or pacify some of the other Europeans being conquered by Germany; Poles, for example, though defined as racially inferior (stupid and bestial, as opposed to the Jewish sly, diseased, and insidiously powerful) were still racially a slot above Jews, whose "darkness" was a given.[29] On the cover of *Degenerate Music, An Accounting*, published in 1938, a black man with bulging eyes and fat distorted lips plays the dread degenerate jazz on a saxophone. On his lapel he sports a huge Jewish star.[30]

According to George Mosse's classic *Toward the Final Solution: A History of European Racism*, in which this and other racialized images of Jews appear, religious and racial anti-semitism constitute two distinct ideological traditions. I am sure I am not alone in occasionally muttering, *who cares which, it's all disgusting and deadly*. But Mosse is making a point. Defining Jews as a race—a pernicious diseased infecting race at that—meant: unsalvageable. Whereas a Christian/religious judgment insists on the possibility of conversion, and thus transformation. Let me not exaggerate this as a positive option. One would prefer to survive, untransformed, as oneself. The psychic cost of assimilation is reflected in the extraordinary suicide epidemic of Jews in the Weimar Republic, with German Jews committing suicide almost four times more than Catholics, and nearly twice as often as Protestants.[31] And the experience of the Sephardi *conversos*, whose difference came to be seen as more and more racial in their lack of *limpieze de sangre*[32] despite their actual or pretended acceptance of Christianity, suggests the increasingly frenetic intertwining of racial and religious bigotry as the modern age unfolds. In many parts of the Islamic world, too, though nothing matched the systematic reach of the Inquisition, crypto-Jews who converted by choice or by force continued to be set apart and persecuted.[33] The accusation of *Judaismo* (Judaizing) could be levied against someone "with no more than one-twentieth of Jewish blood in his or her veins,"[34] a percentage that actually outstrips the Third Reich.[35]

Nevertheless—and this is Mosse's point—the idea that one's religious practice is at fault is consistent with torture and forced conversion, as well as with death for the obstinate; but a racial definition of Jews is consistent with extermination. The racialized being simply is. Extermination is, then, the appropriate final solution.

But in Europe, even pre-Third Reich, the distinction blurs. Periodic forced conversion to Christianity, for example, suggests that Jews could shed their Jewishness, albeit unwillingly. Yet in tricultural Spain, where Jews, along with Muslims, were relatively integrated compared with the ghettos of much of Europe, when mass conversion was enforced, *conversos* remained as a group discrete and mistrusted. The pejorative for *converso* is *marrano*, meaning "pig," whether as sheer insult or in reference to the Jewish taboo against eating pork. But even the flatly descriptive "New Christian" passed down through the generations demonstrates the threadbare nature of the Christian blanket; Jewishness peeps through, defiling, defective, justification for discrimination against anyone of Jewish ancestry. One could argue that the Spanish *conversos* were the first victims of racial persecution in Europe, but in a religion-permeated society, the racial and religious aspects never fully separated.[36] Still, *conversos* unsettled the Jewish Question—*who was a Jew?*—and one of the emerging answers was racial rather than religious.[37]

As Europeans developed racial schema to accompany the colonial enterprise, the placement of Jews was debated. Mosse claims, "Jews were either ignored by anthropologists during most of the eighteenth century or considered part of the Caucasian race, and still believed capable of assimilation into European life." Though some insisted that Jews were "Asiatic," and others acknowledged their confusion, "ideas of cosmopolitanism, equality, and toleration operated for the Jew as they could not for the Negro; after all, the Jew was white." German phrenologist Carl Gustav Carus divided the world into "day people" (Europeans), "night people" (Africans), and "twilight people" (Asiatics and American Indians). Designating day people as superior, and marking the inevitable Jewish nose, he nevertheless included Jews with day people.[38] Similarly the French pseudo-Comte de Gobineau characterized three basic races: white, yellow, black.

> The yellow race . . . was materialistic, pedantic, and taken up with "a steady but uncreative drive towards material property." The blacks [had] . . . little intelligence, but overdeveloped senses which endowed them with a crude and terrifying power. The blacks were a mob on the loose, . . . eternal *sans culottes* who had collaborated with the middle classes to destroy . . . aristocratic France . . .[39]

Is there any doubt that aristocratic France is radiantly white?

According to Mosse, Gobineau's work had impact not in France but in Germany, where by racial default (black and yellow people were scarce), Gobineau's ideas were applied to Jews. Even so, Mosse concludes, "only after the mid-nineteenth century was racism applied to Jews with any consistency." [40]

By the late nineteenth century, according to Sander Gilman, debate about Jewish skin color had modulated into a general consensus in "the ethnological literature . . . that the Jews were 'black' or at least 'swarthy.'"[41] But the debate was hardly resolved. Itzkovitz, surveying a host of scholars, concludes that Jews were most frequently classified as "Asiatic."[42] Crammed into this or that racial category, all over post-Enlightenment Europe the Jew was increasingly seen as physically distinctive, practically a different species. The Jew's body was distinguished not only by circumcision (the Jew is, of course, normatively male), but also by large flat (unmanly, unsoldierly) feet, and by the telltale Jewish nose, evident in iconography from the mid-eighteenth century on,[43] and associated with syphilis, and diseased, darkened skin.[44]

In what I have come to think of as an ecology of hatred, racial anti-semitism kicks in as society secularizes. If a secular society at moments allowed Jews to participate as citizens, no longer totally dehumanized by dint of religious beliefs and practice, racism contravenes this permission by reinscribing Christian fear and disdain as racial. Racism against Jews represents the secularization of Christian anti-semitism, but let not categories obscure essence: difference translated into otherness equals indifference, hatred, and fear.

But if Jews are mongrels and antichrists, how is it that, often enough, no one can distinguish Jews from Christians? How "natural" are differences that can't be spotted or slotted into existing categories? Mosse, again, describes an 1870s German survey that found an estimated 11 percent of German Jews were "pure blonds" and 42 percent black-haired, while (Christian) Germans divided into 31.8 percent blondes and 14.05 percent black-haired. Most striking, however, was the finding that the largest number of both Christians and Jews fit into a "mixed type" category, neither pure blond nor pure black-haired—47 percent of Jews and 54.1 percent of Christians—a similarity that *The German Anthropological Review* found so disturbing that they suppressed the data and fudged, simply reporting that the Jewish population had fewer blonds than the German population. And the Austrians, "always more radical and interested in separating Jew from Gentile, concentrated their survey upon Galicia and

Bukowina, where the Jewish race was said to have maintained its purity. They did find fewer Jewish blonds in that region"[45]—perhaps a relief to folks like the "Viennese prophet of Aryanism," Jörg Lanz von Liebenfels, who in 1905 founded *Ostara, Journal for Blond People.*[46]

Yet lest we focus too heavily on Europe, we should mark the role played by American eugenics and scientific racism in helping Germany develop its master race theory.[47] "The Nazis were avid students of United States eugenics doctrine," notes Nancy Ordover.[48] "American eugenicists, armed with charts, photographs, and even human skulls, were there to provide the visual and mathematical support that rendered racism scientifically valid and politically viable."[49] "Nazi doctors named American eugenicists their ideological mentors at the Nuremberg trials." [50] Publications such as the *American Breeders Magazine* and *Eugenical News* spread the word, and "[w]hen . . . [*Eugenical News*] published the text of Germany's 1933 Hereditary Health Law, an unsigned preface boasted of the influence U.S. eugenicists had had."[51] Laws restricting reproduction and immigration were championed as eugenic victories on both sides of the Atlantic.

APARTHEID/AMERICAN STYLE

Then and now. History and the present. How do we integrate Jews into an analysis of racism?

My grandparents immigrated from Russia and Poland to New York City in the early twentieth century, along with massive numbers of Europeans, including Eastern European Jews. But when I was growing up in New York City in the 1950s and early 1960s, legal immigration was basically at a standstill.[52] During this period, race continued to be seen as essentially a black–white thing.

In 1990, after twenty-five years of living all over the United States— California, Oregon, New Mexico, Maine, and Vermont—I returned to New York, to a neighborhood where I'd lived as a student at City College. Then a cheap slum, now it was mostly working-class Dominican, about to be hit by gentrification with its new identity as "Manhattan Valley."[53] Because of my years away, and because of where I'd been, I saw the city and my old neighborhood with different eyes; but not only my eyes had changed. While I was wandering, people had come to New York from all over the world. Walking around my neighborhood, I saw new configurations, people of all colors and ages in many different roles. Taxi drivers, restaurant workers, small shopkeepers in the groceries, pharmacies, stationery shops that line Broadway were people of color from all over the world, especially Asia, as well as from Latin America, Africa, the Mediterranean, the Caribbean. Rarely African American.

Many of them spoke English wrapped in the vowels and consonants of their mother tongue, while their kids who helped out after school and Saturdays (as I used to help out in my parents' store), were fluently bilingual, good English, as well as rapidfire Spanish, Chinese, Korean, Hindi, Arabic. . . . Many of these kids would go to college. Many would lose their language, their culture. This is the American dream.

Swirling around the dream, I heard contradictory epithets and assumptions about "Asians" collapsing a huge range of culture and history into a single narrative. Even so, distinctive stereotypes were seeping into the mainstream culture: Chinese pegged as the model minority, successful especially in the grind subjects, of math, accounting, computers, but lacking in creativity or indeed personality; (male "Oriental") sexuality

> . . . conceptualized differently from and perhaps even in opposition to, African and African-Caribbean representations in the white imagination. Where the latter are constructed as aggressive, violent and hyper-masculinized, Asians are portrayed as passive, weak and hyper-feminized.[54] [Kobena] Mercer and [Isaac] Julien characterize this orientalist image thus: "The Oriental has no capacity for violence; he is mute, passive, charming, inscrutable."[55]

Indians and Pakistanis were assumed to be racking it up in Silicon Valley, while simultaneously gouging the neighborhood with their cabs and Mom & Pop delis; persistently mocked for their accents and their determination to earn a living.[56] Koreans were seen as Moonies with a greengrocer empire to which only Koreans were admitted; while Arabs and Muslims—assumed to be identical categories—were on the eve of Gulf War I holding down the place of most dread minority, terrorist but also unfairly wealthy, holding "us" hostage to their oil. Meanwhile, Vietnamese, Laotians, and Thai—folks from that part of the world the United States nearly destroyed (and still couldn't win the war)—are invisible, though they are perhaps some of the very poorest of immigrants.

The presence of large numbers of Asians was one change in New York City. The other was "the homeless." In the years I'd been away, between deinstitutionalization and an increasingly inhospitable economy, large numbers of mostly African American men, a few women, were stretched out asleep on the benches and sidewalks, shaking cups, asking, *can you spare some change, I'm very hungry, can you give me something, even a quarter.* It was winter. Some had no shoes. Some had no coat.

As I crossed the neighborhood boundary of 96th Street, the balance of color shifted from brown to white, Latino to yuppie, gentrified, white graduates of elite colleges living in buildings with swimming pools and elaborate doormen, views of the George Washington Bridge; men and women in their twenties whose parents or trust funds bought them apartments costing easily a million dollars. Two million dollars. Lots of old Jews, surviving still in their rent-controlled apartments that will probably turn co-op when they die. Lots of harried thirty-somethings and forty-somethings who had their kids late, split economically between upper middle and middle, and politically between liberals and radicals. Some are insistent about sending their kids to public schools, and some have given up on the public schools, refusing, in their words, to sacrifice their kids to a principle. While in "Manhattan Valley" women tended to be the same color as the children they tended, a few blocks west or south, it was a different story: when I saw a woman and child of the same color, I'd be almost surprised; the norm was women of color caring for white children of working mothers, often professionals, what I've come to think of as the underbelly of feminism. Most of the women were immigrants.

Now, fifteen years later, I see three massive changes: first, the woman–child–color thing cuts two ways: intermarriage and, especially, wide-scale adoption means these days, you might as readily see a white woman—who might be Jewish—with a child or children of color—contrary to the 1950s, when the Louise Wise Services Agency reported almost complete failure in finding white Jewish parents willing to adopt African American babies, even those who were matrilineally Jewish.[57] Second, homeless people are way less visible; they have not been housed but have simply been pushed off the streets by New York's own bundle of meanness, former mayor Rudy Giuliani, and kept off the streets by his mild-mannered but tight-hearted CEO successor Michael Bloomberg. Third, since September 11, 2001, formerly thriving Arab and South Asian communities have been devastated. Those who look like they might be Arab or Muslim are racially profiled, increasingly endangered by street and police violence, by economic hardship, by obstacles to enrollment in schools and colleges. Many from these communities are missing, indefinitely detained, deported.

Back to 1990. The long struggle against South African apartheid was finally bearing fruit. Nelson Mandela had just been released from prison and was about to visit New York. He had publicly embraced Yasir Arafat, and there were those among New York's self-appointed Jewish leaders prepared to picket his visit. The idea that *this* would be the public response of New York's Jews to Nelson Mandela's visit encouraged a process already in place, and the organization Jews for Racial and Economic Justice was formed. JFREJ's first public act was to hold a *shabat* service in honor of Mandela and to raise $30,000 for the African National Congress.

During that time, with the dismantling of South African apartheid fresh in my head, with a vision of economic possibilities open to some of the more recent immigrants, and closed to many who had been in the United States for centuries and in the North for at least decades, I saw an analogy between the structure of apartheid and racism in the United States. South Africa, the Ur-Racist Empire, had three racial categories, not two: white, black and colored, and this last, the buffer category of *colored*, seemed especially useful to contemplate.[58]

But first I need to issue a caveat: It's hard to talk about racial categorization without seeming to accept or even endorse it. What I am describing is air thick with polluting smog, making it difficult both to breathe and to see. At the same time, socially constructed racial categories that shift arbitrarily determine people's opportunities, and can mark the border between life and death. Moreover, even a casual survey reveals division in the monolithic category *people of color*, a division that corresponds suggestively to the three racial categories of apartheid.

One feature of a tripartite system is its nuanced hierarchy of privilege inflected by a shifting buffer class. *Whites* rule. But *colored*, though they will never be white, benefit concretely from not being *black*. They also benefit from the existence of those who are: "blacks" who stand in the racial hierarchy lower than they, the "coloreds." Scholar Roger Sanjek observes that on the West Coast there has been an increase in Asian-white and Mexican-white intermarriage, while

> black–white intermarriage rates remained flat in comparison. It is also worthy of closer historical probing to note that Asian and Mexican intermarriage rates with whites appear to have increased only after blacks became part of the West Coast social order in substantial numbers. . . . It thus appears that Asians and Mexicans . . . became marriageable—and ethnic—to whites only after the U.S. black–white racial regime was numerically and institutionally established in the western states.[59]

I've already noted the post-9/11 explicit and intense targeting of South Asian, Arab, and Muslim communities. In this newly explosive context, a

South Asian friend talks of feeling protected when she is with her African American partner—American, not a foreign terrorist. Yet while these racial categories are unstable, they continue to confer or block privilege. In the United States, the racial benefits accruing to *coloreds* include better jobs, greater access to education, and small business opportunities. These are achieved not only through familial and ethnic networks, but also through some positive stereotyping of Asians as good at math and science, or as having strong family ties. The category "coloreds" comprises a variety of groups, mostly immigrants: Middle Eastern, Chinese, Korean, Vietnamese, Thai, Indonesian, Arabs, Indians, Pakistani, Sri Lankan, Iranians, and so on; people who arrived anywhere between yesterday and a century ago.

This group is lumped together as particularly unaggressive, with the increasing exception of Arabs or perceived Arabs. *Coloreds* are not seen as muggers or rapists, but increasingly, and since 9/11 indelibly, are pegged as irrational religious fanatics, inherently terrorist, given to violence, care-less—unlike "Americans"—of human life. In addition, they are seen as sneaky, sexually perverse; at best, exotic,[60] formerly defined as "white sla-vers" (a phrase that cloaks the "normal" sexual subordination of enslaved African women, such that sexual enslavement of *other* women needs a white marker; while delicately excluding any mention of sex: the accurate term would be "female sexual slavery." As "white slavers" they are thus associ-ated with prostitution, pimping, and syphilis, and, in a more contemporary vein, with sex tourism. Their women: dominated in an unwesternly fashion. Their men, as noted: masculinity suspect, homosexual? sex with camels?

Placement in the hierarchy shifts according to context; for example, British Empire stereotypes of dark males under white/colonial rule, famil-iar from the postbellum U.S. South, turn the plot in E. M. Forster's *A Passage to India,* where an English lady mistakenly charges an Indian man with attempted rape. Yet in the United States, despite actual experience of war with Japan, Korea, and Viet Nam, and the popularization of mar-tial arts, *Asians* as a loose category continue to be seen as effeminate and nonaggressive, not to be feared on the street. They are considered good with money and are assumed to have lots of it derived from mysterious and corrupt practices. Arabs, as noted, form an increasingly distinct sub-category, as the war against Iraq proceeds.

And the bottom of the hierarchy? Native Americans and Latinos might be seen as joining African Americans in particularly onerous oppression. Assumed to be street-dangerous, intellectually inferior, vio-lent and criminally inclined, sexually rapacious, bestial in contrast to the overcivilized effete "coloreds," such stereotypes serve to justify the reality of people's lives: *blacks* are disproportionately unemployed or underemployed, women disproportionately subjected to forced sterilization and sexual abuse, and men to police brutality. The children are more likely to suffer from lead poisoning, to grow up near toxic waste dumps, to be mislabeled mentally retarded, to die in the first year of their lives, to be incarcerated as teenagers, and to be sentenced to death.[61] As I write this, the breaking news—and who should be surprised—is that unemployment continues to afflict the African American community at rates more than double that of the white "community."[62]

Race in this country comprises a range of themes, but six reverberate with particular force: through themes of sex, money, power, intelligence, nationality or culture, and belief system, race is embodied. Potent stereotypes recharge the primal categories that manifest in opposition among *blacks* and *coloreds*, thus dividing the human universe into those who are too much and those who are too little, while whites—white men, to be exact—lodge squarely between too much and too little; too little and too much; whites are exactly the right amount. Presumed, in every way, normal. Unmarked. Don't even require mentioning. The discussion of these themes that follows should be read entirely in quotes, describing not reality but "American" racial fantasy.

SEX   *Black* men are assumed to be bestial and oversexed, studs, rapists or pimps; the women, welfare queens breeding like animals, will-less or way too strong (Sojourner Truth: "Ar'n't I a Woman?"). *Colored* men, on the other hand, are seen as unmanly, perverse and homosexed, associated with prostitution, and syphilis, historically stigmatized as "white slavers," while the women are erotic, exotic, and agent-less (or, alternately, "Dragon Lady"). What remains constant: women and men inside a racialized lens don't perform their gender correctly. Either women and men trade roles, power shifting from men to women in a way that offends white male Christians (and sometimes also offends men of the home community, who want the right to control "their" women). Or else, however weak the men are perceived to be, the women are seen as weaker, outrageously passive: geishas, Miss Saigon, Mme. Butterfly, fantasy Asian women without will, without thought; practically botanical.

Racism and projected distorted sexuality seem to go hand in hand. The racist cosmology of black male=beast (soulless mindless flesh) and white helpless lady (fleshless mindless soul) justifies all sorts of racial apparatus, including the actual sexual abuse of

21

women of color by white men, especially men of wealth and power, and the historical justification for lynching and other repression of black men in order to protect white men's property (which includes white women).

MONEY   *Blacks* are seen as deservedly poor; squandering on fancy cars—it used to be Cadillacs—money earned by and taken from deserving whites; human capital in their formerly enslaved state but today lacking in value or productivity. *Coloreds*, on the other hand, are seen as suspiciously good with money; they have way too much; are sly and exploitative, heartless and godless capitalists, blamed as jobs get exported, and products imported, for stealing the jobs of hard-working white Christians. Arabs share this image of undeserved wealth, and are especially blamed for the rising price of oil.

POWER   *Blacks* are seen as politically powerless but physically strong and violent like nature herself, ready to mug, steal, and riot, dangerously on the verge of rebellion. *Coloreds* are seen as also untrustworthy but sneaky, rather than physically explosive; corrupt, and corrupting, manipulative rather than violent. In the United Kingdom, emphasis on Asian gangs has somewhat erased the distinction commonly drawn in the white imagination between (violent) African Caribbean and (sneaky) South Asian young men.[63] In the United States, September 11 has shifted terrorism whole-hog into the "colored" camp, and even this large scale violence is performed sneakily.

INTELLECT   *Blacks* are seen as intellectually inferior, bell-curve flunkies, perhaps creative as performers, but not as thinkers; *coloreds* are seen as shrewd, academic stars, lacking in true creativity or culture, but their children get diabolically high grades. As with money, *coloreds* are seen as getting an unfair share of accolades.

CULTURE   *Blacks* after centuries on this continent remain outsiders, savage, uncivilized, and cultureless or primitives (sometimes romanticized but always disrespected), while *coloreds* are seen as eternal foreigners, hailing from peculiar and distasteful unwestern "overcivilized" cultures.

BELIEF SYSTEM   *Blacks* adhere to an overemotional Christianity (with undertones of sorcery, voodoo, and a propensity for Christian-hating Islam), while *coloreds* are the archetypal infidels—Muslims,

Hindus, Sikhs, Buddhists, and followers of other religions considered by the Christian west to be foreign, irrational, and disconnected from morality.

What's significant is the division of each strand of undesirable qualities and
values into two poles, and the projection of each of these poles onto "others." Note too the way—at least pre-9/11—"blacks" make "coloreds" look
good; and "coloreds" make "blacks" look like losers. The "Model Minority,"
after all, implies an opposing "Minority from Hell," supposedly proving
that racism is an outmoded fiction, and really it's that inferior "culture
of poverty" or "bell-curve intellect" that's at fault. In addition, the "Model
Minority" trope, by exaggerating the success of Asians, handily obscures
continued discrimination against them.[64]

Simultaneously, as all negativity is projected onto racial "others," culture and style are cannibalized. Where would modern European art be
without African art or American popular music without jazz and blues?
Think of Oprah, Toni Morrison, Denzel. What of the obsession among
privileged middle-class folks with eastern religions, cultures, food? Craft
stores sell dream-catcher kits and white folks long to get down with the
natives. White suburban teenagers wear huge baggy outlaw jeans and track
hiphop. Halle Berry is probably the agreed-upon most beautiful woman
in the United States. From this perspective, racism is a feel-good strategy
to cope with the unpleasant experience of envy.

Of course this racialized tripartite scheme is crude, distorting, yoking
race to class, unequipped to recognize nuances such as the large numbers of black professionals or impoverished East and Southeast Asians,
the West Indian small business owners (who used to be called "the Black
Jews" because of their role as shopkeepers and small landlords). I could
cite many more examples of who doesn't fit. After all, it is racism that collapses the diversity of communities of color into homogeneity.

But this white/colored/black classification suggests how the middle
category—like the middle class—functions: as a buffer zone to protect
wealth, by absorbing blame for the truly powerful who are also usually out
of sight and out of reach. *Coloreds* are blamed—and envied—for making
money; for getting ahead; for their kids' curve-breaking grades, for stealing the jobs of hard-working white Christians. Along with Latinos, with
whom, as immigrants, they are sometimes conflated, they are blamed for
jobs exported from the United States to sites of cheaper labor, and for
products imported from such sites. *Coloreds* are scapegoated for the ravages of global capitalism. Immigrant bashing—whether street violence or

political agendas such as English-only and anti-immigrant rights—becomes a "natural" response to an attack perpetually about to happen.

The category of *blacks* comprises those who, seen as not having money, threaten to rob and pillage hard-working, tax-paying white Christians. In this construct, welfare fits as women's form of robbery; the men are busy mugging. *Blacks* are scapegoated for (perceived) urban violence, and for (perceived) economic need and dependency.

Thus despite the bipolar public face of race and racism in the United States, the submerged tripartite division functions as a safety valve for class rage.

As I've suggested, in the United States one side of the racial–other spectrum, one collection of extremes shifts to Asians.[65] The other side of the spectrum shifts to African Americans, and, insofar as Latinos and Native Americans are considered at all, they are usually subsumed into the category of *blacks*, a blurring eased by the existence of many Latinos who are of African descent. In the eyes of white America, race trumps ethnicity. Even the regional variation and complexity of tripartite division; for example, white–Cuban–African American power struggles in Miami, or Anglo–Hispanic–Native American hierarchy in New Mexico, does not seriously challenge the basic principle of racialized hierarchy.

Where are Jews?

By now it should be obvious. Mongrels to white supremacists; infidels who continue to refuse the true faith; associated historically with white slavery, prostitution, and syphilis; so good with money you could fairly say Jews ARE money; rootless cosmopolitans tenaciously associated with the impulse to control Christians with Jews' ill-gotten gains and clannish plotting, through depraved sexual vices, and a sterile degenerate materialistic culture: Jews lodge somewhere between the categories *white* and *colored,* slipping back and forth according to context.

The middle (*colored* or Jew) serves as a place of blame: stretching beyond horizontal hostility for a vertical encounter with what is positioned directly above. In recent years, the top is often entirely missing, unseen. Black–Jewish conflict. Black–Korean conflict. Though race continues to be perceived as a Black–White binary, conflict is often ethnicized, obscuring and thus protecting white folks from racial or class anger.

The point of this tripartite division I offer is not to reinscribe bigotry but to make plain how this division exalts whiteness. As *blacks* and *colored* are either insufficient or excessive, too little or too much, *whites* are brilliantly perfect—and Jews are splendidly convenient. Jews of color are lumped in with non-Jews of color except to score a political point—Ethiopian

Jews, for example, invoked to demonstrate Israel's magnificent hospitality and lack of racism (ignoring how Israeli treatment of the Beta Israel humiliates and degrades); Iranian Jews cited to prove the monstrousness of the Iranian government. Meanwhile Ashkenazim shift between nonwhite (from a eugenicist racialized white supremacist perspective) and surrogate white; scapegoats and blametakers; superwhites, if you will.

Given that most of the world is completely ignorant of Jewish cultural markers such as *Ashkenazi* or *Sephardi,* stereotypes about Jews are by default usually about Ashkenazim. The diaspora Jew is an Ashkenazi man "represented by European Christian culture as feminized [and/or] queer."[66] From the perspective of Ashkenazim, gender inflects these images so that Mizrahi men are seen either as macho brutes or emasculated, practically women, while *actual Mizrahi women* are seen as primitive and irrational, sexually overactive, or completely repressed and oppressed dwellers in harems. As anthropologist Joëlle Bahloul notes, "Scholars continue to view the Sephardic world as 'archaic' and non-progressive, in large part because of its treatment of women and the extensive sexual discrimination found in it." This concern for women does not include attending to the reality of North African women's lives, their "yearning for modernity," or their significant role in bringing the modern world into their community.[67]

But lest we imagine that any of these categories are racially fixed, Indonesian feminist scholar Saraswati Sunindyo notes how narratives of the 1999 Indonesian crisis repeatedly cited ethnic Chinese as the wealthy elite, whereas the wealth of the [Indonesian] Suharto family went unmentioned. Violence against ethnic Chinese, pogroms, including mass rapes of Chinese women, was, according to Sunindyo,

> not rapes by poor people who hated the Chinese so much—these were orchestrated operations by some faction of the military trying to gain political seats by creating complete chaos. Indonesian academics abroad characterized the rape of Chinese women as "racialized state violence."[68]

Sunindyo explains, too, how the diasporic Chinese had been given a superior position to the "dirty natives," slotted by the Dutch into the minority middle man petit bourgeois position of shopkeepers, pawnbrokers, and associated with money. Anti-Chinese riots have a long history in Indonesia, including during the three hundred years of Dutch power in the archipelago. No surprise that the Chinese are often called "the Jews of Asia."[69]

At the same time, the familiar position of marginality and middleness not only made—and continues to make—the Chinese in Indonesia vulnerable, but also points to some diasporic strengths shared with Jews. Diasporic Chinese, like diasporic Jews, have some common language and culture to draw on, familial connections good for trade and for sustaining a view that stretches beyond the nation-state. The Chinese in Indochina were widely understood as political radicals, perhaps only in part because of the strength of communist organizing and radical education in China itself. Without exaggerating the radicalism of diasporic Chinese, the marginal, middle position might be said to stimulate or at least sustain the production of radicals and create a familiar contradiction: are diasporic Chinese petit bourgeois or wild-eyed revolutionaries? Or both?

JEWS: RACE OR RELIGION?

KATYA GIBEL AZOULAY
(MEVORACH)

When I teach [in Grinnell, Iowa], the first thing I do is to ask the students where their families come from. Given there's almost no diversity in my classrooms, and I mean color or ethnic. . . . So I ask what their genealogy is, it's a way for me to get them to realize, without my having to say it, that they're far more diverse than they thought. If they just say, for example, German, I'll ask "what religion?" Most of the time they don't know, but sometimes they do. Sometimes they come back in the middle of the semester, having gone home and asked, and they found out things they didn't know. The point is to show this unfolding whiteness without having to spell it out in those words on day one and make them feel defensive. Then we can talk about, why do you think Iowa is not only all white, but kind of generic white?

But [even] the Jewish kids will say Russia, Poland, Lithuania. They will not start out by saying "Polish Jews who were forced to immigrate because of pogroms."

—KATYA GIBEL AZOULAY (a.k.a. Mevorach), interview

Where do Jews fit?

Jewish is often trivialized as something you choose, a preference, like tea over coffee. In contrast with visible racial identity, presumptions of choice—as with gayness—are seen as minimizing one's claim to attention, sympathy, and remedy. As a counter to bigotry, *I was born like this* strategically asserts a kind of victim status, modeled on race, gender, and disability: if you can't help yourself, maybe you're entitled to some help from others.

Some Jews will argue that all Jews are people of color, because the alternative seems to be erasure, a polarization of white and color that excludes us. [70] If we have lived in a part of the world for generations, we often look a lot like the others who live there. In 1854, Frederick Douglass understood the obvious. "The Jews, who are to be found in all countries, never intermarrying, are white in Europe, brown in Asia, and black in Africa."[71] But Jews do intermarry, quite widely, and even so sometimes we continue to look strikingly different.

African American/Jew Yavilah McCoy explains,

> When I say "of color," it simply means having dark skin, because in a racialized society, the amount of color in one's skin can often make a difference in the way people see your identity and treat you accordingly. There are many regions of our world where people have dark skin, yet skin color is not the delineator of their identity. Jews come from many of these regions that include Yemen, Morocco, Ethiopia, Egypt and many other countries where individuals of various shades of skin color have been Jewish for ages, and never questioned their Jewish identity in regard to the amount of melanin in their skin. Historically, Jewish identity, for many Jews around the world, of both light and dark skin, has been about religion, culture, practice and a relationship with God. As we encountered racism as a people, and entered societies where racial paradigms were in place, I believe that this began to change. When I walk into a room and say to people I meet "I'm Jewish" often I will get the response "but you're Black." I often want to say "no kidding," but the usual response I give is "Yes, my family has been practicing Judaism for at least three generations, now." The point that I aim to make is that it would make it easier to just "BE" as a Jewish person of color if "black" and "Jewish" identity were not so commonly assumed to be mutually exclusive. Historically, Jews have been multiple skin colors and it's unfortunate that the passive internalization of color consciousness that happens so easily in American society, helped us to forget the freedom from identifying around color that is a part of our Jewish history.[72]

Yet to say, simply, *Jews are not a race*, while accurate, overlooks the confusion, the waffling and uncertainty about Jewish racial identity, and the anxiety created by this uncertainty. Since race emerged as a construct in nineteenth-century biological science, there's always been someone pitching the Jewish race, though not everyone agrees to catch. Still, Jews have been so racialized that subtext overwhelms text: we have been racially hated *as if* we were a race. Even as I assert, *of course, Jewish is not a race*, I come upon "a 1987 Supreme Court ruling that Jews and Arabs could use civil rights laws to gain redress for discrimination against them . . . on the grounds that they are not racial whites."[73]

At the same time, to reduce *Jewishness* to *Judaism* is to forget the complex indivisible swirl of religion–culture–language–history that *was* Jewishness until relatively recently. In eighteenth-century Western Europe, legal emancipation began to offer some Jews the possibility of escaping from a linguistically, culturally, and economically isolated ghetto. Even before Nazi racial definitions reinforced a defensive *only-a-religion* kneejerk from the Jewish community, the lure of partial assimilation led some Jews to define Judaism as narrowly as possible, as religion only: "a Jew at home, a man in the streets,"[74] a private matter, taken care of behind closed doors, like bathing. In Eastern Europe, a Jew was a Jew, marked visually and linguistically, by culture and religion, no Jew-at-home, man-in-street option. In a third variation found in the Islamic world, Jews did not live segregated from non-Jews, and cultural and linguistic interaction was considerable. Yet Jews were not pressed to assimilate or to separate secular and religious identity. Many Jews were encouraged briefly by "Ottomanization," which favored cultural diversity for ethnic minorities, including Jews and other non-Muslims.[75]

Though Judaism the religion does not tell the whole Jewish story, it does provide continuity and connection to Jews around the globe. There is something powerful even for an atheist like myself about entering a synagogue across a continent or an ocean and hearing the familiar service.[76] Even before the printing press made written documents widely available, during centuries of widest dispersion across five continents, most of the Jewish world followed basically the same teachings and worship.[77] A Jewish commonplace goes, "More than the Jews have kept *shabat* (Friday sundown to Saturday sundown, the day of rest and prayer), *shabat* has kept the Jews."

But a Jew is not a Jew only through belief. A Jew need not follow religious practice. A Jew need not even believe in god, not even to become a rabbi—an element of Judaism of which I am especially fond.[78] A non-Jew can become a Jew by embracing Jewish religious practice, but religion offers only one strand, one way of being Jewish. Ironic that it is precisely the Holocaust's depletion of Jews and of Jewish identity, with profound linguistic and cultural losses, that makes imaginable a Jewishness that is *only a religion*—only now, when so much else has been lost. Speakers of Judeo-Arabic, Ladino (Judeo-Español), and Yiddish (Judeo-German) age and die;[79] the Jews who left India, Ethiopia, Syria, Iraq, Yemen, Lebanon, Iran, Egypt . . . watch—mostly in Israel—their children learn to reject and be embarrassed by their rich, frequently matrilineal traditions.[80]

To equate Jewishness with Judaism, culture with religion, is to forget how even the contemporary, often attenuated version of this Jewish cultural swirl is passed down *in the family;* almost like genetic code, as Ashkenazim are genetically marked for Tay-Sachs Disease, Canavan disease, and even (though the genetic-environmental breakdown is not clear) breast cancer. One wonders, given the general amnesia about non-Ashkenazi Jews, whether there are other Jewish genetically linked diseases to investigate.

More provocative is the dazzling DNA discovery of Cohanim genetic makeup among the Lemba in Southern Africa and the Bene Israel of Marathi, India.[81] The Cohanim (Cohens) are the priestly caste, descended, it is said, from Moses' brother Aaron. At the same time, let me stress the obvious: the Cohanim "gene," like Jewishness itself, crosses all races.

But it's confusing, because to say someone *looks Jewish* is to say something both absurd (Jews look a million different ways) and shorthand communicative.

When I was growing up in Flatbush, every girl with a certain kind of nose—sometimes named explicitly as a Jewish nose, sometimes only as "too big"—wanted a nose job, and if her parents could pay for it, often she got one. I want to be graphic about the euphemism "nose job." A nose job breaks the nose, bruises the face and eye area like a grotesque beating. It hurts. It takes weeks to heal.

What was wrong with the original nose, the Jewish one? Noses were discussed ardently in Flatbush, with this or that friend looking forward to her day of transformation.[82] My aunts lavished on me the following exquisite praise: *look at her, a nose like a shiksa* (a non-Jewish woman). This hurt my feelings. Before I knew what a *shiksa* was, I knew I wasn't it, and, with that fabulous integrity of children, I wanted to look like who I was. But later I learned my nose's value, and would tell gentiles this story, so they'd notice my nose.

A Jewish nose, I conclude, identifies its owner as a Jew. Nose jobs are performed so that a Jewish woman does not look like a Jew. The Ashkenazi girls of my generation bleached and shaved, to look less Jewish; the non-Ashkenazi girls bleached and shaved to look more Ashkenazi; more European; less Jewish.[83]

Tell me again Jewish is just a religion.

CHRISTIAN CENTRICITY

Yet in a Christian-centric culture, it is the religious aspect of Jewishness that is articulated. Ethnicity and culture are confused, even for many Jews. We need a word for the system that normalizes and honors Christianity, just as *racism* names the system that normalizes and honors whiteness. Our very lack of a word illustrates the problem. How do we challenge what we have no language to discuss? Christian hegemony? Not very catchy, but the assumption of Christianity-as-norm does exercise a negative impact on Jews, and is erasive and diminishing. Jews usually designate this erasure as a form of anti-semitism, but it's not only a Jewish issue: erasure and marginalization of non-Christians denigrates all non-Christians. We sorely need a term such as *Christianism* to name the system of Christian domination. Such a term would help contextualize Jewish experience as marginality shared with other non-Christians.

Outside the Christian-dominant framework of the West, Christians are sometimes persecuted; in India, for example, or China. But in the United States, where Christianity is the established religion (the doctrine of separation of church and state notwithstanding), Christianity and whiteness are completely enmeshed. Christianity was used to service colonialism and agrarian capitalism/plantation slavery, and was seen as a pacifying tool.

Christians, religiously observant or not, usually operate from the common self-definition of Christianity: a religion any individual can embrace through belief, detached from race, peoplehood, and culture.[84] But while Christianity has also offered people of color a place to belong, to imagine and sometimes even experience equality, I suspect that most white Christians do not feel kinship with Latino evangelicals or Korean Baptists, or with indigenous people converted by colonialists all over the globe.

Doesn't Christianity really, for most white Christians, imply *white*? Think of the massive Christian evasion of a simple fact: Jesus Christ was not, was never a Christian. He was a Jew. What did he look like, Jesus of Nazareth, two thousand years ago? Blond, blue-eyed? I am not minimizing the authenticity or value of Christianity for any believer, nor am I forgetting the liberatory potential of the African American Church or of

Latin American Liberation Theology. But for the most part, *Christian*, like *American*, presents itself as a white man with female and child appendages. At its extreme, as in the Christian identity movement, Christianism merges with white supremacy.

Part of what gives this issue its distinct shape now—at home and around the globe—is the visibility of non-Christians other than Jews. As noted, Muslims are especially under scrutiny, and are widely confused with Arabs, even though surveys of ethnic origins of Muslims in the United States, as defined by regular participation in mosques, indicate that only 25 percent are Arab. The other 75 percent are made up of 33 percent South Asian (Pakistani, Indian, Bangladeshi, Afghani), 30 percent African American, with the remaining 12 percent divided among sub-Saharan African, European, White American, Southeast Asian (Malaysian, Indonesian, Filipino), Caribbean, Turkish, Iranian, and Hispanic/Latino.[85] The racialized Muslim–Arab–infidel blur makes it easy for the United States to wage war on Iraq; to support the Israelis who seem, through the lens of American foreign policy and the eyes of a biased media, moderate para-Western, if not Christian, at least Judeo-, engaged in (normative military) state violence compared with "fanatic suicide bombers." Palestinian religious and cultural diversity is invisible, even though some of the most celebrated Palestinian radicals are (at least were) Christian, such as the late Edward Said, or Arafat's rival for years within the PLO, George Habash, the leader of the Popular Front for the Liberation of Palestine. In this morass, Jewish Arabs are inconceivable.

What I want to note here is the way Muslim hypervisibility creates a tripartite structure of religions, in which Judaism is situated theologically between Christianity and other non-Christian faiths. Parallel to the transition from Europe/biracial to U.S./triracial, we can mark a transition in the United States from dominant Christianity with Jewish deviants, to the present, as immigration swells the ranks of those who are neither Christian nor Jews. While *Judeo-Christian civilization* is a nonsense phrase (since Christians have frequently tried to exterminate the Jews, it hardly represents a joint enterprise), nevertheless, when we factor in all those other faith communities, Jews lodge, again, in the middle: unchristian, yet with a unique prefiguring relationship to Christianity, absorbed into Judeo-Christian, disgorged again as anti-Christ.

You would think that monotheistic Islam, linked to both Judaism and Christianity and thus distinguished from polytheistic faiths such as Hinduism and Buddhism, would occupy a special rung on the hierarchical ladder. Christianity is bound to honor Judaism in order to honor its own origins, though its arrogant theology includes built-in dishonor, regarding Jews as stupidly, sinfully stopping short of the revelation that any decent human would have accepted. One might expect to find Islam a rung below Judaism but a rung above the polytheistic un-bible-based religions. Instead—and only racism/colonialism explains this—we find Islam confused in the Western mind with all the other "Oriental" faiths. The attacks of September 11th have shifted this somewhat, targeting Islam as particularly pernicious among the non-Western faiths, but emphasizing the anti-Christian essence of all those strange dark and dangerous people who hate god-fearing upright Americans.

Despite the extent and complexity of racial mixing in the United States, racial discourse there remains largely bipolar: there is Black and there is White. This binary is far stronger in the East than in the West, where Latinos, Asians and Native Americans are more numerous, more visible, and exercise more influence over the discourse of race and diversity. Still, to a great extent, race in the United States continues to be viewed reductively as two distinct opposites. We could speculate that one reason people clamor to know if Jews are or are not white is they want to understand where Jews fit in the Black–White scheme. Ironically, where Jews fit is often an act of displacement: Jewish replaces/protects White.

[2] BLACK/JEWISH IMAGINARY AND REAL

REAL 1: THE BLACK/JEWISH TANGLE

In attempting to escape the black/white binary in which so much racial discourse is mired, and to situate Jews appropriately in this discourse, I've suggested a tripartite racial scheme based on cultural stereotypes and gradations of privilege that exalt whiteness. But racial reality is not a tidy trinary either. To the extent that race has meaning, it reflects a complicated and intricate history of mixing, from rape to love; or, more abstractly, from distance and detachment to proximity, intimacy, and influence.

The large-scale immigration of Jews from Europe and the Ottoman Empire to the United States was closely followed in time by the Great Migration of African Americans northward.[1] Fleeing a shrinking pool of agricultural jobs and the circumscriptions of bigotry; seeking newly available industrial jobs and the promise of freedom, southern blacks often landed in Jewish neighborhoods. Over the years as many Jews vacated, Jews continued to own property and stores where African Americans resided and shopped. In the late 1960s, James Baldwin pointed out that the white people African Americans mostly encountered were cops, teachers, social workers, landlords and shopkeepers; all but the cops were often Jewish.[2]

"The special relationship"[3] has not been either simple or uniformly positive. Yes, African Americans and Jews worked together for racial justice in the labor movement, especially under the auspices of the Communist Party (CP); but all good communists did the same, as the issue ranked high on the CP agenda.[4] Yes, African Americans and Jews worked together in the civil rights movement; but Jews who went south for—say—Mississippi Freedom Summer numbered only a few hundred, hardly legions of allies. One might as readily characterize the relationship as frequently out of touch, periodically at odds, with both sides often failing to understand each other's point of view. African Americans are more likely to be focused elsewhere, while a fair number of Jews may be heard swearing that they understand how it is: *Weren't we slaves in Egypt? Haven't we suffered? Aren't we just like you?*

In addition, those Jews who are politically progressive may respond to African Americans they encounter—or wish to encounter—with a hunger for approval. In some circles, the presence of African Americans at a meeting or demonstration marks success or failure.

One example: In New York during the winter of 1994, Chinese Staff and Workers (CSWA) put out a call. Restaurant workers were on strike at Chinatown's Silver Palace and they needed to increase visibility and pressure. Jews for Racial and Economic Justice (JFREJ) responded, along with several other organizations. It was a vicious winter, but people showed up every Sunday to add our bodies to the picket line. This went on for months. Important alliances were built, and the workers finally won some concessions from the restaurant owners.[5] Yet throughout this time, there were JFREJ members calling up to chastise us, as though we had been waylaid by the wrong struggle. *Aren't you working with African Americans?* they'd ask incredulously, as though that were the sole measure of antiracist activity. When we'd explain the solidarity work we were doing, some callers would react with anger or wistfulness: *But don't you have any black-Jewish dialogue groups?* The complaining phoners couldn't see the struggle for racial and economic justice in front of their faces; nor did they notice that the clamor for dialogue groups was noticeably louder among Jews, while African Americans were much more apt to seek concrete action or relief.

African Americans and Jews *have* had a distinct relationship born of proximity, as people of the cities; of some powerful shared biblical tradition; and even (though we should not exaggerate likeness) as outsiders. Yet—for example—as leadership of the often idealized International Ladies Garment Workers Union (ILGWU) remained firmly in the hands of white, mostly Jewish men, the tales of discrimination against the union's increasingly female black and brown membership could turn your stomach. The stakes were high, including not only jobs and decision-making, but also subsidized housing; and the ILG leadership pumped considerable money into workers' housing, from which people of color were routinely excluded.[6]

"How could this happen in a union that is supposed to be so liberal?" asked one union member in the early 1980s. "The blacks, Hispanics, the Chinese are the workers. The dues come from these people, but the housing is all white and middle class. These were union pension funds."[7]

If discrimination and exclusion were not bad enough, spurious charges of anti-semitism were bandied about, in an attempt to evade the issue of racial discrimination.[8] As Herbert Hill points out, in the early 1990s, a period rife with African American-Jewish media-exacerbated tension, "the current conflict between the two groups was preceded by an older ongoing discord within the labor movement."[9]

Yet we would be off track should we flip too hurriedly into assumptions of apathy or hostility. One of many examples: in the United Auto Workers, leftist Jews supported a major attempt over a period of years to elect an African American to the UAW International Executive Board.[10] Even the charged history of African American women working as domestics for Jewish families has conflicting outcomes. On the one hand, those with class privilege who grew up being cared for by African American women (or other women of color) often expect that women of color are here on earth to tend to white people's needs.[11] On the other hand, it was a Jewish woman in Kansas—Esther Brown—who initiated *Brown vs. Topeka Board of Education*, the 1954 Supreme Court decision that outlawed segregated schools, because she "resented the fact that her housekeeper's children were receiving an inferior education. She persevered though harassment and threats, her husband losing his job and a cross being burned on their lawn."[12] Anecdotal evidence suggests that this story is hardly idiosyncratic.[13]

Transformative as such encounters—and the stories of such encounters —must be, they are entangled with issues more complicated than an occasional act of personal kindness or even of political commitment. When have we been allies and when have we failed? This chapter attempts from a number of directions to demythify a story girded in myth.

Mythology blocks clarity: You could almost say that's its job. The black–Jewish imaginary in the United States springs from a mostly Jewish-conjured, pre-conflict paradigm, a garden of Eden in which Jews and African Americans—primarily under the auspices of the ILGWU and other labor unions, the National Association for the Advancement of Colored People (NAACP), and the CP—lived together in beloved community. Didn't Rabbi Abraham Joshua Heschel march from Selma to Montgomery beside Dr. King? Didn't Dr. King call Heschel "my rabbi"? Indeed, rabbinical support for civil rights was such that in 1968 when King, about to speak at the Rabbinical Assembly of the Conservative movement, "entered the hall, he was greeted by 1,000 rabbis singing 'We Shall Overcome' in Hebrew."[14] From that golden age, the fall from grace, Black Power enforcing exile from the Civil Rights movement. Ocean Hill-Brownsville. Crown Heights. Jesse Jackson referring to New York as "Hymietown."[15] Louis Farrakhan calling Judaism a gutter religion. Accusations that Jews dominated the slave trade.[16]

Through all this, any negative incident got endlessly recycled in the media. The flip side of fantasized unconditional love is, of course, the assumption that African Americans are particularly anti-semitic;[17] while

Jews are especially racist. Or else Jewish liberals fantasize the rage of the oppressed, and swim in the gully of guilt and fear that accompanies privilege.[18] Chances are an African American hearing a Jew utter the words *Aren't we just like you* finds it ridiculous. Any African American walking around a shopping mall, or trying to secure a mortgage, or DWB (Driving While Black) on the New Jersey Turnpike; or worrying not only about the daughters out late but also the sons; these folks would tell you: being black and being Jewish are very different. . . .

But look what I've done linguistically, what we do constantly: assume that African Americans and Jews are absolute impenetrable opposites. Assume *black* means *not-Jewish* and *Jewish* means *not-black*. The alacrity with which African American/Jewish opposition is imagined results in a perpetual disappearing act, whereby those who are both black and Jewish become unimaginable. African American Jews in the popular imagination don't exist. Even when they announce themselves with a prayer book, a tallit, or other marks of Jewish practice, they will be subject to inquiry: "Are you Jewish?" Or else they are repeatedly reduced to the rarest of minorities, so tiny as to be insignificant. While I was working on this book, any time someone asked about the title, I braced myself to hear how they felt about Sammy Davis, Jr., or how they once knew a black Jew. Yet the same person might fail to notice in her/his own apartment building live two African American Jewish families, and who knows how many down the street or around the corner or for that matter in synagogue.

As Yavilah McCoy said, and it bears repeating, "It would make it easier to just 'BE' as a Jewish person of color if 'black' and 'Jewish' identity were not so commonly assumed to be mutually exclusive."[19]

The implication of a binary in which Jewish stands in for white, and black stands in for non-white, is presumed opposition, separation, distinction; the possibility of overlap is rarely raised. Katya Gibel Azoulay points to

> the prolific attention given to Black–Jewish *relations* which accentuates either group polarization or coalitions but remains silent on the personal fusions resulting from these relations. . . . In particular, in the United States, the union of Black and Jewish identities has been alternately neglected and negated in part because of the slippage of Jewishness into whiteness.[20]

Still, Jewish–African American conflict becomes much more complex if we recognize the estimated 200,000 people in the United States who are both Jewish and of African descent.[21] However we understand the racialization and deracialization of Ashkenazim, the struggle against racism shifts and opens differently as we absorb the fact that many Jewish sisters and brothers are by anyone's definition people of color. As Navonah, a graduate student and a Hebrew Israelite, said most eloquently, "If Jews of color and white Jews were working together to fight racism, this would change the way racism was fought."[22] We would begin to understand Jewish categories on their own terms and grasp—not shallowly but profoundly—the multiracial, multicultural nature of Jewish community.

REAL 2: AM I POSSIBLE?

YAVILAH MCCOY

I went to a Hasidic elementary school, and in my elementary school was where I learned the word shvartse . . . *I was told that it was just the Yiddish term for "black" but I knew it was a derogatory term because of the way it was used. (I sometimes ask friends today who make the same argument to think of the last three contexts in which they heard the term* shvartse *used and to determine whether any one of these contexts were flattering.) Early on, I noticed that my classmates feared the young men and women of color in our neighborhood because it was a routine practice for a group of girls I was walking with to cross to the other side of the street should they see a black person coming in our direction. I remember being angry on many occasions and even sometimes stubbornly walking forward alone, and rejoining my group at the next corner, to prove that there was nothing to fear, but inside, feeling like I was waging a losing battle against a myth that I could not change.*

Our school building was next door to a very large public high school, and at afternoon recess the girls would sit at the window and make fun of the kids coming out of the next door school, calling them "monkeys" and poking fun at their behavior. I remember one day asking in frustration for the group to stop their comments because it offended me, and getting back the reply from a classmate that I shouldn't be so sensitive because they weren't talking about me and my family but the shvartse. *"We don't mean you—we mean them." Hearing the racism that lurked in my classmate's comments and trying to make sense of how being a "Jew" was somehow supposed to inoculate me from the harshness of its presence was always a struggle. The hardest thing was knowing that racism had become a part of the culture that my parents had so trustingly come to in search of truth, and realizing that the admission of one, eight, or twenty people of dark skin to "the fold" of the community we lived in, had not changed any of the preconceived notions around race, that existed and were upheld by members of the community.*

More recently, people have suggested that with the growing numbers of people of color in the American Jewish community, racial prejudice must be on the decline. My answer has been that awareness of the presence of Jews of color is growing, yet, it continues to be a challenge. The small number of Jews of color living in various communities around the U.S., cannot, by presence alone, contradict the practice of "exceptionalism" in regard to uprooting racialized thinking. In the face of long-held prejudices, it is too easy to see and treat one or two Jews of color as exceptions to otherwise true negative rules regarding race and cultural stereotypes, and we must be willing to work on this subtle area of our thinking as well in order to eliminate racism from our communities. They don't have to reckon with their treatment of people who are dark-skinned who are not Jews. They just have to accept this new dark-skinned Jew. But *not marry that Jew.* But *not touch that Jew. I had kids cry in my classes . . . they would make us hold hands on trips, and kids would cry rather than touch my hand. They were afraid I would turn them black. There was very, very harsh racism.*

—Yavilah McCoy, interview

CAPERS FUNNYE

I was drawn to Judaism as a spiritual quest, a lack of spiritual fulfillment I found in other faiths. I tried on Islam for a while. But Judaism just seemed to fit my soul. Judaism is not just something folks are born into. Some, yes. But don't the kabbalists tell us that each human being has a spark and those sparks go into the world. They can go into any soul. Many people feel that when some people come to Judaism they were Jews already, they had a Jewish soul, a calling to Judaism. Julius Lester said that.[23] Many years after I converted to Judaism, became very much a practicing Jew, I started digging into my family's history. My mother's mother's name before she was married was Rosella Cohen. Her mother's name was Tamara Cohen. And her husband's name was Cesar Cohen. Is there a connection? I can't prove that definitively but the names suggest it.

From the black/Jewish perspective, Christianity was not the religion of choice of the greater majority of African Americans, particularly those whose ancestors had anything to do with the Middle Passage and the slave trade. Christianity was a faith system where the very people who were enslaving you were now going to give you God. And so for black Jews that just seemed an impossibility. The connection with Africa is that many of the African people who were transported through the Middle Passage to the Western Hemisphere were of Hebraic stock from the Ashanti and the Ibo of West Africa, who have distinct connections with Judaism in their past. The more we study the more we learn of these connections. So our return is a return to the worship of our forefathers, not necessarily trying to immolate or imitate Ashkenazi Jewry.

My wife and I first went to Africa in 2002 and it was interesting that everyone there could pronounce our name—FUNNYE. Everybody in Cameroon and in Nigeria said "Fu-nay." My wife looked at me and she said "Do you notice that they know how to say your name?"

So I asked the guide and he said this is a common name: It's Ofunnye in Nigeria.

I've been involved with the Jewish community since 1978–79 when my wife and I first enrolled our oldest daughter in Jewish dayschool in the nursery program. As Jews we were very opposed to having our children attend public school because although public school is not supposed to promote any religion in fact it does, particularly around Christmas holiday and Easter. In the black Jewish community there's vehement opposition to these holidays being foisted on our children.

Since many black Jews were converts to Judaism from Christianity they understood full well the significance of these Christian holidays and how they were infused into the school system. We did not want our children being confused. Once the children reached 6th grade they in fact did have to attend public schools. But I wrote letters and went to the school and talked with the teachers and met with the principal and let him know that these were days when my children would not be in school [the Jewish holidays] and that my children could not be forced to sing Christmas carols or to participate in Christmas plays or making Easter baskets. The principals and teachers, every year we developed that understanding.

And the children my children went to school with would ask, what did you do for Christmas, so a couple of teachers asked if I could come to class and explain Hanukkah to the children. So I'd do that from time to time. All of my children attended the school, and after three years or so I was invited to join the Board of Directors of the school and in another few years people asked me to run for Vice President of the Board. And then Chair of the principal selection committee and then the curriculum committee. . . .

So that was my entry into Jewish community. I also attended Spertus Institute for Jewish Studies to take some classes in Hebrew and that grew into two degrees and eventual employment with Spertus as business manager for several years. I did not imagine I would wind up becoming a rabbi.

—Rabbi Capers Funnye, interview

I don't know why I felt the attraction but I know it was there from a very young age. . . . In the early '70s Levy's Rye Bread had an ad campaign with head-shots of people of different cultural backgrounds taking a bite out of a piece of bread, with big smiles on their faces. The caption said, "You don't have to be Jewish to love Levy's!" The first ad I saw, in a subway station, had a little black boy. I remember seeing this ad, and the way I interpreted it was that you don't have to be white to be Jewish. That made me feel good for some reason. I actually felt relieved.

—Toni Eisendort, "An Ethiopian Gilgul"

I was born into law and I grew up to practice of the Old Testament observing the law. I would go to the temple and observe Rosh Hashanah, Hanukkah, Yom Kippur, Passover, all the high holy days. I grew up going to temple as part of my life. It's my faith, it's something I maintain and carry with me as a major part of who I am.

But I don't call myself Jewish. For two reasons. First, biblical. I was taught that white people were from the line of Esau and people of color from the line of Jacob. People at the temple referred to themselves and each other as Hebrew Israelites. There's a lot of Hebrew Israelites in Chicago who make more of a political interpretation of the bible: they offer classes, they talk about black Americans, especially. But I go to the temple to worship.

The term "Jew" I associate with white people. I have some conflicting emotions about that. If I say I'm not Jewish because Jewish people are white, it's as if I'm accepting that all Jewish people are white people. Yes, not all Jewish people are white people, I do know that, but at the same time the term "black Jews" doesn't work for me either because it seems to assert that Jewish people are "normally" white. You have these terms, these labels that other people give you, that don't quite work for you, and so you establish your own terms, and those terms are sometimes in reaction to terms that already exist.

My mother was a Hebrew Israelite—she is actually fluent in Hebrew. My father converted when he married my mother. My grandfather on my mother's side was a Hebrew Israelite, he came into law in his life-time, and he converted to Judaism. I think at one point he was Christian. He just wanted some kind of meaning with his faith and he wasn't getting that. So he decided to search for the faith that spoke to him. He did research and studied the bible and how it related to the African descendants.

My grandfather was dating my grandmother when he came into the law, and then she converted with him. Once they got married, they practiced, and then they taught their children. So their children were born and raised in law, as was I. I don't know if that was an issue for their families. I need to talk to my grandmother about this. I remember one conversation about how her sisters-in-law frowned upon her because she didn't come to family gatherings around Christmas—my grandparents honored conflicting holy days. But it wasn't like my grandmother's family disowned her. They just said, oh, that's what you want to do, okay. You're still our child.

In my school community, I didn't see many people of color who practice Judaism, but I found a community of Hebrew Israelites when I went to the temple. I'd see there were actually other people my age and of color who practiced Judaism. On high holy days, our temple had about fifty-one hundred people. For the Sabbath, more usual would be twenty-five, thirty. Growing up as a Hebrew Israelite, I didn't have any connections in my immediate community besides my siblings.

When you're a kid you hear about all these Christmas presents and your classmates phone and ask, what'd you get? When I was in 6th grade—I'll never forget this—a classmate of mine asked me what was I getting for Christmas, and I thought, let me see what will happen if I say I don't celebrate Christmas. That was the first time I said it. I don't celebrate Christmas. And she said, "Why?" And I said, "I celebrate something else." And she said, "What do you celebrate." "I celebrate Hanukkah." And she said, "Don't white people celebrate Hanukkah??"

"Black people celebrate Hanukkah too."

I would always be under scrutiny at my school because I didn't celebrate these highly normalized Christian holidays. For years I didn't talk about it. I would ask myself, why is it people don't know about this? When I got into high school my friends would talk about their holiday and what they were doing; or Ash Wednesday, they have to get something on their forehead. And they would ask me, why didn't you get anything on your forehead? I'd say, that's not what I practice; it's not what I believe.

By now I've made some peace with it. One thing about my decision not to mention anything about my spirituality, my practice of Judaism—it caused me to question myself. Why couldn't I just tell them, no, this is what I practice. Because I realized, maybe I'm afraid of what they would say if I told them. Also I don't always want to have to explain myself. Why should I have to?

I've always seen my faith as possibly interrupting alliances with other people of color because I haven't met a lot of people of color who practice Judaism or call themselves Hebrew Israelites. Sometimes it's really tough. Part of me says accept that Jewish people are supposed to be white and come to grips with being a Hebrew Israelite. Part of me consistently feels that my faith is too sacred to put into the political realm and debate about. I'm not going to give it to anyone to scrutinize or talk about.

White Jews are usually surprised when I say "I practice Judaism." It's like, "What? You do?" Why are they so shocked or so resistant to that thought? In the temple we would say that Jewish people are our cousins, Esau and Jacob again. But even in college I just didn't see any connection. One day I decided to *venture out with a friend who was also of color and a Hebrew Israelite. We went to a temple at my university, and there were a lot of white Jews. We felt very isolated and unwelcome. I would say we left within twenty minutes. That's partly why the numbers of Jews of color are so underestimated. They're not welcomed so they're not in Jewish institutions to get counted.*

It's not like I'm hostile toward white Jews, I don't want you to think that. The white Jewish people I speak to who know about other Jewish people of color are usually very open-minded. Open to telling me—for example—where I can buy a mezuzah. My advisor, who happens to be Jewish—I told her, I practice Judaism and I need to get a mezuzah. And she told me where to go. But when I went to the synagogue to buy the mezuzah, the people there looked so skeptical. They weren't cold, they just looked at me like they were mystified. Like I didn't belong there. I asked if this was a synagogue where I could purchase a mezuzah and they asked if I was lost. Like at Passover, when I eat my matzoh I'm so visible.

I'm constantly dealing with assumptions. My sister and I are working on strengthening our faith. But we also need to prob-lematize the terminology we use, and the representation of Jews. You don't see people of color on the matzoh boxes. If we could diversify the production of images and work on redefining our over-simplistic notion of what it means to be Jewish, then I think we'd be working towards something more accurate.

I would like people to understand that the Hebrew Israelite culture is complex. Once we recognize Judaism as multi-cultural, we could start building alliances. There's so much potential in understanding the multiculture that surrounds Judaism. And if Jews of color and white Jews were working together to fight racism, this would change the way racism was fought.

—Navonah (pseud.), interview

I was born in Ethiopia and grew up in Israel. I came to New York a few years ago and I was looking for an apartment in Brooklyn, in Boro Park [an Orthodox Jewish neighborhood]. First they spoke to my [white] Israeli friend and the apartment was available. As soon as they saw me, the apartment was no longer available. I think some of the Jewish communities need to open themselves to different Jews. They need to understand that Judaism is not only European, Judaism has different dimensions and different colors.

43

If you're Reform they might not consider you a Jew as well. But I don't think it's a religion thing. God never said hate anyone who doesn't look like you.

—Beejhy Barhany, interview

REBECCA WALKER
Courtesy David Fenton

Late one night during my first year at Yale, a WASP-looking Jewish student strolls into my room through the fire-exit door. He is drunk, and twirling a Swiss Army knife between his nimble, tennis-champion fingers. "Are you really black and Jewish?" he asks, slurring his words, pitching forward in an old raggedy armchair my roommate has covered with an equally raggedy white sheet. "How can that be possible?"

Maybe it is his drunkenness, or perhaps he is actually trying to see me, but this boy squints at me then, peering at my nose, my eyes, my hair. I stare back at him for a few moments, eyes flashing with rage, and then take the red knife from his tanned and tapered fingers. As he clutches at the air above him, I hold it back and tell him in a voice I want him to be sure is black that I think he'd better go.

But after he leaves through the (still) unlocked exit door, I sit for quite a while in the dark.

Am I possible?

—Rebecca Walker, *Black, White, and Jewish*

Jews of African descent include children of mixed parentage, like writer Rebecca Walker whose Jewish white father and African American Christian mother (writer Alice Walker) married in the civil rights movement, or journalist Robin Washington, also a civil rights baby, who founded the African American Jewish Alliance in Chicago in 1995. It is estimated that some twenty to thirty thousand African American Jewish children, now adults in their twenties and thirties, were born from "civil rights marriages."[24] There are also Beta Israel such as Beejhy Barhany, who went from Ethiopia to Israel to Harlem. There are those mysteriously drawn to Judaism as children, like Toni Eisendorf or writer Carolivia Herron.[25] There are children of parents, even grandparents, who chose Judaism, like graduate student Navonah, maintaining her practice of Judaism in harsh lonely conditions. Multicultural educator Yavilah McCoy is raising a fourth generation of Jews, herself raised Orthodox in Crown Heights, an imagined locus of unbridgeable division.

As the rate of racial intermarriage continues to rise, it seems, anec-dotally, that a disproportionate number of the white people in racial intermarriages are white Jews marrying non-Jews of African descent. A Teachers College study conducted in 1960—i.e., pre-mass civil rights activ-ity in the North—suggests this, at least in New York.[26] In the North, African and Jewish Americans met not only through individual encounters, but also through political engagement; two of the very few integrated institu-tions in the United States in the 1920s to the 1950s were the NAACP and the Communist Party, in which African Americans and Jews participated in large numbers. People met, fell in love, married and had children. The generation of the 1960s and '70s repeated and increased this pat-tern, in the civil rights movement and in colleges where Jews and African Americans met and socialized. In the Peace Corps, in study abroad, and with the new influx of immigrants, the "color" of the U.S. Jewish commu-nity has deepened, by anyone's measure. One study found that 59 percent of Americans born to white wives in interracial marriages are likely to be Jewish;[27] another, that one-third of whites in New York City who were mar-ried to or sexually intimate with African Americans were Jewish, mostly Jewish women.[28]

At the same time one suspects that this is the very group—in New York, at any rate—least likely to affiliate religiously. In the same Teachers' College study, "the majority of couples reported no religious affiliation."[29] Some of those leftist, civil rights, and union babies were born to secular parents who rejected religion. Some were born into Jewish families or communities that rejected the black parent and the children born of these unions, or, as in Rebecca Walker's case, alienated the grandchild through their racism. But questions remain: Does the new generation of African American Jews reject their Jewishness altogether? Do they reject the reli-gion but maintain a secular Jewish identity? Or, as Gibel Azoulay recalls, though her own family identified strongly as both black and Jewish, other such families she knew in the 1960s

> de-emphasized their commitment to the Jewish community pre-cisely because the Jewish parents refused to accept the marriage. The contradiction between their parents' behavior and the lib-eral tenets of Jewish ethics motivated the couples to sever ties altogether rather than finding alternative contexts in which to reconcile this gap.[30]

Yavilah McCoy likewise reports growing up among other African American-Jewish families, most of whom didn't stay connected to Jewishness. James

McBride wrote in *The Color of Water* about his mother Rachel, who left her rejecting father and Judaism for the welcoming community of an African American church. Hettie Jones, wife to Amiri Baraka (the former LeRoi Jones), was rejected by her parents, and raised her two (African American–Jewish) girls in the embrace of her ex-husband's family.[31]

But the story of African American Jews did not begin yesterday or even in the 1960s. In 1896, in Lawrence, Kansas, William S. Crowdy founded the Church of God and Saints of Christ, preaching "a heterodox version of Judaism based upon his assertion that black people were descended from the ten lost tribes of Israel."[32] By 1919–1931, "there are records of at least eight Black Jewish cults [*sic*] that originated in Harlem."[33] The literature provides vigorous and inconclusive debate about numbers—and about what those numbers represent. Some congregations identify only as Jewish, some mix with Christian elements; some connect with white Jewish congregations, some say black Jews are the only true Jews.[34] Some carefully keep kosher (some define kosher uniquely; e.g., no frankfurters), observing *shabat* and all Jewish holidays.[35] The Israelite Board of Rabbis identifies six member congregations,[36] but additional black Jewish congregations worship all over the United States and Africa—North Africa, Ethiopia, Uganda, Nigeria, Ghana, and Kenya, all have Jewish communities, some ancient, some newer but with ancient heritage.[37] In 2006, Nigeria alone had at least thirty congregations.[38]

In addition to observant Jews who are black, and blacks who observe Judaism (and I have no interest here in jumping in with the rabbis to decide who is and isn't really a Jew),[39] there are those who simply have a Jewish mother, which makes them halakhically/by Jewish law Jewish; or a Jewish father, which may make them Jewish by family, practice, or culture.

On the cover of the catalog for the first exhibition ever of African American art at the Metropolitan Museum of Art in New York (1976) is a painting by Jules Lion (himself the child of a white father and African American mother), a portrait of a German Jew (Ashur Moses Nathan, 1784–1862) with his mixed race legally adopted son Achille. Graenum Berger comments, "Dr. Regina A. Perry, the first black woman in America to hold a doctorate in art history, who organized the exhibition said 'It's the first painting known to American art history in which a white man openly displays affection for his black child.'"[40] Berger continues, "But the evidence is clear that neither the mother nor the children ever became Jews."

How clear? By mid-nineteenth century there were already many ways of being Jewish. Moreover, a child born to a Jewish parent might not at a given moment observe or even identify Jewishly, but might, over time, change. And if not the child, perhaps the grandchild.

IMAGINARY 1: EXODUS

Jewish and African Americans have carried heavy symbolic weight for each other, not just in the recent past but back many decades:

> As early as 1900, Negro preachers were traveling through the Carolinas, preaching the doctrine that the so-called Negroes were really the lost sheep of the House of Israel. There is no reason to think, however, that such reflections did not begin much earlier, in fact during slavery itself. . . . In 1800, a well-planned insurrection of slaves, under the leadership of a slave named Gabriel, was discovered near Richmond, Virginia. Franklin Frazier's account of this event notes that Gabriel . . . made use of the Bible to impress upon the Negroes that they as the Israelites could throw off the yoke of slavery and that God would come to their aid.[41]

Everywhere one looks in the language of bondswomen and men, and of the freed Africans, Exodus looms:[42] the story of the Jews, God's chosen people, and of the emancipation that would come in the promised land— the North more often than Africa. Moses was Harriet Tubman's nom-de-guerre. Nationalist Marcus Garvey was often referred to as "Black Moses."[43] Self-identified black Jew Arnold Ford tried (without success) to persuade Garvey to adopt Judaism as the religion of African Americans.[44] Early Pan-Africanist Edward Wilmot Blyden, "one of the very few black thinkers 'to make a significant impact on the English-speaking literary and scholastic world in the nineteenth century,'"[45] published a pamphlet called *The Jewish Question* in which, far from trashing Jews (as such titles usually portend), he examined Jewish history, calling Zionism "that marvelous movement."[46] Carolivia Herron, African American Jew by choice, writes of feeling thrilled at a very young age by the possibility that her neighborhood butcher was a Jew because she thought Jews and Hebrews were the same and "If Hebrews exist somewhere they must be far away with Moses, getting free."[47]

Finding parallels is one thing. Watching a supposed opposition flip at times into a double identity, a both/and, is something else. The theme of the black Jew, the Jewish black, emerges early. Were some of the slaves owned by Jews converted to Judaism? What of African Americans who saw in Judaism a religion that felt true and right and chose to follow it, or to reconstruct? or invent? a history in which it was always theirs?

Theories of origin include the original Jews, the lost tribe, the Ethiopians or Abyssinians. According to Harold Brotz, one theory "somewhat suggested by the fact that so many . . . [black Jews] were from the West Indies, is that they were descendants of slaves of Sephardic Jewish slaveholders in the West Indies."[48] But this point is contentious. Brotz argues that Jewish slaveholders "in fact . . . did not Judaize [convert to Judaism] their slaves."[49] Likewise, Graenum Berger explains that Southern Jews did not try to convert their slaves because a Jewish slave could not then be sold to gentiles or made to work on the sabbath,[50] and points to explicit rules disseminated by a [Jewish] congregation in Charleston, South Carolina about accepting proselytes, "provided he, she, or they, are not people of color."

On the other hand,

> According to the astute black historian C. L. R. James, in the islands the great majority of Jews treated their slaves in accordance with the fundamentals of biblical law. . . . James states that "Except for the Jews, who spared no energy in making Israelites of their slaves, the majority of the colonists religiously kept all instructions, religious or otherwise, away from their slaves."[51]

In other words: the subject needs more research. But listen to the following story of burial, resonating with the story I told earlier of the mixed race baby whose body was almost dug up by the church deacons.

> It is not known whether Lucy Marks, a member of the congregation Mikveh Israel [in Philadelphia], was the descendant of one of the black Jews who came up to the islands or was a former slave of Rachel Marks. She was a devout observer of the precepts of Judaism. . . . In the prominent Marks family, in whose household Lucy lived, she was an accepted member. Upon her death, the Marks family applied for a customary permit for burial in the historical colonial Spruce Street Cemetery. This was in accordance with congregational practice, which entitled Lucy to a place in the burying yard, providing that her induction into Judaism met with rabbinic dicta. Horrified that a black woman would lie eternally in consecrated ground among the old Jewish aristocracy, a number of members protested. But the Marks family and their supporters were successful in providing a Jewish burial for Lucy.[52]

IMAGINARY 2: MEDIA COVERAGE

If many people of African descent saw their own story writ large in Jewish texts, Jewish American culture in the early twentieth century was relatively obsessed with African Americans. Certainly every generation of progressives has found some Jews (and other whites) imitating African American culture, longing to "get down with the people." As hard evidence of Jewish focus, historian Hasia Diner details mountains of coverage between 1915–1935 from both the Yiddish and the Jewish English-language press about African American issues.[53] The Jewish English language press covered almost nothing that was not specifically Jewish—*except* for African American issues; while the Yiddish press, covering a much broader scope for its Yiddish-literate readership,[54] paid virtually no attention to other ethnic or racial communities, again with this single exception. Both English and Yiddish papers offered considerable coverage of African American synagogues in Harlem.[55]

As with the better-known Jewish involvement with the civil rights movement of the sixties, it is the disproportionate engagement of Jewish journalism with African American news that strikes us. The surprise is how far back dates this sense among many Jews that the experience of African Americans was relevant to their own. Yet why should we be surprised? Leo Frank, an Atlanta factory owner and a Jew, charged with the murder of a white Christian woman, was lynched in Atlanta in 1915. Fredric Jameson finds the connection in

> more primary experience, namely that of fear and of vulnerability.
> . . . this experience of fear in all its radicality . . . is surely the very
> "moment of truth" of ghetto life itself . . . : the helplessness of the
> village community before the perpetual and unpredictable immi-
> nence of the lynching or the pogrom, the race riot.[56]

I would argue that whatever its source, its "moment of truth"—and I assume there are multiple moments and complex truths—Jewish identification with at least some aspects of African American experience did not demand much of a stretch.

Diner is clear that this Jewish preoccupation reveals more about Jewish issues than about black experience, and her analysis posits an explanation that is part ethics, part displacement. Through attention to the issues confronting African Americans, Jews could express their own anxiety about discrimination, discuss racism without calling attention to anti-semitism, and explore this new society with its promises, lies, and confusions. Diner's discussion asks, essentially, why do Jews focus on African Americans?[57] She does not explain Jewish attention to black concerns as due to Jewish virtue or a Jewish antiracist gene. Instead, she argues,

> Jewish ends were served by involvement with blacks. . . . For Jewish leaders in the early twentieth century, the issues of black America provided an attractive and appropriate forum to adapt and blend their cultural heritage with contemporary realities.[58] [For example, i]t was thus with more than empathy that the American Jewish periodicals reported on the expulsion of Roscoe Conklin Bruce, son of Mississippi's black reconstruction senator, from Harvard's Dormitories in 1923,[59]

resonating as it did with recent quotas imposed on Jewish applicants. Similarly, both the Yiddish and English Jewish press widely reported race riots, describing them frequently as pogroms; St. Louis, after the 1917 riots there, was referred to as Kishinev.[60] The *Forverts*, socialist and anti-Zionist, even-handedly reflected its antinationalist politics in opposition to African American nationalism, while the Zionist *Tageblatt* and *Morgen* with equal consistency favored nationalist politics, for Jews and blacks alike.[61]

Even in 1934–35, when black Harlem residents organized against Harlem's Jewish merchants, and Jewish nerves were rubbed raw by the rise of Nazism in Germany, the Yiddish press bent over backwards to distinguish the boycott leader (referred to as the "Black Hitler") from the masses of Harlem residents, and refused to interpret even the riots as anti-semitic.[62]

That Jewish papers covered black news as it spoke to their Jewishness is evident noticeably in the coverage of the Jewish English language publications, which

> never discussed discrimination against blacks in its most constant forms. No discussions of segregated streetcars, segregated public facilities, or political disenfranchisement graced the pages of these magazines. Those particular issues did not link up to the problems Jews themselves were facing.[63]

At the same time, during this period, the Arbeter Ring/Workmen's Circle, a Yiddishist mutual aid society

> refused to become chartered in seven southern states because the incorporation papers stated that membership must be limited to whites. It was not that they wanted, or even expected, blacks to

join the Arbeter Ring, but they did not want to sanction racism in
even the most minor way.[64]

It was the largely Jewish socialist ILGWU and, to a lesser extent, the
Amalgamated Clothing Workers of America, that deliberately sought to
organize African Americans, whether on the job or sent in during a strike
as scabs: this at a time when African American workers desperate for jobs
were frequently brought in as strike breakers. As noted above, as the garment industry's constituency shifted to comprise mostly women of color,
while the leadership remained mostly white, Jewish and male, the story of
the union is less inspiring, but should not obfuscate the earlier achievement, almost alone in acting on the understanding that African Americans
situated as scabs were also workers.

Indeed, Diner's chapter on "Our Exploited Negro Brothers" is a virtual
love fest between African and Jewish American labor luminaries such as
A. Philip Randoph, Sidney Hillman, the Harlem Labor Committee, and
others, including ILGWU leader Rose "Bread and Roses" Schneiderman,
who insisted that Local 62, the Undergarment Workers, hold meetings in
English instead of Yiddish, so that African American women workers could
participate.[65]

Diner identifies five themes that dominate Jewish press coverage
of African Americans: oppression and racism (always very sympathetic
and outraged), criminality (explained in terms of economics), African
American achievement and heroism; Jewish and African American relationships; and African Americans as the American Jews. Racism among
Jews was explained as economic and shameful. Anti-semitism among blacks
was barely cited, but also explained as economic—not really anti-semitism
but resentment of shopkeepers and landlords. Diner's analysis allows us to
see how the fates of the two people—those who were slaves in Egypt and
in the American South, those led to freedom by Moses, those who were
hated by the Klan—were perceived by at least some Jews as intertwined.
Jewish-African American conflict or collaboration tends to symbolize the
possibility—or impossibility—of alliance across lines of race.

IMAGINARY 3: MEDIA HYPE

For the half-century beginning in 1915 (the year Leo Frank was
lynched and Booker T. Washington died)[66] there thrived a presumption of
Jewish and African American alliance and affinity around a common left-
of-center politic. We can link the end of that assumption to the late 1960s

and the rise of nationalism, a point to which I'll return: Black nationalism, often linked with Afrocentrism, on one hand, and Zionism on the other. The time is 1967–68, the Six Day War and Ocean Hill-Brownsville.[67]

I think I can assume bare-bones knowledge of the Six Day War, but Ocean Hill-Brownsville? In New York (and New York is certainly the paradigmatic center of African American–Jewish interaction), Ocean Hill-Brownsville has become code for the split between two communities previously seen, or imagined, as allies. Those fighting for community control of the schools, a city-wide initiative in response to parents disturbed at what was happening to their children's schools, clashed with the United Federation of Teachers (UFT) over the power to hire and fire. Ocean Hill-Brownsville is a predominantly African American district in Brooklyn. The UFT, with a mostly white membership, many of whom were Jews, many of whom feared they would lose their jobs, called a city-wide strike. Some UFT members, including Jewish and non-Jewish whites, crossed the picket line, an excruciating choice for many between the union and racial justice. Perhaps some Jews of color were also UFT members; perhaps some parents of color were also Jews.

The strike and the conflict lasted for months. Antagonism and betrayal stored up over the years exploded, exposing the rifts between the two communities. *Ocean Hill-Brownsville* as shorthand can evoke deep bitter feelings to this day among New Yorkers who lived through it.

This earlier presumption of alliance and linkage has since the late 1960s up through the 1990s been displaced by a contradictory axiom of discord and antagonism between the two communities. The predominant assumption now is that African American politics remain mostly progressive, explicitly pro-Palestinian and *therefore* anti-Jewish, while Jewish politics are seen as shifting ever rightward, obsessively focused on Israel, inherently anti-Palestinian, and, at best, indifferent to issues of racism because they—Jews—are not under siege. Similarly, a casual assumption has dominated popular culture and media, as well as academia: the idea that African Americans are especially anti-semitic, more so than, say, white Christians; and that Jews are uniquely racist, more so than non-Jewish whites. Bolstering this assumption, we find an unnuanced knee-jerk identity politics. Popular media seem unable to locate any African American or Jew who thinks outside the box, thus reinforcing an unvoiced premise that the two communities are inherently disconnected, as opposite as possible.

Here is an example of how the media can massage African American–Jewish antagonism into The Truth. Albert Raby, who died in 1988, was the organizer who brought Dr. King to Chicago; who ran Harold Washington's successful campaign in which Jews and African Americans worked together to elect Chicago's first black mayor; who co-chaired a group of African Americans and Jews formed to deal with conflict between their communities. Albert Raby was an important man in the history of African American struggle, of Chicago, of black–Jewish relations, and hardly anyone outside Chicago has heard of him. Yet even while he was alive and helping to make history, he was nearly invisible at a time when Louis Farrakhan was commanding headlines.

How has this played out in public life? In 1992, Johnnetta Cole, then president of Spelman College, a historically black women's college in Atlanta, was being considered for a position in the Clinton cabinet. Dr. Cole's African American identity, coupled with her connection with Cuban solidarity groups, and her sympathy with Palestinian aspirations, triggered an alarm for the Jewish establishment, as if these automatically proved that she was bad for the Jews. The tiniest bit of probing would have revealed exactly the opposite: Dr. Cole had worked closely with the Atlanta Jewish community, by whom she was much beloved.[68] In fact, Dr. Cole was withdrawn from consideration not because of Jewish opposition, but because she was widely seen as too radical.

Andrew Young, as Ambassador to the United Nations, dared to meet with representatives of the PLO and was forced to resign. For years, Young and Cole continued to be cited as proof that Jewish power undermines African American aspiration.

More recently, Georgia State Representative Cynthia McKinney was defeated by a vicious nationally financed campaign, because she had been outspoken in criticizing Israeli policy and calling for cuts in U.S. aid. That such evidence is taken as "anti-Jewish" is common enough slippage in this historical period, but extra suspicion rests on the assumption that progressive African Americans are especially anti-semitic. Yet according to African American historian Marshall Stevenson, Jr., "anti-semitism has never been as strong among blacks as among the mutual enemies of blacks and Jews."[69]

Media, more interested in sound bytes than in accuracy, have played an extremely destructive role in recycling and strengthening these assumptions. Cooperation is no longer newsworthy, and what dominates the shallow present is hype. Jewish and African American media, as well as the mainstream outlets, headline and exaggerate points of tension as a way to increase sales.

Take Crown Heights, Brooklyn, summer 1991, headlined as one more instance of black–Jewish conflict. A black child accidentally killed by a Jew;

a Jew killed by a black mob. Are we even? Is this inevitable? But the story is knotted with complexity. Gavin Cato, a Caribbean American child, was killed by a car driven by a member of the ultra-Orthodox Lubavitchers.[70] Yankel Rosenbaum, a Hasidic rabbinical student, was killed by a mob shouting "Kill the Jew." The media unanimously erased the specificity of an unusual neighborhood, two distinct communities living side by side: mostly Caribbean—including middle-class, middle-aged homeowners, long-term residents with children in college, as well as a more recent younger and poorer immigrant community; and a smaller, ultra-Orthodox separatist community of Jews. Despite its uniqueness, "Crown Heights" was repeatedly invoked as *the* black–Jewish paradigm: fanatic, clannish Jews attacked by rioting, uncontrolled blacks. Only enraged, polarizing voices were sought and reported. Hardly anyone noted that Yankel Rosenbaum, stabbed during the riots, died in the emergency room of a New York City hospital because he did not receive prompt, competent care. Crown Heights was also an untold story about inadequate services and terror for both African Americans and Jews.

Yet the Jewish and African American narratives of Crown Heights have rarely been synchronized.

1998: I am teaching at Brooklyn College, and give a lecture on Jews and whiteness. I talk about Crown Heights. During Q & A, a man, clearly a faculty member, white, wearing a yarmulke, raises his hand.

"In Crown Heights in 1991 blacks weren't cowering in their homes for days."

Shannon Short, one of my students, raises her hand, a young African American. She's so nervous her voice shakes and I have to ask her to speak a little louder.

"I live in Crown Heights and we were scared," Shannon says. "My mother wouldn't let us go outside for three days. Everyone was scared. People put signs in their window, like to signify black or Jewish."

"Nonsense," says the Jewish professor.

Nonsense? I'm so shocked I say mildly, "I want to point out that you've just denied someone else's experience," but another of my students, Jumaane Williams, child of civil rights activists, is way ahead, on his feet. "See," he says calmly, "you're speaking from a place of privilege . . ."

The professor interrupts, yelling at Jumaane with uncontrolled scorn. Chaos erupts. I'm shouting from the front, trying to restore order, until Leslie, my organizer girlfriend, yells to me to take the mike. With the mike it's easy to shut him up, but then he leaves, claiming a prior engagement.

For the rest of the discussion, people keep talking about how the professor spoke to Shannon with such disrespect, how he just walked out. What most stunned people was his arrogance.

At our next class this group, which has experienced its own, never acknowledged, racial divide, is united in anger at the professor's disrespectful treatment of our Shannon. Even Larry, my unregenerate reader of the right-wing *Jewish Week*, who refuses to clip articles from the *New York Times* because it's too liberal, keeps repeating, "What hurt me is his talking like that to Shannon, because I know Shannon would never lie."

How many Jewish college students—or professors—have had the opportunity to hear, or the will to listen to, Crown Heights from an African American perspective? Anna Deveare Smith's *Fire in the Mirror* tried to bring together Jewish and African American voices to tell the story of Crown Heights, but what emerges is a montage, not a coherent narrative.

Similarly, Freddy's Records, a popular African-owned shop in Harlem, 1996. Freddy's was being evicted by a Jewish store in which it rented space. Protests in support of Freddy's included some anti-semitic content. Most horribly, an African American man shot into and firebombed the Jewish-owned store, killing eight people including himself. Media treated this as "yet another black–Jewish incident," ignoring the following complexities:

- The motivation for eviction was a steep rent increase for the Jewish store levied by the African American church that owned the building.

- Most of the store's employees, and thus most of the victims of the violence, were people of color.

- The employees, along with the store owner, fearing the potential for violence, had repeatedly sought police protection, which was not provided.

• Finally, the killer, a former street vendor, had been pushed over the edge by a ban on street vending from New York's now lionized mayor, white, non-Jewish (though frequently sporting a yarmulke as a kiss-up to conservative Jews), Rudy Giuliani.[71]

Ocean Hill-Brownsville, Johnnetta Cole, Crown Heights, Freddy's—a few of many possible examples—are invoked and reinvoked as proof of inevitable African American–Jewish hostility; used, reduced, distorted to stigmatize Jews as superpowerful, controlling, racist exploiters, or African Americans as irrational, bitter, dangerous, anti-semitic losers.

Yet any of these incidents can be fleshed out or deconstructed to reveal greater complexity, obscured class issues, and—in most cases— many people from both communities working very hard across lines of race and culture to promote justice and harmony. Even at the peak of actual conflict, the Brooklyn Women's Coalition in Crown Heights continued to meet, including African Americans and Caribbean Americans, secular Jews, and Lubavitch women. Even the teenage boys were playing basketball together, and a black-Jewish rap group performed inside and outside the community.[72]

Marshall Stevenson has remarked that the violent explosions of New York have mostly not occurred in other cities.[73] What did occur in several cities was the formation of African American–Jewish coalitions (I know of Seattle, Philadelphia, and St. Louis) and women's dialogue groups (I know of New York and Pittsburgh)—and campus after campus bringing together students and speakers of Jewish and African descent.

What is this exaggeration and fondling and repetition of conflict about? Why in a complex multiracial society in which most marginalized groups are at odds with one another, do we even talk about *Jewish–black conflict* as something unique? Because harping on conflict disrupts and— to coin a word—*impossiblizes* alliance across racial/quasi-nationalist lines. Not for nothing did German Socialist August Bebel dub anti-semitism "the socialism of fools." The odd hyperemphasis encodes class struggle and urban chaos in racial/cultural terms, similar to the Apartheid scheme sketched above. African Americans, scapegoated for crime and urban violence; Jews scapegoated for the ravages of capitalism, identified as the ones who make, steal, and spend all that money while decent Christians lose their jobs, as the eggheads and elitists who design social welfare policies that hard-working whites pay for. By substituting Jews for wealth and blacks for poverty—by racializing wealth and poverty—the structures of wealth and poverty are obscured and thus protected. From both angles, the subtextual message flashes neon: *Successful alliance across racial lines is impossible. Don't Bother.*

REAL 3: SOLIDARITY

Without valorizing African Americans as braver and more ethical than other people, and without idealizing the Jewish people as antiracist warriors, let me return to significant historical instances of cooperation, solidarity, and victory. In the 1920s, 1930s, and 1940s, in the NAACP and the Communist Party-USA, as noted above, African Americans and Jews worked together to combat racism, to organize as workers and as consumers. (It bears mentioning that the NAACP was not always thrilled by this proximity to the Party.) They worked together in the early 1930s to defend the Scottsboro boys, nine African American Alabama youths, ages thirteen to twenty-one, charged with raping two white women in a case that was enormously important—in the African American community and in building racially integrated activism inside and outside the CP. They worked together to elect African American communist Ben Davis to the New York City Council.[74] As Nazi power manifested, it was an African American newspaper—the *Pittsburgh Courier*—that first called for a boycott of German goods. In the Civil Rights movement of the early sixties, (presumably white) Jews—less than 3 percent of the population—comprised more than half the white Freedom Riders, nearly two-thirds of the white Mississippi Freedom Summer volunteers.[75] Given that many young Jews did not participate through Jewish organizations and were probably not counted as Jews, actual Jewish participation was probably even much higher.[76] Not that the Jewish people en masse worked for civil rights; it's the lack of participation by other whites that make Jewish percentages loom so large. But Jews did contribute numbers that had an impact not only on the struggle but on that whole generation of Jews who participated, and on their children, a fair number of whom are Jewish and African American.

In 1999 Amadou Diallo, an unarmed young African immigrant was gunned down in the entrance to his apartment building by four New York City cops who fired a total of forty-one bullets. In a time when not much was happening in the streets, the waves of coordinated protests, launched by Reverend Al Sharpton's National Action Network, were astonishing. Over a two-week period, more than 1,200 New Yorkers participated in civil disobedience at New York City's Police Headquarters. Among the protesters, an explicitly Jewish contingent of more than 120 was organized by Jews for Racial and Economic Justice, in addition to the many Jews who got arrested with their neighborhood or union, as queers or as students, without getting counted as Jews, including Carolyn Goodman, whose son Andrew was one of the three civil rights workers killed in Mississippi during the summer of 1964.[77]

On every social justice issue, one continues to find a predictably high level of participation by African Americans and Jews. In an article claiming "Jewish–Black Ties Loosen Over Years," Rachel Pomerance quotes Rabbi David Saperstein, director of the Reform movement's Religious Action Center, and a member of the board of the NAACP, "There isn't a day that goes by that the Black and Jewish caucuses on Capitol Hill don't work together." Pomerance continues, "According to Saperstein, collaboration among blacks and Jews is strong across the country, and his own group's black–Jewish activities are as robust as he can remember."[78] Based on some of her sources, Pomerance might well have titled her article "Jews and Blacks Still Connected." But information about positive connection, cooperation, solidarity is not treated as newsworthy; somehow it is not seen as either black or Jewish, as if we are only black or Jewish when we are at odds.

Nationalists from both communities often belittle this history of cooperation. African American nationalists sometimes view it as a story of debilitating paternalism, and read Jews as one more untrustworthy group of whites. Jewish nationalists dismiss the civil rights experience with hurt feelings at "their ingratitude" (a sentiment I have noticed expressed most commonly by people who did not themselves actually participate in the movement) and hunker down into "we made it, why can't they," citing racist theories of inferiority about why "it didn't work."

Progressives in an identity-focused period always struggle with contradictory impulses: the desire to gather, concentrate, and represent one's own community vs. the need to work with others across differences, boundaries of race, class, gender, culture. Imagine the possibilities of groups that do not divide along identity lines because they are intrinsically bi- or multi-identified, with all the subtlety and nuances multiple experience can afford. Imagine the possibilities of conversations that include and express the perspectives of those who are both Jewish and black, conversations about economic and social crises, about race relations, even about the Middle Passage / Slavery and the Holocaust. African-Anglo scholar Paul Gilroy, while careful "to resist that idea that the Holocaust is merely another instance of genocide . . . [comments,]

There are a number of issues raised by literature on the Holocaust which have helped me to focus my own inquiries into the uncomfortable location of blacks within modernity. However, it seems appropriate to ask at this point why so many blacks and Jews have been reluctant about initiating such a conversation.[79]

Perhaps one reason why such cross-cultural discussion might make Jews anxious is that we are so accustomed to identifying with our victimhood. One of our grand defenses is uniqueness. Our diaspora. Our genocide. Our religion. The chosen chosen chosen.

From 1967, the words of the late James Baldwin echo timely as ever:

A genuinely candid confrontation between Negroes [*sic*] and American Jews would certainly prove of inestimable value. But the aspirations of the country are wretchedly middle-class and the middle class can never afford candor.[80]

How do we mobilize candor? How long is the list of conversations that need to happen?

How do we jump start the conversations—not as pure talk, dialogue without legs—but as vehicles for change? Gilroy again suggests

the concept of diaspora can itself provide an underutilised [*sic*] device with which to explore the fragmentary relationship between blacks and Jews and the difficult political questions to which it plays host: the status of ethnic identity, the power of cultural nationalism, and the manner in which carefully preserved social histories of ethnocidal suffering can function to supply ethical and political legitimacy. These issues are inherent in both the Israeli political situation and the practices of the Africentric [*sic*] movement.[81]

Imagine the impact of a multiracial Jewish council, community group, city-wide coalition, with members rooted in different locations. People of Color. Atheists. Orthodox. Reconstructionists. Children and grandchildren of communists and civil rights workers. Children and grandchildren of Holocaust survivors. Those who hail from Sepharad, from Mizrahim, from Ashkenaz. From B'nai Jeshurun, one of New York's oldest and most progressive synagogues. From the Commandment Keepers, New York City's largest African American Jewish congregation.[82]

Not that there aren't obstacles. Some people refuse to recognize multiple identities. Jewish Conservative and Orthodox leadership still won't permit ordination for open queers; Orthodox leadership still refuses to ordain women. Many traditional synagogues reject the Commandment Keepers and other Israelite congregations. Some Orthodox black Jews feel more connected to other coreligionists of whatever race than to Christian or Muslim blacks. Some children of African American–Jewish parents don't feel connected to their Jewish side, and see themselves as mixed black–white.[83] Many light-skinned Jews feel disconnected from their Jewishness, and see themselves only as white.[84]

Not to mention—while I'm listing obstacles—garden variety racism and anti-semitism.

Even so: the conversations would encourage an exploration of complexity, multiplicity; would discourage easy polarizing assumptions that prompt us to "stick to our own kind," for we discover our own kind all over the globe.

REAL 4: NATIONALISM AND FEMINISM

Identity. Our own kind. A concept hauntingly beautiful and potentially deadly. And a little weird, once you think about it, for nationalism taken literally, as in the nation state, or more broadly, as in separatism, glosses over all other differences among "our own kind"; and does so purposely. A fervor of brotherhood can obscure class difference, for example. In a similar vein, Gerald Horne argues persuasively that anticommunism "created favorable conditions for the rise of narrow nationalism and xenophobia in both the African American and Jewish communities; it is this dual narrow nationalism that has led directly to the present crisis in race relations generally, and in black–Jewish relations particularly."[85]

Another of those differences glossed over by nationalism is gender. As Cynthia Enloe has observed, "Nationalism typically has sprung from masculinized memory, masculinized humiliation, and masculinized hope."[86] The rhetoric surrounding liberation struggles evokes the male defending the honor of his woman or his nation (usually the motherland) against the would-be rapist. Of course women have participated in liberation struggles, but this participation, when acknowledged, is most often depicted as brave but tragically, aberrationally imposed by the exigencies of history. The desired outcome is triumph over the enemy so the little lady can zip back home (or at least back to the file cabinet or coffee maker) where she belongs.

As feminist sociologist Saraswati Sunindyo has pointed out, "Nationalism thrives on crisis."[87] Often our sense of group identity sharpens under attack, as danger sends us scuttling back to a community we hadn't even known we wanted. Jewish identity often crystalizes or finds strength in moments of crisis, current or remembered (the Holocaust being the most potent example of remembered crisis). Power seekers exploit this desire for safety. In both African American and Jewish communities, the lure of the nation state has sought to restore manhood, to relieve the humiliation of oppression. Jewish nationalism—Zionism—seemed to promise state normalcy, protection, and transformation from the shtetl Jew (and, later, the Holocaust victim) into the Uzi-toting Israeli or the kibbutz-born sabra. Similarly on this point, African American nationalism as solution to the problem of racism seemed to promise dignity, liberation, and autonomy: Liberia, Marcus Garvey, Elijah Mohammed and the Nation of Islam, and of course Malcolm X;[88] Black Power, Afrocentrism; Stokely Carmichael morphing into Kwame Ture. African pride frequently linked to anti-semitism on one hand and masculinity on the other.

Naturally, then, there are those in both communities who embrace conflict—especially conflict with an enemy whose power is, after all, limited; and reject diaspora and diasporic culture as inauthentic, emasculated, effeminate.

Where do real live women enter this discussion?

Perhaps the most famous image of African American–Jewish alliance is a photograph of Dr. Martin Luther King, Jr., and Rabbi Abraham Joshua Heschel marching side by side. Without in any way belittling these truly great men, the "great man" model excludes the masses of common people who effect social change, including many women. But in particular, leadership in both Jewish and African American subcultures, as in the dominant culture, is depicted as overwhelmingly, aggressively male. In response to the masculinized humiliation of which Enloe speaks, bolstered by religious traditions in which morality and patriarchal authority merge, and by the sense of emasculation that manifests—however differently—in each community, Jewish and African American men have countered with masculinized versions of strength: combative, absolutist, contemptuous of compromise.

Most commonly, the public face even on positive Jewish–African American relations has been inscribed as largely male. Michael Lerner and Cornel West,[89] though they mention gender, do so in booming patriarchal voices. It took years before they invited a woman to join their public conversations, and though their choice of partner—Susannah Heschel, Director of Jewish Studies at Dartmouth and daughter of Rabbi Heschel— is apt, might not the gentlemen have also included an African American woman? What about an African American Jew? Similarly, Paul Berman's

1994 anthology *Blacks and Jews*[90] contains nineteen essays, only three by women, though appropriate women's voices were not hard to find in 1994. The purpose of inclusion, let me stress, is not a mindless "political correctness," but accuracy and completeness.

We can see the male domination of African American-Jewish relations played out on college campuses, one of the few places in our very segregated society where Americans of Jewish and African descent come into potentially fruitful contact. Again and again, a black student group, usually male led, invites a prominent black nationalist—almost always male—sometimes publicly associated with anti-semitic remarks. The result, usually, is a polarized campus, with mostly men speaking out against each other; African American students pressured to present a united front, to suppress dissent amongst themselves; Jewish students pressured to choose sides between those who identify with Jews and are concerned about anti-semitism, and those who identify as progressive and are concerned with racism, as if these were mutually contradictory concepts. This split must be felt most painfully by those who are both Jewish and African American;[91] but also by those who are either but care about the others. Or by those who just plain care about justice and know we need to work together.

Perhaps equally destructive (though ignored by media) are the multitude of programs organized by Jewish student groups that focus on exclusively Jewish concerns and rarely connect with the crises in racial and economic justice with which African American communities are struggling. That Jewish campus programming is often paid for by off-campus funders[92] only reinforces the sense of Jews cutting their own deal, and of Jewishness and fighting racism as mutually exclusive concerns.[93]

Several times I have been invited to speak at campuses riven by such conflicts, brought in, usually by a group of women, to mop up.[94] The gender dynamics were pretty obvious. It was tough, cool to support African American nationalists who stood up to the Jews—especially since anti-semitism demonizes Jews and inflates Jewish power. It was tough, cool to insist that Jews should turn their backs on others, should only care about their own, forget that bleeding-heart liberal—and they don't quite say, but they mean—*sissy* stuff.

Yet on every campus I visited I met Jews and African Americans, often women, concerned about both racism and anti-semitism. Some of these visits were deliberately organized proactively to talk about working together. Often I was explicitly partnered with an African American woman.[95]

Without essentializing gender, we can ask: what happens if we bring women's voices into the public arena?[96] Looking again at Dr. Johnnetta

Cole, who would, I suspect, have been largely supported for a cabinet position by Jewish *women,* as Lani Guinier—another African American (and Jewish) woman proposed and abandoned by Clinton—was endorsed by the National Council of Jewish Women, while mainstream (read: male-dominated) Jewish organizations opposed her.[97]

Another example, from San Francisco State University, where, in the spring of 1994, a mural of Malcolm X was unveiled that included several Jewish stars with dollar signs. The media of course were off and running, their so-profitable black anti-semitism rearing its head again, a polarized campus, victimized Jews, ungrateful blacks—as though the artist automatically represented an entire community. But acts of resistance, opposition, or lack of support for the mural were simply not reported. Most strikingly, a few sources noted that a professor had painted STOP across the mural and had been arrested. Few of the news accounts reported that the professor—Lois Lyles—was a woman, and none reported that she was African American, or that she took this bold and personally risky action because she felt that attributing anti-semitism to Malcolm defamed his memory.[98]

Or, look at affirmative action. Repeatedly waved between our communities as a red flag of difference, a racialized prediction of attitudes toward affirmative action disintegrates if we factor in gender. I know that Jewish men are not unanimous in opposition to affirmative action, though you might think so to hear the positions of the major Jewish organizations. But Jewish women overwhelmingly support affirmative action, and not surprisingly, since we have so benefited from it. The point is, to depict Jews as monolithically opposed to affirmative action is to discard (at least) half the community.

Nor have Jewish men completely forsaken progressive positions. In the 2004 election, for example, as African Americans voted overwhelmingly (88–90 percent) for John Kerry, Jews were next, at 75 percent. Without muting issues of privilege and political differences, turning up the volume on Jewish women's voices would help shift the priorities, agenda, and weight of the Jewish community such that the presumption of black–Jewish opposition would be seriously challenged.[99] Jewish *women's* agenda and the agenda of the African American community correspond on many critical issues: reproductive rights, public entitlements, housing, education, employment, health care, affirmative action, and violence against women and children. Even recognizing how often mainstream feminism has fallen short of its aspiration to be a multiracial, multicultural movement, we still find among women more grassroots awareness of these critical issues than we are likely to find in a male-led movement. Jewish women have risen into leadership of some Jewish communal organizations and synagogues, and we find "the" Jewish community speaking out for choice, gay rights,[100] and many economic issues. If we examine sites of Jewish social justice or coalition work, we find a disproportionate number of women leaders. This is no accident. Our experience as women and as feminists brings us to the struggle against racism and poverty, incites us to contradict the destructive masculinist xenophobic voices that claim to represent us.

For example, Alain Finkielkraut, a French intellectual, repudiates his past commitment to socialism and liberation struggles, as if these commitments had been inauthentic refusals to be fully Jewish.[101] I, on the other hand, interpret these same commitments on the part of my younger self—civil rights, anti-imperialism, women's liberation—as foreshadowings. I would say, I *was* being a Jew without claiming it, without knowing it. I think this is more than a personal difference between myself and Finkielkraut. Since the civil rights movement, Jews are commonly assumed to have moved to the right, but this shift—to the extent that it exists—is sharply gendered. I do not hear the same sarcasm, pessimism, rejection, and dejection in the voices of leftist Jewish women of my generation—or of the generation of women now in their twenties and thirties, who have their own history of activism. Jewish men such as Finkielkraut are trying to cut a deal with the larger Christian society. They identify with a sort of —victim-privilege of Jewishness, a *we've suffered so we have no responsibility* form of Jewishness, blurring the time lapse between mid-century and the present, standing apart from contemporary struggles for peace and social justice.

Women cannot stand apart from these struggles because women *as women* are in struggle, connected to the struggles of other women. We recognize our common oppression by gender. In addition, many of us understand—some from our own experience and location, some through the experience of those we love, and some through education in why and how to be allies—where oppression by gender, race, class, and sexual orientation intersect and reinforce each other.[102]

Thus, while many Jewish men aspire, with some success, to occupy center stage, many Jewish women are still marginalized—I am tempted to say, *are still Jewish*, as the margins have offered such a determining and valuable vantage point in Jewish diasporic life. When I ask, then, why Jewish women are proving so important to Jewish renewal, to feminism, and to progressive political movements, I try not to answer essentially, *because we're so cool;* but analytically, *because we're so positioned.*

Since September 11, 2001, assumptions about African American–Jewish conflict continue to waft over the airwaves, but given the endless war on Iraq, Israel's relentless occupation of captured Palestinian land, the dominant paradigm of conflict in "the" Jewish community has mutated. Jewish/African American has shifted out of focus.[103] Reality has done nothing but get worse; African Americans are as poor, unemployed, and above all as locked up as ever, but they are off the symbolic hit parade of hopes and fears. I still run into Jews angry at "African Americans' ingratitude," who'll justify anything on the grounds of Louis Farrakhan. But another paradigm has emerged to dominate Jewish thought since September 11th: Jewish–Arab, Jewish–Muslim, Israeli–Palestinian conflict. In this subtext, Jews/Israelis are simultaneously innocent victims attacked by Arab terror, and models of dominance: an unfettered military, soldiers who do whateverthefuck they please, never mind that bleeding heart garbage about human rights.[104]

[3] WHO IS THIS STRANGER?

LOOLWA KHAZZOOM

As we go story by story through the history and heritage of the Jewish people, we find that Judaism is rooted deeply in the Middle East and North Africa: Abraham and Sarah, Moses and Miriam, the Talmud, the first yeshivas, and the Hebrew language all come from the Middle East and North Africa. Purim tells the story about Iranian Jews. Passover tells the story about Egyptian Jews, and so on. So whether your family is from Poland, Syria, Germany, Spain, India or Ethiopia, the Middle Eastern and North African Jewish heritage is a part of your Jewish heritage.

—Loolwa Khazzoom, "Jewish Multiculturalism"

One thing that has always been challenging for me, in regard to the current Arab–Israeli conflict, has been the equal sign that I have seen placed between "Arab" and "Anti-Jewish." Over the course of my life, I have had experiences that taught me to love the Arabic flavor of the culture and language of many Sephardic Jewish communities. My father had always gone to all sorts of different synagogues around New York—on Sabbath, he would grab my sister and me and we would walk all over the place. He would sit in these different synagogues and learn their songs, and so we have a repertoire of lots of beautiful cultural songs. When I was ten, he started studying with a rabbi who was from Baghdad. He became the spiritual influence in my father's life. So from the time I was ten until I was an adult and left my house, our neighbors were Sephardic, we davened in the Sephardic shul, and we kept the cultural and religious traditions of the Jews of Baghdad.

In this circle, there was a lot of overlap between what people might call Arabic culture and Jewish culture. There were sounds, foods, melodies, the form of chanting, the Hebrew itself . . . where you could feel the influence of our growth in Arabic lands. In our community, there were many stores that were owned by Arabic-speaking people and my father would speak to them in Arabic when we went to shop, greeting them with "Asalam Aleikum." I remember, very early on, feeling a comfort with Arabic culture that was not foreign to my Judaism. As I got older, and learned about the history of the establishment of the State of Israel and modern-day Zionism, I noticed that I was sensitive to the places where I felt "Arab" and "Jewish" were being juxtaposed against one another, almost as opposites, without taking into account that there were many "Arab Jews."

Now I know that there is a deep history of anti-semitism in Arab lands, that cannot be ignored, but I never felt that there was enough information offered in my Jewish education about the history of alliances between Arabs and Jews and the times and places where Jews and Arabs lived together peacefully. Many of my father's friends grew up in families where they and their Arab neighbors ate together, shared family celebrations, and had close relationships. Depending on the ruler/leader of the time, Jews had both good times and bad times in Arab lands, and I've always felt that the history of Arab–Jewish alliance did not get enough good press in charting the path toward peace in the future.

—Yavilah McCoy, interview

My father and my uncles came from Morocco and lived in France. In 1947–48 they went to do their bit for the development of the Jewish state and they all had stories of being discriminated against, getting called shvartse. *None of them wanted to stay in Israel because they had not come from some village, they had lived in France, they had some education, they were multilingual. They were working-class, blue-collar types, not intellectuals, but they had some world experience. And they didn't want to be treated like that.*

Growing up in L.A., my Jewish culture was always Ashkenazi. The writers I admired were Hannah Arendt and Kafka, and the Americans Bellow and Malamud. They're all great. But no one took the time to introduce me to Edmond Jabès or Elias Canetti.

—Jordan Elgrably, interview

Our Judaism which [in Ethiopia] we kept for 2,500 years, they said was not Judaism.

—Avishai Yeganyahu Mekonen,
in the film *Judaism and Race*

I'm not religious but I am Jewish.

—Nissim Behar, in the film *Adio Kerida*

Who are the Jewish people?

By the mid-sixteenth century, "Jewish communities could be found in countries as far-flung as Jamaica, Brazil, Yemen, Afghanistan, Ethiopia, India, and China, as well as in many countries in Europe . . . today the World Jewish Congress identifies 120 countries with a Jewish community."[1] Since so few people, including Jews, know about Jewish histories and communities around the globe, this information comes as a salutary shock, followed—I hope—by a shift in perspective.[2]

But as Lewis Gordon, Director of the Center of Afro-Jewish Studies at Temple University, points out:

> What's complicated is there are certain myths that dominate the way we study migratory populations. One such myth is that people migrate and their descendants remain exactly the same. And that's not true. The people we see today in Northern Europe who call themselves Jews—their ancestors didn't look the way they look. Similarly—what's interesting—is we're seeing a living example of this today. In my research I come across so many Jewish communities. Not only Ashkenazic and Sephardic. I come across the Abayudaya of Uganda, the Lemba Jewish community of Southern Africa, on and on. I just came back from Brazil, where I began to see not only the presence of Moroccan and Ethiopian Jewish communities but also some of the lay rituals. I've seen people on the street who reflect the West African Jewish community who may have come over through slavery. But no one is asking those questions so the research hasn't developed yet.[3]

Mizrahim (or *Maghribim*) from the Middle East and North Africa, Sephardim from the Iberian Peninsula, Ashkenazim from Western and Eastern Europe—but these *froms* represent diasporas centuries old, and descendants live all over the globe. These terms may suggest but cannot predict color or appearance. By one estimate, 13.5 million Jews in the world break down into an also-estimated three-plus million Mizrahim/

Sephardim and ten-plus million Ashkenazi.[4] But where are we counting the Hebrew Israelites?[5] The *conversos* who fled to the new world? The Jews in Nigeria, Uganda, India, Iran, Turkey, . . . Jews of color in the United States, invisible, unwelcomed, thus, undercounted, . . . undercounted because unwelcome?

In the United States, the number of Jews is estimated at about 5.9 million. This includes—or should—people of every race who were born into Judaism through one or both parents; people of every race who chose Judaism; people of every race who were adopted. There are multiple paths to Judaism, some of which have nothing to do with religion. While Conservative and Orthodox Judaism, and the Israeli Law of Return, recognize only the matrilineal passage of Judaism, the Reform practice of welcoming as Jews children of a Jewish father is likely to spread, given the concern for Jewish continuity and the rising rate of Jewish intermarriage. And, as Lewis Gordon points out, sometimes the oldest Jewish traditions are patrilineal.[6] In any case, religion is only part, not the whole. Children of a Jewish father with a Jewish family may in reality grow up way more Jewish than a child of two nominally Jewish parents who are alienated from their Jewishness.

Rabbi Angela Warnick Buchdale, a mixed heritage Korean/Ashkenazi, gave the following sermon to her congregation on Martin Luther King, Jr.'s, birthday, 2001:

ANGELA WARNICK BUCHDALE

The idea of a multi-racial, multi-ethnic Jewish congregation makes a lot of Jews in our communities uncomfortable. Ethnic identity has always been important to the Jews, and today, for many Reform Jews, "cultural Judaism" is the centerpiece of their Jewish identity [which] usually means a common heritage tied to Jewish immigrant life: parents or grandparents who lived in Forest Hills or the Bronx, ate knishes and spoke Yiddish, who lived among Jews, married other Jews, and had Jewish children. They aspired up, and uptown, ultimately to Jewish nirvana: the Upper West Side. For some cultural Jews, their entire Jewish identity can be distilled down to the comfortable use of *schvitz* or *schlep* in daily discourse. Cultural Judaism is popular because it's effortless; it's as easy as remember who your mother and father are, what they look like, and how they talk.

For some of us, though, it's not so easy. Our parents spoke other languages, ate different food, prayed to different Gods. And our Judaism threatens cultural Jews in several ways: First it seems to dilute collective Jewish cultural memory—what happens when half the congregation has no relatives from Brooklyn? Secondly, multi-ethnic Jews may seem to taint the purity of Jewish ethnic culture by introducing elements of different traditions into the Jewish community. Lastly, and perhaps most difficult of all, because many multi-ethnic Jews have had to base their Jewish identity on foundations entirely separate from ethnic affiliation, they call into question the very validity of cultural Judaism, because they demonstrate a Jewish identity based solely on actively chosen, religious affiliation.[7]

While this emphasis on religious identity makes me, a secularist and a cultural Jew, squirm, it also helps me confront the Brooklyn Jew in me who thinks I am real because I was born this way. Sometimes I need to be reminded that almost everything Jewish I know, beyond *schvitz* and *shlep* and the ambiance of childhood, I have had to learn as an adult. Being a Jew is an exercise in pluralism.

For example,

> *My grandfather, as a young man, was drawn to Jewish concepts, to Jewish practice. He was a firm believer that the journeys of the people of Israel through the stories of the Bible were a powerful paradigm for both the struggles and liberation of African Americans in this country. In the early points of his life, this belief made him a Hebrew Israelite, and he lived and observed what laws he could discern from the Bible with other Hebrew Israelites that he helped to form into a community. As his family grew and my grandfather's work in the labor unions increased, he became close friends with many Jewish colleagues who shared with him their knowledge of traditional Jewish custom and practice and my grandfather melded what he learned of Sabbath and holiday observance, kosher dietary laws, and other practices into his choice to embrace what he called the path of the "most high God" and to live an upright life in the study of Hashem's ways. My grandfather never chose the path of a formal conversion to Judaism but raised my mother and her siblings with a "Jewish"*

71

identity that was reinforced by the solidarity she shared with a small number of other Jewish students, in her predominantly Italian High School, who also took days off from school for the observance of Jewish holidays.

Through witnessing the two worlds that my grandfather traversed as both a Hebrew Israelite and a Jewishly observing union "comrade," my mother eventually developed questions of her own regarding Jews and Judaism. Both she and my father describe themselves as seekers of the truth, and as having a desire to connect with the history and philosophy of practice that was behind the beautiful traditions that my grandfather taught them. They came to the Orthodox community looking for answers and, in converting, felt that they had made a spiritual link to the past and future of the Jewish people. I was raised in a family of eight Orthodox black Jews. Two parents, six children. I was reared in the yeshiva system from age four to seventeen and my growth into my own Jewish identity has been about appreciating the various entry points that there can be for "Jewish" identity and noticing, through the model of my grandparents, that being "Jewish" does not always begin with a ceremony or the trappings of a recognizable Jewish exterior, but on the inside in the choices people make regarding how they will live their lives. Of the many things I will always be thankful to my grandparents for, I find that I have daily opportunities to be thankful to them for showing me by example what "Jewish" looks like on the inside.

—Yavilah McCoy, interview

HILARY THAN

One Jewish experience from one Jew who grew up Jewish. Someone who chose to become Jewish, on the other hand, might not seem to other Jews or feel to her/himself very Jewish initially, but after years of practice living as a Jew, this feeling would shift. The *mikveh*—ritual bath—is part of the conversion ceremony, but *mikveh* only symbolizes a larger immersion in Jewish history, a process that develops over time. As Hilary Than, born in Malaysia, "raised in the Chinese religion of many gods," describes it:

I did not feel Jewish those first years
after my conversion. I felt I was wearing
a new mask over old masks, I was dancing
a new dance, miming the moves. I felt like a fraud
in synagogue, mouthing a lie when I said,
"God of our fathers." I wish I had known
what I know now: we are our memories.
I did not feel Jewish for I had no memories yet
of living Jewish, being Jewish.
The convert's mind
is a brand new culvert that does not
know the feel of water until the doing
fills it with memory, floods it with rain.[8]

Yet images of washing, filling up, and flooding mask a critical truth: the person one has been does not—and should not—disappear. Hilary Than does not become a Brooklyn Jew; she becomes a Jew from Malaysia who knows the Chinese religion of many gods. Moreover, if she is encouraged to share this knowledge with her Jewish community—as I suspect she is too seldom encouraged to do—the Jewish community has much to gain.

THE CULTURES OF JEWS

The Eurocentric story of the Jews begins with Abraham leaving his native Ur and settling in the promised land. Other milestones include the destruction of the Second Temple—and now we leave the Middle East, as though no Jews stayed; the Expulsion from Spain (usually the only recognition of non-Ashkenazi experience); and now it's Europe all the way: Blood Libels, Emancipation and Enlightenment, Pogroms, Immigration, the Holocaust; and escaping Europe, the crowning glory, the founding of the Jewish state of Israel, in which—almost like Columbus with America— the Zionists, having almost discovered Eretz Israel, defeat the savage indigenous people who aren't really there, and make the desert bloom.

To turn Eurocentrism inside out, we should begin with the Arab world, a strategy that has historical accuracy to recommend it.

MIZRAHIM

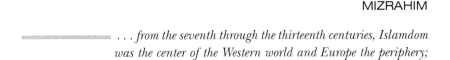

. . . from the seventh through the thirteenth centuries, Islamdom was the center of the Western world and Europe the periphery;

correspondingly, the Jews of the Muslim world were the world's leaders in wealth, culture, and intellectual achievement. They were also the bulk—generally estimated at 90 percent—of the world's Jews. The Jews did not blunder into the Muslim world as immigrants or exiles. They were part of the population of Western Asia, North Africa, and Iberia, now called al-Andalus, where medieval Arabo-Islamic culture developed as an amalgamation of Arabic language, Islamic religion, and local culture. Jews were an intrinsic part of this culture.

—Raymond Scheindlin, "Merchants and Intellectuals"

The Jews who are today called Mizrahim or Maghribim[9] are those who lived in the Arab world and Turkey (what was once the Ottoman Empire), as minorities in Muslim rather than Christian culture. Some converted to Islam but secretly retained Jewish practice (they are called the *Donmèè*). Their mother tongue often is/was Arabic or Judeo-Arabic. *Mizrahi* means "Eastern," commonly translated as "Oriental," and is used by and about Israelis often interchangeably with *Sephardi,* a point to which I will return. The confusion between categories is only partly due to Ashkenazi ignorance or arrogance, lumping all non-Ashkenazim together. Partly this slipperiness is the result of Jewish history: some Jews never left the Middle East, including Palestine; some returned as Ladino-speakers after the expulsion from Spain. Some kept Ladino, some lost it, some never had it. There was considerable intermarriage. Mizrahim are usually defined as people of color, though they may range from fair to dark; Eastern rather than Western, colonized rather than colonizers. *Mizrahi* is less about race and color, everything about geography and history.

The Jews of Morocco date back more than two thousand years, fortified by Jews expelled from Iberia in the late fourteenth–fifteenth centuries. Turkish Jews go back even further; in the fourteenth century, Turkey provided safety for Jews fleeing Europe. Every country has its own Jewish history, though Turkey is one of the few—Iran being another—with a Jewish future, a sizeable community of Jews who still live there. (In the mid-twentieth century, most Jews left Morocco, Algeria, Libya, Tunisia, Egypt, Lebanon, Iraq, Syria, and Yemen—mostly for Israel, though France, Québec, Britain, and the United States attracted those who could afford a choice.)

During this prosperous and ascendant period in the Islamic world (seventh through thirteenth centuries), Jews were relatively protected, integrated, and free. Non-Muslims were relegated to a formal second-class citizenship with legal protections, *Dhimmi* status that Christians found grating. But for Jews, being *Dhimmi* might have been experienced as a relief, conferring rules and limits,[10] as opposed to the violence and oppression that often defined Jewish experience in Europe. Clearly Jewish life in the Islamic world was distinct from what is conventionally presented as "the Jewish experience."[11] As historian Raymond Sheindlin notes, "In general, whenever Islam was in a state of strength, as it was until the tenth century and as it would again be in the Ottoman Empire in the fifteenth and sixteenth centuries, Jews living within its territories would be able to live with dignity, interacting easily with Muslims."[12]

When I was a small child [in Egypt], it seemed natural that people understood each other although they spoke different languages, and were called by different names—Greek, Moslem [sic], Syrian, Jewish, Christian, Arab, Italian, Tunisian, Armenian.

—Jacqueline Kahanoff, in Alcalay, *After Jews and Arabs*

ELLA SHOHAT

My [Iraqi] grandmother, who still lives in Israel and communicates largely in Arabic, had to be taught to speak of "us" as Jews and "them" as "Arabs." . . . For those of us from the Middle East and North Africa, the operating distinctions had always been "Muslim," "Jew," and "Christian," not Arab versus Jew. For us, the assumption was that "Arabness" referred to a commonly shared culture and language, albeit one with religious differences.

Generally, as Iraqi Jews, we were well-integrated and indigenous to the country, forming an inseparable part of its social and cultural life while retaining a communal identity. We used Judeo-Arabic[13] in hymns and religious ceremonies. The liberal and secular trends of the twentieth century engendered an even stronger association of Iraqi Jews and Arab culture, which brought Jews into an extremely active role in public and cultural life. Prominent Jewish writers, poets, and scholars played a vital role in Arab culture, distinguishing themselves in Arabic-speaking theater, in music as singers, composers, and players of traditional instruments. In Egypt, Morocco, Syria, Lebanon, Iraq, and Tunisia, Jews became members of legislatures, of municipal councils, of the judiciary, and even occupied high economic positions.

—Ella Shohat, "Arab Jew"

[Pre-state, in Old Jerusalem] Jews and Muslims had common courtyards, just as if we were a single family. We grew up together. Our mothers revealed everything to the Muslim women and they, in turn, opened their hearts to our mothers. The Muslim women even learned how to speak Ladino and were adept in its saying and proverbs. We didn't live in shelters for the needy like the Ashkenazim and there were no large estates separating our houses from those of the Muslims. . . . All the kids played together and if anyone else from the neighborhood bothered us, our Muslim friends would come to our defense. We were allies.

Our mothers would nurse any Muslim children whose mothers had died or were unable to attend to them, just as they would care and watch over them if their mothers were busy or otherwise occupied. And the same was true the other way around . . .

—Ya'aquob Yehoshua, "Childhood in Old Jerusalem"

What needs to be stressed, repeated, hammered home is the shared Judeo-Arabic culture, the rich cultural flowering and the intimacy. In light of my discussion of nationalism and masculinism, we should consider the role played by gender. In any case, the experience of those who "made aliyah" (emigrated to Israel) does not always reflect triumph. Ella Shohat again supplies a corrective: "the impossibility of ever going [back to Baghdad] . . . once led me to contemplate an ironic inversion of the Biblical expression: By the waters of Zion, where we sat down, / and there we wept, when we remembered Babylon."[14] Not for nothing does Shohat riff off Edward Said's now-classic "Zionism from the Standpoint of Its Victims"[15] by inserting Mizrahim into the story: Shohat titled her 1988 essay "Sephardim in Israel: Zionism from the Standpoint of Its Jewish Victims."

Listen to a news article from 2006, reflecting the longing of contemporary Iraqi Jews for their home—not Zion but Baghdad or Mosul:

> Iraqi-Israeli Jews who were born in the now violence-plagued city of Mosul will make a trip to Iraq to 'return to their roots' this spring [2006]. This trip, promises the sign, will include visits to the grave of Jonah the Prophet [which is in Mosul], the grave of Rabbi Nahum al-Kushi of Mt. Sinai, the cave of Abraham our Forefather, and the grave of Noah (of Noah's Ark). . . . Despite the bombs, the kidnappings, and the curses on their adopted homeland—Israel is widely believed by Iraqis in Iraq to be behind the U.S. invasion and occupation of their country—Iraqi-Israelis are rushing to sign up.

"I'm going no matter what," said Nahum Ballush, 72. "I want to go back and see the river, the Jewish quarter." His voice trailed off. . . .

Over 120,000 Jews left Iraq during the early 1950's. Those still alive are yearning to return to the sights, sounds, and scents of the place they loved and left before it's too late.[16]

The longing for home is benign, even if surprising in view of the Zionist narrative in which only Israel is the beloved homeland and every other place is dangerous or grim. But listen to the humiliation of aliyah for many Mizrahim in the early years of statehood.

We were wearing our Sabbath clothing. We thought as the plane landed that Israel would welcome us warmly. But goodness, how wrong we were! When the plane had landed at Lod airport, a worker approached us and sprayed us all over with DDT, as if we were lice-infested. What sort of welcome was that? We felt they were spitting in our faces. When we disembarked from the plane, they herded us into a train, which was so crowded that we were stepping on each other and our fine clothes were dirtied. My husband was crying and so was I. Then the children started crying and our sobs went up to heaven. . . . Since it was a freight carriage it had no electric light, but as it sped along we thought of the death trains which had taken European Jews to the Nazi camps. Finally we reached the "Sha'ar Ha'aliya" camp and we were taken in with other families, then they wrote down our names and "gave" us new Hebrew names. .. [The] camp had been a British army detention centre before it had become an immigration camp. The Israeli security authorities had reinforced the camp's security by doubling the height of barbed wire around it and installing a direct telephone link to the Israeli police in Haifa port. There was a police force of sixty constables, four sergeants and an officer to supervise the immigrants, who were housed in tents or tin-roofed barracks. . . . As I wandered amongst these tents, an elderly Iraqi waylaid me. "I have just one question," he said. "Are we immigrants or prisoners of war?" My tongue was tied and I could not reply.

—Anonymous, in Alcalay, *After Jews and Arabs*

Humiliation and grief.

My father's family had left Baghdad for Israel in 1951, along with most of Iraq's Jews. I always knew that they had endured a number of painful and traumatic years in the "transit camp." . . . In moving to Israel, they suffered a fall in socioeconomic status and dignity so severe that a majority of women and some of the men in the family suffered chronic depression.

I was eight years old when I first learned of this bleak fact. During a visit to Israel we were invited to dinner by cousins near Nahariyya, near the Lebanese border. As we entered the grassy area of their backyard, we were greeted by two long banquet tables bearing piles of food whose delicious scent wafted in the light of the summer moon. I had never seen anything like it.

Behind these tables three fleshy matrons watched us with sad smiles and dull eyes. . . . Ever since that visit to Nahariyya, I have been haunted by the sight of the three dull-eyed women poised behind the tables, so anxious that we partake of their food. That food was more than the product of two straight days of cooking: It was the last hope for continuity, the sole element of their age-old culture that survived uprooting.

—Lital Levy, "How the Camel"

Or listen to the words of this Yemenite women's song from Israel from which the title of this chapter is drawn:[17]

I shall begin to sing, of You O Lord,
Above all firmaments!
O Lord, my true support,
My heart is full of longing
And full of signs.
O mother, I will not tell the sorrows,
Like a camel lying on my heart
And like daggers stabbing.
O my mother, my family,
How they abhorred me.
They sent me to a land
I do not know, nor am I known here.
To a distant land they sent me
And abused me indeed!
When I walked atop the roof
Others said: "How voluptuous and delightful!"

And when I came down to the yard
They said: "Who is this stranger?"

Sephardim in Israel were made to feel ashamed of their dark olive skin, of their guttural language, of the winding quarter tones of their music, and even of their traditions of hospitality. Children, trying desperately to conform to an elusive "sabra" norm, were made to feel ashamed of their parents and their Arab countries of origins. At times the semitic physiognomies of the Sephardim led to situations in which they were mistaken for Palestinians and therefore arrested or beaten. Since Arabness led only to rejections, many Sephardim internalized the Western perspective and turned into self-hating Sephardim. Thus not only did the "West" come to represent the "East," but also, in a classic play of colonial specularity, the East came to view itself through the West's distorting mirror. . . . Oriental Jews have to be taught to see the Arabs, and themselves, as Other.

—Ella Shohat, "Sephardim in Israel"

While it is commonly assumed that statehood improved the educational level of the "primitive Oriental" Jews—Israeli scholars point to a downward trajectory for Mizrahi who made aliyah: the educational level of adolescents, the third generation, measures poorly against what their grandparents achieved in the countries they left.[18] No wonder: beyond shame and stress, "[during the crucial formative years of the 1950s, . . . as many as 60 percent of the transit-camp children did not attend school."[19]

In a series of ideological and material gambits surely familiar to those who have witnessed bell-curve justifications of poverty, race naturalizes class. Ammiel Alcalay explains:

Middle Eastern Jews were typecast in the role of "primitive survivors" of an archaic past, and Israeli educational, social, and cultural institutions stigmatized them, reinforcing the boundaries of a class society based on ethnic, culture, and linguistic background. . . . The very idea that these communities possessed densely textured and creative public and private intellectual lives ran against every stereotype embedded in the institutional structures and common rhetoric of the new state. In this context the intellectual life of these Middle Eastern Jewish communities—initiated at the dawn of the technical age and forged in the cauldron of colonialism and nationalism—was almost unimaginable.[20]

Shohat summarizes: "The Jewish experience in the Muslim world often has been portrayed as an unending nightmare of oppression and humiliation. I in no way want to idealize that experience; there was tension, discrimination, and violence. On the whole, however, we lived quite comfortably within Muslim societies."[21]

SEPHARDIM

To be a Sephardi, I discovered, is to see the world as mystery, so that even ordinary events are infused with the sense of otherness. . . . Sephardim are prone to be polyglot and multicultural from infancy, as they crisscross religious and ethnic boundaries with deceptive ease. . . .

To be a learned Jew or Muslim in Al-Andaluz presupposed more than the mastery of Arabic and Hebrew, and the ability to discourse in flowing ornamental phrases on astronomy, theology, medicine, literature and the ancient Greek classics. The honing of language into a civilizing instrument that is at once dulce et utile epitomized the Jewish Golden Age in Spain.

The degree to which Arabic and Hebrew cross-pollinated would be difficult to exaggerate and, given the present antagonism between these two Semitic peoples, impossible to reconstruct. And yet a Sephardi is still marked by the inner dialogue between the ancestral Jew and the Christian and Arab "others" who inhabit his [sic] psyche.

—Victor Perera, *The Cross and the Pear Tree*

AMMIEL ALCALAY

In my immediate background or family there were commonly four–five languages around and a wide range of experience between the generation of grandparents down to the generation of my parents—in which people had generally lived in at least three countries and may have gone to school in a different language than the language in which they grew up—that was fairly typical—and had some other language they used for traveling. I had a great aunt whose purpose was to travel around and collect jokes; she spoke eight or nine languages. I didn't really identify it with anything other than my family . . .

—Ammiel Alcalay, interview

1985. In Northern New Mexico there are people who light candles on Friday night and don't eat pork. They have names like Rael, which some say comes from Israel. Physically they are indistinguishable from their neighbors. Only some of them know why they do certain things and they know it is dangerous to tell. When I lived in Northern New Mexico in the early eighties I didn't know any of this; I was just hungry for Jews. My first Hanukkah in Santa Fe I made a menorah and lit the candles and said the blessing, alone but picturing Jews all over the world also lighting and blessing candles. Imagine my shock when, years later, on a return visit to Taos, I meet at a brunch a woman named Diana who grew up in Questa, twenty-five miles north. She tells me about the large number of Jews, more and less hidden, who live and die here. She indicates our host: "His mother lights candles on Fridays," she says; "he doesn't like to talk about it." Later I drive to Questa to find a cemetery Diana told me about. I walk through the graveyard. There, among the crosses, every so often, a headstone with no cross. Many with the family name Rael, first names like Isaac, David, Sarah, Rachel, Moises, Aaron, Eli. On a few headstones the small stones which signify a Jew has visited a Jewish grave.[22]

Sephardic Jews are those whose mother tongue is/was Ladino (Judeo-Español), and whose religious practice and diaspora path can be traced at some point through the Iberian Peninsula (Spain and Portugal). There, during the European "Dark Ages," they enjoyed a tricultural Golden Age and, in the Jewish lexicon, substantial freedom, unghettoized, interacting culturally, intellectually, politically, and economically with Muslims and Christians. As Victor Perera pursued his own family history, he learned,

> [u]ntil the arrival of bloody-minded Almohade Berbers in 1146, bent on implanting Islam in all of Europe, Spain's Jews generally lived at peace with Muslim rulers and their Christian subjects; and they thrived culturally and commercially as never before or since.[23]

This peace persisted until the Christian conquest of Iberia and the Inquisition, "a holocaust stretched over centuries,"[24] which included forced conversion, torture, death or expulsion of Muslims and Jews alike. The Inquisition was driven by such practical matters as money and power, but racial bigotry played its part, dehumanizing and demonizing. The year 1492 marks not only Columbus's voyage, but also one of the major expulsions of the Jews from Spain; Portugal would be next.[25] (Several crew members, perhaps even Columbus himself, are thought to have been *conversos*.)[26]

Risking robbery, rape, and murder, Sephardim migrated far. They lived for generations and even centuries in Holland, Germany, Italy, France, Yugoslavia, and Greece, as well as North Africa, the Middle East, the Caribbean, and the Americas. Sephardic communities in Europe were decimated by the Holocaust.[27] But while Ashkenazim collectively continue to be haunted by the Holocaust, Sephardic Jews are more likely to dwell on the pain of exile, the expulsion from the beloved *Sepharad*. Centuries later, Cuban-born Ruth Behar is perfectly in the Sephardic tradition as she transforms this longing (for Cuba, rather than Spain) into a love song, the film *Adio Kerida* (Goodbye Dear Love), and writes about coming home with her ancestors' huge clanging keys to the courtyard of her home.[28]

The first Jews in the New World were Sephardim, some seeking religious freedom, some living for centuries as secret Jews. Another wave came in the second and third decades of the twentieth century from Turkey, on the heels of the Young Turks rebellion.[29] Some Sephardim considered themselves to be the aristocrats of the Jews, and looked down on the Ashkenazi history of ghettoization and persecution. In the mid-eighteenth century, it was reported that intermarriage with Ashkenazim resulted in banishment from the synagogue and "from the [Sephardic Jewish] Nation."[30] Some looked with contempt on the *must 'arab*—the Arabic-speaking Jews: "Just as Western Europeans viewed the peoples of the Middle East as exotic, these Jews viewed their brethren to the east and in Asia in the same way."[31]

Spanish Sephardim sometimes resent the blurring of distinctions between themselves and Mizrahim, reacting with pride in their history and with Eurocentric bias against non-Europeans, referring to themselves as "true" or "pure" Sephardim.[32] In religious terms, Sephardic rabbinical authority and religious practice tends to be far less polarized, less confrontational than either Ashkenazi orthodoxy or the reform movement that challenged it. Prominent Sephardic rabbis of the nineteenth and twentieth century reveal most commonly a stance of flexibility even towards *Halakhah* (Jewish law), emphasizing common sense and the ability to formulate new rulings, and the need to synthesize religion with science and technology, self-defense, secular education, and modern political values such as democracy and solidarity.[33]

Like the Mizrahim, Sephardim run the gamut from fair to dark. As early as 1663, an English traveler noted the range in skin color of the Sephardic Jews of Amsterdam: "The men are most of them of a tawny complection [*sic*] with black hair; some have clearer skins, and are scarce discernable [*sic*] from the Dutch."[34]

Jews who came from Iberia shared with Jews in the Islamic world a common religious culture, yet "[t]he Jewish upper crust had little to do with the indigenous *must 'arab* Jews."[35] Often the subtext is class manifest in culture. "Wherever they arrived, the Sephardim would quickly assume the reins of leadership in politics and the economy. Their knowledge of Europe and European languages made them attractive business partners and diplomatic agents for local Muslim rulers."[36]

By the nineteenth century, a Sephardic bourgeoisie would dress in European style, and would speak French or English along with the local Jewish vernacular, as well as, for religious purposes, Hebrew. These Jews, because of their social and economic positioning as outsiders, sometimes would welcome colonial powers, whether from Europe or the Ottoman Empire. Many were educated at the Alliance Israélite Universelle, schools created by French Jews in response (twenty years later) to the Damascus Blood Libel[37] and to a general sense of the "degraded condition" of their coreligionists. Not so coincidentally, these Jews were educated to fill slots in the colonial administration a generation or two ahead of the Arabs, so that as Arab nationalism surged, these Jews became caught in the middle with mixed loyalties.[38]

Ashkenazi recognition of "other Jews" may extend to the Sephardi, the Jews of Iberia, who are seen as European, but stops short of the Mizrahi, who are that impossible blend of Arab and Jew, though, as noted, the term *Sephardi* is often used to refer to both groups. As Ilana Halevi remarks, "these vaguenesses of vocabulary, reservations and obstructions reflect in reality the shifting character of the barriers themselves, and the fact that the language is not ready for the social reordering that is underway."[39] Ammiel Alcalay argues,

> At this point it's an academic question because all these iden-
> tities have changed so drastically. You're talking about people
> having been defined through Israeli categories and definitions. I
> think you can't talk about anything at this point without thinking
> through these categories. Because they've redefined everything.
> Yes, one can make the distinction, but you're talking about a really

tiny group of people who retained any kind of Spanish-centered tradition. But to begin with, there's kind of a false distinction: How do you get to Spain? You get to Spain through Iraq, that's how the migration moved. The kind of Spanish Sephardic element who in many cases became very hispanified and lost more of the Arab element—even though that is implicitly in the Spanish—the people who are more Spanish centered, expelled in 1492 and go more towards Europe, rather than people who went to Syria or Palestine or North Africa.[40]

1990. Ofra, a new acquaintance, has just moved to Washington, D.C., and is eager to meet Jewish lesbians. I am visiting D.C. for a friend's birthday party, and so I invite her. Ofra is a beautiful woman with olive skin and smooth even features; her family comes from Turkey.

Not five minutes after Ofra arrives at the party, as she and I are filling our plates from the enormous buffet, my birthday friend's mother, Rose, a woman of eighty-some years, approaches us.

"Hello," Rose smiles pleasantly at Ofra, but staring—my radar goes off but I am way too slow. Without missing a beat, Rose asks, "What are you? You're so exotic." It occurs to me that she thinks she's paid Ofra a compliment.

Ofra's face closes up and I can see this is a familiar experience. She changes the subject and leaves shortly thereafter.

Later I think, I could have teased gently: "Rose, Ofra probably thinks you are exotic." I could at least have taken Ofra aside, cut through her protective change of subject, and apologized for Rose who reflects exactly the thinking of the Ashkenazi community that doesn't even know it is not "THE Jewish community," does not even know it is Ashkenazi. Someone perhaps too old to learn.

Not to be melodramatic or self-aggrandizing—people fail in these ways all the time, no big deal, you might say. Ofra seemed a sturdy person, more than capable of making her own way—no one died, no one even cried, probably. But still I recognize a series of failures. I failed Ofra, who came, hopeful, to connect with community in her new city and got reminded of her status as an outsider. Failed myself—I

liked her, had wanted to make friends, and came off looking clueless and timid. Failed the Jewish lesbian community
Ofra sought and which she well might have enriched. Even
failed Rose who was perhaps not, after all, incapable of hearing something new.

Researching for this book, I discover that Rose's error is an historical
phenomenon called "Coethnic Recognition Failure," and that—in the
early 1900s, when the new wave of Sephardi came to the U.S.—as now, it
caused considerable pain.[41] For example, "a number of Ashkenazic Jews
of the Lower East Side protested the presence of the 'Turks in our midst,'
and petitioned the Mayor . . . for their removal. Upon learning that these
'Turks' were actually fellow Jews, the Ashkenazim withdrew the petition."[42]
Did the Sephardi's Jewishness neutralize their alienness? What if they had
actually been non-Jewish Turks: was that a crime warranting expulsion? Is
there something called "Cohuman Recognition Failure?"

POST-COLONIAL JEWS

The Jewish Diaspora has created an incredibly diverse Jewish world.

Chinese Jews, for example. Jewish arrival in China is estimated to begin
"at least by the 7th century,"[43] with the largest and most articulated Jewish
community found in Kaifeng, thought to be the largest city in the world at
that time).[44] Not anti-semitism but a complicated history of civil war, floods,
and impoverishment devastated the Kaifeng Jewish community.[45]

The Jews of India who "lived among the predominant Hindu and
Muslim population for millennia, making Judaism one of the oldest religions in India. . . . Unlike many parts of the world, Jews have lived in India
without significant violence of anti-semitism. . . ."[46] It's a quick jump to
connect the lack of violent anti-semitism with the weak minority status
of Christians. "Even so, economic factors, among others, have prompted
many Jews to emigrate to Britain . . . , Israel,"[47] and former British Empire-
mates. India still houses some five thousand Jews in four separate Jewish
communities,[48] created by distinct waves of migration. Some of these Jews
'began' as Sephardi or Mizrahi or some other racialized category.

The oldest group is the Cochin Jews (Malabar Jews) in modern Kerala,
said to date from the time of Solomon, "successful merchants [who] had
slaves who were converted to Judaism and then emancipated, *Meshuhararim*
or "released" in Hebrew. Most have left India, but many of the old people

continue to live in what is still called Jew Town. The Bene Israel, centered around Mumbai, is the largest Indian Jewish community, also very ancient, said to be descended from Jews stranded by shipwreck in 175 BCE as they fled the depredations of Antiochus Epiphan. In the nineteenth century, Cochin and Baghdadi Jews participated in educating the Bene Israel in Judaism. Their Indian population has declined drastically through emigration. Baghdadi Jews, relative babes, date from the eighteenth century when mostly Mizrahi came not only from Iraq but also from all over West Asia, settling in Mumbai and Calcutta. Largely merchants and businessmen, they sought to foster trade and avoid religious persecutions.[49] B'nei Menashe, the newest of India's Jewish communities, believe they are descended from the tribe of Menashe. They are thought to have migrated very early across the Silk Road to China, losing many of their customs but maintaining an oral tradition, including poems about crossing the Red Sea. Eventually many migrated back to Northeast India, where they came together in the 1970s, to reclaim what they call the religion of their ancestors.[50]

In contrast to the knowledge base about Euro-Jews, or even Indian Jews, the relatively paltry state of research about African Jews is striking. Lewis Gordon calls for rigorous study on Jewish migration in Africa.[51] As Tobin et al. argue most persuasively,

> The African story parallels that of other groups of Jews throughout the Diaspora. . . . there are long-standing communities with greater or lesser degrees of continuous practice, depending on how safe they were. There are those who have Jewish heritage and now practice other religions. Either through assimilation or through forced conversion, some may live as Christians or Muslims, yet are proud of their Jewish ancestry. There are also those who discovered Judaism and decided to convert. . . . Whether ancient or new, a distinctive trait of African communities results from historical isolation from rabbinic Judaism. Their Judaism has either been passed on through oral tradition or is practiced as pre-Talmudic Torah-based Judaism.[52]

Jews of Africa include those from North Africa (Morocco, Tunisia, Egypt, Algeria), but also from East, West, and Southern Africa: the Beta Israel of Ethiopia, and the Lemba of Southern Africa, the community that has within it a priestly cohort whose DNA follows the same patterns as those of other Cohanim. Communities who claimed or embraced Jewish roots in the twentieth century, including the Abayudaya in Uganda, the Rusape in Zimbabwe, and the Sefwi in Ghana.[53] The response of the Jewish mainstream to these communities has varied, from support to denial. In addition, of course, there are European Jews who immigrated to Africa, including the Jews of South Africa, who were disproportionately represented in the anti-apartheid struggle and in the post-apartheid government.

FEMINIST RITUAL

In 1997 Flora Samuel, a Bene Israel women's organizer and leader of an Indian women's group in Israel, heard about a new American Jewish ritual for naming a baby girl, and responded by publishing "The Bene Israel Cradle Ceremony: An Indian Jewish Ritual for the Birth of a Girl." The ceremony, called *barsa,* was created by Bene Israel women "adopting a Hindu custom" to celebrate the birth of a child. The ceremony is mostly for women and children, and came into being, Samuel writes, as a home social custom, not as a ritual for synagogue that would have only included Jews. As Samuel writes, "Now what about the non-Jewish neighbors and friends who also wanted to see the newborn and bring him or her presents?"[54]

Aside from the earthy charm of the custom described in some detail— at one point, for example, "the mother picks up the coconut and while she is sitting on the bed, she pushes it back under the bed between her legs. She is jokingly chided by the other ladies to push it as far back as possible so the next pregnancy won't be too soon"—its origin and purpose shed light on Indian acceptance of cultural difference, the importance accorded relations between Jews and non-Jews, the place of women in the Bene Israel community, and the Bene Israel's openness to other cultural influence.

ASHKENAZIM

"At last," someone at this point is sure to say: "the regular Jews; the real Jews."

When we talk about white Jews, or European Jews, we are talking mostly about Ashkenazim, estimated at about ten million of the world's thirteen million Jews;[55] and about half the Jews in Israel.[56] Many people, including many Ashkenazi Jews, think they know about these Jews, but the knowledge rarely goes beyond shallow factors: a food item, a *didl didl* melody, an accent associated with an inherently comical grandmother; and of course the Holocaust, about which people also think they know something.[57]

Ashkenaz comes from the word for Germany, and Ashkenazi are those Jews whose religious practice and diaspora path can be traced through

Germany. Their *mameloshn* (mother tongue), Yiddish—Judeo-German with lots of Hebrew and Slavic mixed in—means, simply, "Jewish," the language of *Yidn* (Jews). The highly assimilated Jews of Germany proudly spoke German, shunning Yiddish, which they considered to be "ignorant jargon," "not a real language." The small wave of German Ashkenazi who migrated to the United States in the nineteenth century looked with dread and shame upon their impoverished, jargon-babbling, superstitious horde of coreligionists (also Ashkenazi) arriving at the turn of the twentieth century from Russia and Poland.[58]

Ashkenazim migrated to the far points of the globe—North and South America, Australia, Africa, Asia, so that a Mexican or New Mexican Jew might have an ancestry that traces back to Berlin or Brooklyn instead of Spain. Because of diaspora, current location is only one anchor of identity.

Ashkenazi also names a religious practice that may include Jews of any race. Sephardi practice never split into denominations, while Ashkenazi culture is characterized by division and extremes: fundamentalists, on one hand; on the other, in-your-face anarchist Yom Kippur balls organized in deliberate violation of religious practice. Even religion is strongly polarized into camps of Orthodox, Conservative, Reform, and the smaller Reconstructionist denomination, while the Orthodox denomination is split into Modern Orthodox and Hasidism, Jewish fundamentalism.

The Ashkenazi communities of Europe were nearly exterminated by the Holocaust. Given this, there is powerful irony in the frequent casual absorption of Ashkenazi Jews into the category of "European." At the same time, the tendency to view the sojourn of Jews in Europe as one big pogrom culminating in the Holocaust—what historian Salo Baron dubbed the "lachrymose" view of Jewish history—belies decades and even centuries of fruitful interaction.[59]

What is rarely known except by scholars is the range and variety of the pre-Holocaust Ashkenazi communities of Europe: traditional, socialist, communist; Orthodox and secular; capitalist and worker; Yiddish-speaking and/or fluent in the vernacular of wherever they lived: Russian, Polish, French, Czech, German. . . . There is a whole literature, not just Nobel Prize winner Isaac Bashevis Singer, or Sholem Aleykhem whose Tevye stories hit Broadway as *Fiddler on the Roof*, but also brilliant narrative writers and experimental poets such as Chaim Grade, Kadia Molodowsky, Anna Margolin, Mani Leyb, Itsik Manger, and a host of others.[60]

Just as Ammiel Alcalay explains the intervention of the Israeli state in challenging definitions of Mizrahi and Sephardi, so does Rabbi Lynn

Gottlieb invoke immigration to the United States as challenging the meaning of Ashkenazi:

> I don't know if Ashkenazi works anymore. Me, I'm sixth genera-
> tion American, my son is seventh. Am I still Ashkenazi? I would say
> that I'm an American Jew, not Ashkenazi, though Ashkenazi is cer-
> tainly my heritage—German Jewish and the Austrian/Hungarian
> empire, but that was the 1840s![61]

DE-ASHKENIZATION

The widespread unarticulated assumption that all Jews are Ashkenazi
has scholarly as well as political and cultural implications. In sites of Jewish
education, where scholars, rabbis, and Jewish communal leaders are
taught, where the relatively new interdisciplinary field of Jewish Studies is
burgeoning—with more courses, more programs, more majors and minors
—the question of *how* Jewish history and culture are conceptualized is
critical.

For example, *The Jew in the Modern World*, published in 1980,[62] is an
otherwise excellent documentary history. While it includes a few documents about Sephardi in Europe and New Amsterdam, it contains nothing about the Middle East, Asia, or Africa. Sections are either generic (on
religion, science, identity, anti-semitism) or geographically and culturally specific (The Process of Political Emancipation in Western Europe
1789–1871; East European Jewry; the American Experience; Zionism; and
the final section, the Holocaust).

What is missing? Anything that recognizes "the modern world" outside of Europe or Euro-America. One example, and it is a glaring void:
even the section on the Holocaust includes no documents from Salonika,
Macedonia, or Rhodes, where Sephardic communities were ravaged at a
rate topped only by Lithuania, Poland, and Germany,[63] a fact few know.
How often have you heard of the deportation of Tunisian and Moroccan
Jews? or of Germans sending Libyan Jews to concentration camps and
Tunisian Jews to slave labor camps?[64] Pogroms in Baghdad and Basra sent
the cities' Jews fleeing across rooftops. In Morocco, the King promised to
protect Jews, but in spite of this, many were shipped off to the European
death camps.[65]

Mizrahim responded in a variety of ways to the threat to their own
communities, as well as the communities of other Jews. Egyptian Jews
boycotted German goods; Persian Jews intervened to help Jewish children

escape from Poland.[66] The documentary history might have included something about the pro-Axis Jerusalem mufti, or the popularity of *Mein Kampf* in Cairo in the 1930s; or about the role played by WASP eugenicists in the United States in developing Nazi eugenics; or with something that addresses the complications of anticolonial, anti-British sentiment.

Why isn't this part of the story?

When I turn to the book's fascinating demographic appendix, I find "on the entire European continent [by the fifteenth century] there were probably fewer than 300,000 Jews; in the entire world there were fewer than a million, most of whom were concentrated in the Near East."[67]

Why does Europe come first, when the majority of Jews were clearly elsewhere?

A newsletter published by Ivri-NASAWI—an organization founded by Sephardi/Mizrahi writers, artists, and intellectuals—cites gross examples of "Ashkenazism" (an article in a mainstream Jewish publication profiles Tunisia as "Jewish backwater"), and depicts Tunisians as ahistorical, and exotic. Ivri-NASAWI comments, "No intellectuals are interviewed for the story; the implication is that there are no Tunisian intellectuals [the writer] can talk to."[68] Another example in the Ivri-NASAWI newsletter focuses on an event at the Los Angeles Workmen's Circle: the topic was relationships among Jews, Chicanos, and Latinos in L.A., but the event neglected "Spanish/Ladino-speaking Jewry in the city, and an examination of the deeply significant links between Jews and Hispanic culture over the centuries."[69] Beyond ignorance, this is a fine example of shooting oneself in the foot, losing an opportunity to forge the very connections the event was created to foster.

Too often anthologies, performances, booklists, conferences, or seminars titled *Jewish culture, history, experience* . . . include only Ashkenazi culture, history, and experience. In most Jewish courses, anthologies, seminars, series, studies . . . at best, there is a small postscript for diversity, into which the one or two Sephardi or Mizrahi items are tokenistically slotted: as though Sephardic and Mizrahi Jews are diverse, while Ashkenazi Jews are what? Normal?[70] As Shoshana Simons, a Jew of mixed Sephardic–Ashkenazi heritage, has remarked, "Often I'm asked to speak as a Sephardic Jew at progressive events. I feel like I'm the spice to add flavor and multicultural legitimacy to events whose dominant perspective is, tacitly, Ashkenazi."[71]

Simons wrote these words as part of a thoughtful commentary on the Teach-in on Radical Jewish History, organized by Jews for Racial and

Economic Justice in 1993, which we had named *In Gerangl*, Yiddish for "In Struggle."[72] I had invited Simons to join one of the panels, which she graciously accepted, even while explaining that our use of a Yiddish title signified to her that the event was not about or for Sephardic Jews.

At first when I shared this observation with our organizing committee, some simply dismissed its relevance, on the grounds that the vast number of Jews in the United States are Ashkenazi (usually estimated at somewhere between 85–97 percent). Yet even the high end, 97 percent, leaves three percent Jews who are *not* Ashkenazi, greater than the percentage of U.S. residents who identify as Jews of any sort (about 2.5 percent). As Jews, whose inclusion in multicultural events and in democratic process depends on a commitment to minority—even small minority—representation, we should have magnificent sensitivity to the politics of inclusion.

Ten years after the first *In Gerangl*, as I write this, I am pleased to note how retro these responses seem. We know the issue and we know of at least some resources, partly because Shoshana Simons struggled with us; because prominent Sephardic leader Edward Alcosser spoke so eloquently at the teach-in, sharing with us his understanding that time and history move differently in the Sephardic world.[73] Each step can also be a doorway.

But let me stress a basic point. If in our planning we excluded a whole community of Jews, we failed—not as bad people, or politically incorrect, or any of the guilt-and-shame apparatus that obscures the real problem with certain political choices. We failed ourselves because Jews who are cultural and ethnic minorities in an Ashkenazi-dominant context or who span more than one culture can be enormous assets in helping the Jewish world enter a multicultural arena girded appropriately for the struggle against racism and anti-semitism.

This challenge to Ashkenazism doesn't mean that we shouldn't have events focused on Yiddish culture or history. I am as impatient as the next Yiddish-lover with dismissals of Yiddish on the grounds that it is "just European" (while valorizing Sephardic culture as "non-white"). The revival of Yiddish language and culture is a splendid phenomenon. What is the point of rejecting a culture that—almost miraculously—has survived? The problem is the assumption that Yiddish is *mameloshn* for every Jew.[74] Not all Jews have Ashkenazic roots, and assimilation has left even many Ashkenazim alienated from their Yiddish heritage. And what about those who choose to adopt Ashkenazi culture? I am discomfited by folks drawn to cannibalize the cultures of others, but I believe that those who seriously learn, commit, and practice inside a culture—through the flow of history, as Jew-born-in-Malaysia Hilary Than depicted it in her poem, might earn the right to—humbly—call it their culture.

But a movement that includes all of us can't assume *yidishkayt* as our common culture. Even when we turn to the relationship of Yiddish culture to contemporary progressive Jewish politics, we cannot assume *yidishkayt* as *the* Jewish cultural norm that accompanies Jewish progressive politics. People often equate radical Jewish tradition with the Jews of Eastern Europe. But a great many Ashkenazi Jews were apolitical or traditional: not every Brooklyn Jew was a communist!

Moreover, there's much to learn about radical Jewish traditions that are not Ashkenazi. We may not find information about these in a tidy volume titled *Radical Sephardim* or *Mizrahi Dissent*, though the time for such volumes is perhaps not far off. In the present, we need to be on the lookout for clues; for example, historian Yosef Kaplan notes an outsider tradition among *conversos* who fled from Spain to Portugal, in the years before 1492 (when Portugal began forcing Jews to convert):

> The great majority of them assimilated into Iberian society, though
> . . . their particularity marked their intellectual, theological, and
> literary work in Spanish and Portuguese, *which often expresses a subversive attitude toward dominant values in Iberian society such as honor and pure Christian lineage* [emphasis mine].[75]

Just a whiff: subversion of dominant values, especially Christian/racial purity.

Closer to our own time, we find more than a whiff: Ammiel Alcalay points to Mizrahi "extended and deep involvement on the part of younger people with various Arab nationalist, communist, and socialist movements, as well as with branches of the Zionist movement itself."[76] Alcalay cites, among others, Sami Mikhael, "an extremely popular and well-regarded Israeli writer originally from Iraq," whose work "deals in a highly personal way with the complex relations between Jews and [non-Jewish] Arabs within the Communist Party in both Iraq and Israel."[77] There is abundant evidence of widespread Jewish involvement with the communist parties in Egypt and Iraq, which also document years of Mizrahi political involvement and intellectual activity.[78]

Radicals abound among those who emigrated to the United States and edited the Ladino press, such as self-proclaimed socialists including New York's Moise B. Soulam (*La Vara*) and Maurice S. Messim (*La Bos del Pueblo*). *El Progreso*, another New York Ladino paper, was also openly socialist. Among those who emigrated to New York were numbers of young male intellectuals from Salonika "imbued with socialist and humanitarian ideals."[79]

I don't claim it's simple. The shape of most thinking on progressive Jewish history and culture has been defined by Ashkenazi experience. For example, for the next JFREJ teach-in, we tried to find the equivalent to *In Struggle* in Ladino.[80] *En lucha* someone said, the obvious Spanish equivalent, but when we finally tracked down someone whose Ladino was idiomatic rather than bookish, she howled with laughter. *En lucha,* she said, conveyed wrestling. She told us, *Con peña* (though later we learn it should be spelled *kon pena*), and that's what we used, but I notice as most people talk about these annual teach-ins, *in gerangl* has stuck and *kon pena* has dropped out of the shorthand. Similarly, the title of JFREJ's tenth anniversary celebration, *Menches in the Trenches,* reveals both the wit and creativity that characterizes JFREJ's best work, and the Yiddishist bias that is alternately confronted, avoided, and forgotten; honoring a tradition of radical Jewish activism, JFREJ also reinscribed Yiddish as "the" language of progressive Jews.[81]

Nevertheless, in the process of searching for *in struggle* in Ladino, we discovered an old phrasebook for Yiddish-speaking trade unionists trying to organize Ladino-speaking workers, in which Yiddish is translated into Ladino and English, all of it—including the English—in Hebrew characters. Unfortunately for us these predecessors did not feel the need to say "In Struggle." But we made contact with the department of Sephardic Studies at Yeshiva University and with a number of Sephardic women,[82] we got on some mailing lists, and were able to include many Sephardic cultural and community events in our newsletter, and even cosponsored some. We can also draw on a larger pool of Sephardi contacts in planning our events, thus taking us another step forward toward authentic multiculturalism.

At the Association for Jewish Studies conference in 2003, at a Roundtable on Integrating the Sephardi/Mizrahi Experience,[83] scholars examined the reasons for disproportionate focus on Ashkenazim, or on emphasizing only the Sephardim, neglecting Mizrahim. Historian Marina Rustow explains: "Scholars are still more comfortable with Europe. This is not mere Eurocentrism [but] . . . is also a question of languages and access to training, . . . bibliographies and primary sources in translation, . . . intellectual and literary history . . . [84] Historian Sarah Abrevaya Stein offers a less generous explanation: "laziness" or, "a profound resistance to reconceptualize." Stein raises the challenges of how historical eras and themes are defined or imagined, and argues that the conventional frame of Jewish Studies doesn't work for Sephardi/Mizrahi experience. She cites the traditional polar doublets *assimilationist vs. nationalist* or *religious vs. secular,* as oppositions that don't really hold for Sephardim/Mizrahim. As another example, Stein cites "Emancipation and Modernization," a dominant theme in Jewish/Ashkenazi history. Legal emancipation in the eighteenth and nineteenth centuries, often linked to modernization, is assumed to be an essential event. Sephardic/Mizrahi Jews were not legally emancipated. Ergo: the theme excludes them.

However, Stein points out, the largest numbers of Jews, who lived in Eastern Europe, weren't legally emancipated either. Yet the experience of these Ashkenazim is not ignored; they are even credited with exercising creativity and resistance in the face of nonemancipation. In contrast, Sephardim/Mizrahim are simply omitted from the discussion.

Another, and more complicated, example is provided by the date 1492, a year that had a huge impact on Iberian Jews (expulsion), but not on Mizrahim. By emphasizing the significance of 1492, scholars homogenize non-Ashkenazi experience. (An analogy might be collapsing the experience of all non-white people into the experience of African Americans.) This homogenization then justifies future ellision: "after 1492 nothing really happens in the non-Ashkenazi world, except for outbursts of messianic fervor," which are usually mustered to denigrate the intelligence and sophistication of the Mizrahim.

Stein discusses the complexities of integrating Sephardi/Mizrahi experience of the Holocaust. Of course, the Holocaust had a much greater impact on Ashkenazi Jews. But as noted above, the impact on Sephardim and Mizrahim was not negligible; it was just distinct. At the same time, discussion of Jewish communal disruption and trauma regularly ignores the fact that for most Arab Jews, disruption of *their* ancient communities came as a result of the founding of the Israeli state, not from the Holocaust. This disruption is largely treated as deliverance, a factor that ignores the experience of many immigrants.

Falling outside the framework, not fitting the paradigm: these experiences will resonate with scholars of women's studies and ethnic studies, as our early efforts to expand the academic disciplines to include us are recognized. Another speaker at the Roundtable, Hebrew Union College's (HUC) Mark Kligman, remarks, "Sephardic Studies now for us is where feminism was twenty years ago." Kligman further notes that while Jewish history is usually pretty well-integrated up until 1492, the modern period is a hole that acts as if nothing happened after the Expulsion. Kligman suggests the creation of a new core focused on: Sephardim in the Western World, including the New World; Sephardim in Israel; and Judaism and Other Religions, including mysticism.

As part of his presentation, Kligman distributes a document from HUC titled "Sephardic Studies Curriculum Vision Statement," which explains the program's focus:

> The Sephardic Studies Curriculum aims to contextualize the Sephardic tradition into the larger picture of Jewish life acquired by HUC-JIR students. In educating rabbis, cantors, educators and communal service professionals, HUC-JIR is dedicated to developing in each student a commitment to Judaism and exposing each to the diversity within the Jewish tradition. The Sephardic Curriculum seeks to enhance and develop students' knowledge of pluralism, diversity, tolerance and cultural interaction.

The document includes thought-provoking "Guided Questions," such as

> Which factors produced the rise of the Golden Age of Spain? What has Sephardic culture preserved . . . from the Golden Age? Discuss the Sephardic Model for cultural interaction, tolerance, and pluralism in the past . . . Given the richness of Sephardic history and its intimate connection to Islamic and Christian life . . . how does this model of cultural interaction help you to conceptualize Jewish history? . . .

This document—while a huge step forward—defines *Sephardic* strictly in terms of Iberia, until the expulsion, when the Sephardic diaspora spread to areas that had already been inhabited for centuries by Arab Jews. Elsewhere this brief document mentions "Middle Eastern traditions" and "liturgy of various traditions . . . Moroccan, Middle Eastern (Syrian, Turkish, Greek)." Clearly some level of inclusion of Mizrahim is intended, but the intention is faintly realized. It needs to be said: Sephardic experience from Spain or Portugal does not cover the field nor does "Sephardic" necessarily mean "European"; Spanish and Arab culture are deeply entangled.

Shortly after the Roundtable, I asked scholar Ammiel Alcalay what he thought of the need to integrate Mizrahi/Sephardi experience into Jewish Studies. His response was characteristically large:

> I think the whole idea of Jewish history has to be reframed. The discipline as such has kind of suffocated itself because of ideology blinders and lack of contextualization, and a kind of Judeo-centric view of history. I have an increasing problem with

the idea of Jewish history as such: you have to look at geography, you have to look at time, at very basic interactions.

So you include Mizrahi history into Jewish history, but then you have to go much further and put Jewish history within human history—and that I find happening really rarely. One of the things that was implicit in what I was doing in *After Jews and Arabs* was redefinition of Europe. If you have all these people who were in Europe for eight hundred years or so, in Spain—are they European? All these categories really need to be interrogated and turned up on their ear somehow to get to something a little more real.[85]

Similarly, Ella Shohat argues for understanding the situation of Arab Jews as an opening:

The case of Arab Jews is just one of many elisions. . . . Mizrahi/ Sephardi peace movements, from the [Israeli] Black Panthers of the 1970s to the more recent East for Peace and Oriental Front groups in Israel, Perspectives Judeo-Arabes in France, and the New York-based World Organization of Jews from Islamic Countries, not only call for a just peace for Israelis and Palestinians, but also for the cultural, political, and economic integration of Israel/ Palestine into the Middle East and North Africa. They thus call, as do I, for an end to the binarisms of war, an end to a simplistic charting of Middle Eastern identities.[86]

What is essential to grasp and internalize: the dominant conception of "Jewish"—light-skinned, European, Yiddish-speaking—is in fact a subset. But let's not replace the mono-Ashkenazi with an Ashkenazi-Sephardic binary; not even with a Mizrahi-Sephardi-Ashkenazi triplet. Not all Jews fit any of these categories, and besides there is significant overlap and interplay among categories, beginning perhaps with Spain, where Europe and Africa met. What we need to do is pull the thread of Ashkenazi dominance so that hierarchy collapses into an appropriately global construct.

So we move past simplistic dichotomies. Jew vs. Arab? More than one million Israeli Jews and a significant number of Canadian and French Jews are both. Arabs hate Jews? Moroccan King Muhammed V resisted the Vichy regime in the 1940s, stating "There are no Jews or Arabs in Morocco; there are only Moroccans."[87] (Wouldn't the film classic *Casablanca* be enriched by this tidbit, instead of depicting—as it does—Moroccans joyously bursting into *La Marseillaise*?). I have already drawn extensively on Ammiel Alcalay's brilliant scholarly exploration, *After Jews and Arabs: Remaking Levantine Culture*, which demonstrates the entwined culture and history, and the impact on Europe of the two "natural opposites." Whose interest does the assumption that Jews and Arabs are automatic enemies serve? Once again, Jews stand in for the West in what is seen and named openly in the White House as a holy war against the infidel. Arabs/Muslims are blamed and targeted indiscriminately for all political violence, all terror, all the ways in which people in the United States now feel unsafe.

In the 1940s, Rachel Wahba's family left Iraq, traveled through Mumbai, where Rachel was born, to Japan, where the parents remained for twenty years before joining Rachel, who had arrived in California ten years earlier.[88] Another family in, say, Holland, perhaps Sephardic in origin and in culture: one sibling might have escaped to the United States, another to Argentina, a third to China, and a fourth to South Africa. Were they Dutch? And are the survivors and their families now, respectively, American, Argentinian, Chinese, and South African? In 1933, Lily Golden's communist parents, a Polish Jew and an African American, moved to the Soviet Union to escape U.S. racism and to help build the Soviet Revolution. Are Golden and her daughter Yelena Khanga Russian Jews?[89] My friend Dalia's grandparents, early Zionists, left Eastern Europe for then-Palestine, but could not survive economically and so moved to Egypt, where Dalia was born: an Egyptian Jew?

Listen to Katya Gibel Azoulay:

> My children's genealogy encompasses three continents—my mother came to America as a refugee from Nazi Austria where her *race* was listed as Jewish; my father emigrated from Jamaica and his ancestry is Afro-Cuban-Caribbean with a Scotsman (not married to his maternal ancestor) among his (mutually) unacknowledged forefathers. I was born in New York City where my birth certificate lists my mother as "white" and my father as "Negro." My children's father was the second of four children born in Jerusalem after his parents immigrated to Israel from Morocco in North Africa with three children.[90]

Only respect for the full range of Jewish experience can prevent the loss and distortion that is racism. Moroccan writer Ruth Knafo Setton, whose family immigrated to the United States, was asked as a child by her teacher in front of the class, "Is it true you eat people in Morocco?"[91] That this came from the Jewish community toward a Jewish child is only part of the significance; the other part is inextricably bound up with racism against Africans, Jewish and non-Jewish alike. Similarly, the editor who read Knafo Setton's novel—*The Road to Fez*—in manuscript and requested,

"Next time try writing about the real Jews,"[92] devalued both Setton's Jewish life and her Arab life.

Devalued her Arab Jewish life.

The significance of this extends far beyond racist deletion of this or that Jew, as unacceptable as that deletion is, and extends to the roots of what and who is a Jew. If some Jews are Arabs and some Arabs are Jews—and have been for centuries; if al-Andalus is Europe and Arab Jews live all over the world; if Arab and Jewish cultures and languages and food and music and art and film are at times intertwined; if "when Jews wrote in Arabic, they ordinarily referred to God as 'Allah'";[93] if Arab and Jew are distinct but not opposing categories; most importantly, if one can be both, as, we have seen one can be black and Jewish, then the inevitable impossible-to-bridge binary vanishes and we stand on seriously common ground.

What if we recognize and welcome those of us who are both Jewish and Arab? What if we learn about the shared foundational history of Judeo-Arab culture? What might that common history and culture do to assumptions of inherent inevitable conflict? to the swallowing of Judaism into "Judeo-Christian" culture?

Turning inside out has a dual function: when we situate the excluded experience where it rightfully belongs, we see the formerly dominant experience differently. If Ashkenazi/Europe is not all there is, then even Ashkenazi experience in Europe bears reexamination. Assumptions about Europe, as nothing but ghettos and segregation, fail to explain, for example, the language. How is it that the Ashkenazis developed Yiddish, a language so close to German that Yiddish and German speakers can converse? David Biale suggests, "For every period of history, interaction with the non-Jewish majority has been critical in the formation of Jewish culture. Even those Jewish cultures thought to be the most insular adapted ideas and practices from their surroundings."[94] Biale points to periods of high interaction followed by more internal periods, so that those Jews who spoke Ladino/Judeo-Español in Spain communicated easily with Castilians; they spoke the same language. But when they continued to speak it in Serbia, Salonika, Palestine, Turkey . . . it was quite another story. Similarly the Yiddish-speaking Jews who moved into Eastern Europe did not develop, for example, Judeo-Polish or Judeo-Russian, but instead integrated Polish and Russian into Yiddish. Focused in this way, a different pattern of Jewish history emerges. Mix, separate, mix, separate. Each mixing a change so that when time for separation comes around, what separates out is not the same. Paul Gilroy makes a similar argument about blending, unrecognized interaction, and cross-fertilization between English/black culture/history. "This blending is misunderstood if it is conceived in simple ethnic terms, but right and left, racist and anti-racist, black and white tacitly share a view of it as little more than a collision between fully formed and mutually exclusive cultural communities."[95] As Gilroy knows: nothing is fully formed. Nothing is mutually exclusive. On neither side is it the same. In fact, are there sides?

Or, in the language of Jewish aspiration, ingather, wander, ingather, wander.

U.S. JEWS

Emily Schnee is an Ashkenazi Jew married to a Nicaraguan Christian. Their twins, Benjamin and Camilo, were beginning to grapple with being Jewish and Christian, Latino and white.

CAMILO AND BENJAMIN TORUÑO

When my kids must have been about 3½, we went by Garfield Temple and they were just figuring out what churches are, their school is in a church, and Camilo asked, Mommy is that a church? I said, No, it's a synagogue and he said what's that and I said it's a church for Jewish people. So he said, what's Jewish? which made me feel like I was a total failure in Jewish education.

The other day Camilo says to me— we're reading all this Passover stuff and all of the references are in the past, *when we were in Egypt*—he says, We were Jews, right? I said, No, we *are* Jews, and he said, We're still Jews?

They were happy yesterday getting picked up early from day-care for the seder, and they told their teacher why, and they said, we're Christian and Jewish. They seem to like saying they're both. Like they say, we're from New York and Nicaragua. Today I put matzoh with cream cheese in their lunchboxes. There have been situations previously where one of their teachers didn't know what some food in their lunchbox was, some health food, dried papaya. Camilo loves the stuff but he didn't want me to put it in his lunch-box any more. Around the matzoh I perceived their first anxiety as a minority: they wanted to know, will the teachers know what it is? I said they'll know what it is. But the kids went through a mental checklist of all the other kids, who would know and who might not know what matzoh was. One thought their Latino teacher would know, the other wasn't so sure. They were talking about their friends, and I'm not sure they know who is and isn't Jewish, or how they decided who would know what matzoh was.

Recently I was reading to them a book about the underground railroad. The book doesn't talk about black and white, but in the pictures, all the slaves are black and the masters are white, and the people who help are also white. I had anxiety that in learning about racism, they might believe some racist ideas. But then we started reading about Passover and I realized how different it is when you, your people have been enslaved, and that made me feel so much more comfortable as a white person because they were learning that Jews had also been slaves, so they weren't going to accept that there was a good reason for any people to be slaves.[96]

What is the racial makeup of the Jewish community in the United States? Mostly Ashkenazi, yes; but what does that tell us? Neither the *National Jewish Population Survey 2000–2001* nor the *Jewish Community Study of New York 2002* seems to have asked even one question about race.[97] Tobin et al. summarize the difficulty of counting Jews of any race: census counts do not ask about religion or culture; the diaspora means exactly that Jews are "highly dispersed," thus difficult to find; and "some Jews do not want to be found."[98]

In an earlier stage of research in 2004, Gary Tobin estimated the number of Jews of color at about 400,000 out of 6 million Jews, and this total does not include Sephardic Jews, who represent about 6.67 percent.[99] However when researchers begin to complicate their findings—with Israelis in the United States (whom they estimate at 50 percent Mizrahi or Sephardi); with those who describe themselves as Jewish-and-other (rather than white); with the 120,000 foreign-born Jews whom they assess as more than 50 percent of color; with the common underestimation of Sephardi ("Millions of people have Jewish ancestors, especially those of Portuguese, Spanish, and African descent, but are unaware of it"). Imagine, too, the bi- and multiracial Jews who might be disproportionately uncounted because they are alienated from Jewish community. Do the math: according to these calculations, the number of Jews of color jumps to "at least 20%."[100] Even if this figure is overprojected, what is clear is this:

The number of Jews of color is large enough that Jewish whiteness should never be assumed.

Should we say it again?

The number of Jews of color is large enough that Jewish whiteness should never be assumed.

Through intermarriage, adoption, conversion, reimmersion, and reclaiming: The number of Jews of color is growing both in the United States and worldwide.

Imagine the internal migration that might take place if the Jewish community were open and welcoming, so that alienated Jews would choose to engage or reengage with other Jews. Imagine if intermarriage brought people warmly and automatically into the Jewish community instead of requiring conversion. Imagine if a recent study on interracial marriage among Jews did not indicate a persistent and powerful bias against African Americans. More than half the respondents agreed (strongly or somewhat) with the statement that "Most white Jews would be comfortable with their child marrying a Jew who is Asian; or a Jew who is Latino." Yet when the prospective spouse shifted to specify "a Jew who is black," the rate of agreement dropped to 15 percent.[101] This is a *shande*. It's critical that Jews not follow conventional racial progress, which is to mainstream Asians and Latinos, jumping ahead in the queue of upward mobility, while maintaining the bottom for blacks.[102]

What about the widespread practice of adoption? Demand for Jewish babies is high. Some will remember the scandal of hundreds of Yemeni Jewish babies taken in the 1950s from their parents in Israel on pretext of illness; these children were reported dead and sold to Ashkenazi Jews in and out of Israel.[103] In the past twenty years or so, most Jewish would-be parents have simply adopted non-Jewish babies, many of whom are of color, many of whom are virtually purchased in the international market. Some raise their children as Jews; some don't. Some convert the children as infants, a practice I confess makes my skin crawl for reasons I find hard to explain. Perhaps it's the nonvolitional aspect (but babies never get to choose their religion), or the lack of need, in my book (if you're raising them Jewish, they're Jews). I wonder, too, how many make the effort to raise these children biculturally, as both Jewish and whatever else they are. As Rabbi Angela Warnick Buchdahl, a mixed heritage Korean/Ashkenazi Jew, has remarked, a Jewish family that adopts a Chinese baby needs to understand: "You are now a Chinese Jewish family."[104]

In fact, the dramatic increase in transnational adoption is beginning to have a huge impact on the racial and ethnic identities of Jews now in their teens and even twenties. The Farbrangen Cheder cooperative Jewish Sunday School in Washington D.C. has a student body consisting of about 25 percent children of African descent.[105] Among my Jewish friends I number an American-Belgian couple (heterosexual) who gave birth to one child and adopted a second, from Peru (they moved from an East Coast industrial city to the Southwest, so that the whole family could root in Latino/Jewish culture). Other friends include a U.S. couple (heterosexual) who adopted a child from Paraguay and gave birth to a second child (they spend months at a time in Costa Rica). A lesbian couple, one born Ashkenazi/Jewish, the other a Jew by choice, who adopted two African American girls. A lesbian couple, one Jewish, one Italian, who adopted a girl from Peru (they spend time in Mexico whenever possible). An Ashkenazi Jewish man and a Latina woman, who just gave birth to twins. An Ashkenazi Jewish woman married to a Nicaraguan man, also had twins. An Ashkenazi Jewish man partnered with a South Asian woman planning to have children. A lesbian couple, one Guatemalan Sephardi and one U.S. Ashkenazi who gave birth to a daughter through insemination by sperm deliberately chosen from a Latino. Some of these children are being raised in a consciously Jewish context; some not.

Add up the racial diversity I've just described. But for the most part, look around the room at Jewish events: at services, at celebrations, at cultural happenings—odds are the room will not reflect this racial diversity. The sparsity of color in the organized Jewish community is at least partly due to the lack of welcome, the blankness, the weird blend of invisibility and hypervisibility that people of color encounter. In a word, racism. People fear it. People experience it.

Witness the controversy in Israel (and in the U.S. Orthodox Jewish community) over whether some Ethiopian Jews were "really Jewish." As Hagar Salamon notes, in coming to Israel, Ethiopian immigrants "found themselves singled out as 'blacks' for the first time in their history." She continues: "The contrast between the silence on the racial question among Israeli Jews and the vocal mention of the issue by their fellow Jews in the Diaspora [is] . . . striking. The Ethiopian Jews have formed the focus of attempts by Jews outside Israel, particularly those in the United States, to disprove allegations that Judaism is racist."[106]

The rejection of Beta Israel's "authenticity" mirrors Jewish denial: if Jews are white, then are nonwhites really Jews? There was/is far less concern over the authenticity of Russian Jews, despite the fact that most Ethiopian Jews are religiously observant, while most Russian Jews are not and moreover know almost nothing about Jewishness. Besides, as is widely rumored, a fair proportion of the Russians claiming Jewish ancestry for purposes of making aliyah (immigration) are not actually Jewish.

This difference in community response is explained partly by orthodoxy: there's some rabbinic anxiety over the religious practice that developed in Ethiopia, separated for centuries from the Judaism that developed elsewhere under rabbinic control. Katya Gibel Azoulay warns us against glib acontextual explanations of a broad array of Jewish custom, observance, and so on, as racism. She notes:

> somebody posted an article that said black Jews had trouble finding spouses. As the controversy unfolded, it turned out the people having trouble—a small number—are converts. . . . Their issues are not the issues of, say, Ethiopian Jews. One can't just talk about black Jews. . . . One important point missing from the email exchange was that Brooklyn [the location] is filled with Persian Jews, Syrian Jews, Iraqi Jews, African Jews, a few from Ethiopia, Yemenite Jews, Jews who fit into that broad rubric of people of color, though they don't necessarily identify as people of color. . . . But these are not people who are necessarily going to embrace someone who's converted unless through very traditional orthodox circles. The discourse of American tolerance and liberalism means many people are saying—and I'm not saying if I agree or disagree—that if anyone wants to identify as Jewish, that's enough for me. That's fine. But then you're talking about something entirely different. You want to wake up in the morning and decide you're Jewish, attend synagogue, find a rabbi, bring your own cultural traditions into it, recreate a new type of Jewish identity, that's fine. But that does not necessarily guarantee acceptance, and the lack of acceptance may have almost nothing to do with color. . . . There are expectations at times put on certain Jewish communities that are not the same ones that would be put on another group. Of course there is still a question of color prejudice, but I don't think everything is reduced to color prejudice.[107]

But it's hard to explain otherwise the openhanded outreach to the Euro-origin Russians vs. the shaming insistence on conversion for the Ethiopians, including circumcision of grown men.

Or the 1996 revelation that Israeli blood banks "had for years been routinely disposing of blood donated by Ethiopians," for fear of contamination by HIV.[108] Or the news that in 2002 a leading Conservative rabbi charged two Orthodox kibbutzim with racial discrimination "after they refused to admit two Ugandan Jews to their language program."[109]

Some Jewish parents sit shiva for a child who marries a *goy* (non-Jew)—though with the rate of Jewish intermarriage perhaps as high as one in two, one suspects that this has become quite rare. Is the mourning especially deep for those who marry a nonwhite *goy*? Consider the impact of this disinheritance and exclusion on a community that bemoans its shrinkage and loss of Jewish continuity.

Rebecca Walker asked, "Am I possible?" What is *possible*? People used to "know" that the sun circled the earth. As more data was collected, more and more elaborate theories evolved to explain the data in ways consistent with earth-centrism. But at some point a vast collective sigh must have been released along with a massive simplification: ah, yes, the sun is at the center—and all the dangling data falls into place. It is exactly this disorientation I seek by decentering Europe in the Jewish experience. How hard it is to let go of what you think you've known all your life. Letting go of the familiar, learning to embrace—at least to stand next to—the strange. Recognizing that to many Jews, I, my accent, my foods, my smells are strange. Letting go of the unconscious comforting assumption on which I was raised: we are the real, the normal Jews, and those others are other. This decentering has several phases: who represents, who speaks for, who is seen as, who is welcomed: Who shapes and mobilizes the Jewish future?

[4] PRAYING WITH OUR LEGS

JENNY ROMAINE

We believe that to kvetch is human, to act divine.

—Progressive Jewish Alliance, Los Angeles

The late Rabbi Abraham Joshua Heschel is reported to have said, of the famous 1965 Selma-to-Montgomery civil rights march, "I felt like my legs were praying."

In cities across the nation, Jews have created locally based, visibly Jewish antiracist, antipoverty initiatives. These groups emerged as progressive Jews grew collectively troubled by the Jewish right wing presenting itself as *the* voice of U.S. Jews, while Jewish progressives, broadly active in progressive movements, were mostly invisible *as Jews*.

In response to an increasingly fractious self-proclaimed Jewish right, progressive Jews have visibly mobilized Jewish organizing around racial and economic justice. Although most of these groups are locally created, defined, and controlled, some have had significant contact with each other. In several instances, older and more developed groups have offered trainings and consultations to the newcomers.[1] Some of these consultations were funded by the Jewish Fund for Justice (JFJ), which in 2000 created the Jewish Social Justice Network precisely to support this sense of connection and cooperation among those Jewish social justice groups that had received some funding from JFJ.[2]

The Network folded in 2004 for lack of funds, but the concept of attempting on occasion to speak with a strong united voice has found a different format. In April 2004, the Jewish Council on Urban Affairs (JCUA; Chicago), the grandparent of us all, assumed leadership, creating a conference on working Jewishly for social justice. In December 2005, with curriculum designed by the much younger but fast-growing energetic Jewish Community Action (JCA; St. Paul–Minneapolis), in Chicago, under the auspices of JCUA, some sixty activists were trained in community organizing. In addition, JCUA has facilitated working with UNITE/HERE and other unions, honoring the Jewish historical role in the needle trades specifically and labor movements more generally.

But largely the groups work to visibly and Jewishly confront racism and fight for economic justice. What is the theory and practice of such groups? What are they good for? What makes them Jewish? What is the relationship between this antiracist work and Jewish racial and ethnic diversity?

In pursuit of these questions, I interviewed the leaders of four such groups: Jewish Council on Urban Affairs in Chicago; Jewish Community Action in St. Paul; Jews United for Justice in St. Louis (JUJ); and Jews for Racial and Economic Justice in New York (JFREJ). There are many others I might have chosen. (In the following chapter, I interview leaders of groups focused specifically on Jewish diversity.)

Many of these groups deliberately evoke a framework that goes something like this: *Jewish history teaches us to welcome the stranger, reminds us of the dangers of racial hatred, and instructs us to pursue justice.* The following, from the website of Minneapolis's Jewish Community Action (JCA) is typical:

> "Love the stranger because you were strangers in the land of Egypt." (Deuteronomy 10:19) Because you once knew how it feels to be a stranger, you should know better! The admonition to love the stranger occurs 36 times in the Bible, many more times than Sabbath observance rules, dietary laws, or admonitions against stealing, lying or coveting. Why the stranger? Because the stranger is weak, defenseless, alone—scorned, wronged, and in need of protection.
>
> Our grandparents were "strangers." My grandfather came to this country in 1883 as a young boy of 13, all by himself. Somebody met him at Castle Gardens and brought him to a family. I know where he lived, a tenement on Essex Street on the Lower East Side in New York, because I searched for it and found it. He was taken in as a child, made a life and raised a family. This is my story. Your story is likely to be similar. If your grandparents or great-grandparents were not embraced as strangers, you would not be here today.

Likewise the assertion that Jewish religion, ethics, and/or values instruct us to pursue justice. From the website of Chicago's Jewish Council on Urban Affairs (JCUA):

> *Tikkun Olam* commands Jews to reconstruct the world by reaching out to those in need. *Tzedakah* comes from the Hebrew word *tzedek* which translates as justice. According to the 12th Century Jewish

sage Maimonides, the highest form of *tzedakah* is helping people to help themselves. Since our inception, these principles have led JCUA to pursue social and economic justice and build a better quality of life for all of Chicago.

Jews for Racial and Economic Justice in New York City (JFREJ), as part of its campaigns for immigrant rights, signs off its e-mail alerts as follows:

> Jewish tradition teaches:
>
> You shall not oppress the stranger, for you were strangers in the land of Egypt.
>
> You shall not oppress a worker, whether s/he is of your community or a newcomer in your land.
>
> There shall be one standard of law, for citizens and strangers alike.

Washington D.C.'s Jews United for Justice created the following text based on comments from participants at their founding meetings:

> BECAUSE in the early morning hours we wonder if we're longing for a Jewish left or left Judaism & we often feel not quite at home in the communities we create & we worry that anti-semitism is too strong a word & we have more than one favorite deli and they're both the best & we know in our souls what a ghetto is & we come in all colors and orientations & we're surprised that progressive politics and Judaism can be un-entwined & we know where talk of penny-pinchers, bankers, and unsuccessful garage sales leads & it is worth knowing if your mother was from Lodz or Riga or Cairo & we often notice Saturdays & we've learned that you can always choose your own response to any situation & Judaism is an infinite resource & it aches not to bring our Judaism to our justice work & our homes must be places of refuge and sanctuary lest we never forget & locks reminds us of bagels not keys & our elders often fear yellow Stars of David are the reward for a local Jewish presence & we were fourteen year old girls working in sweatshops and leading textile strikes & contradictory and mutually exclusive have never been obstacles for stereotypes & we've never spoken only one language & our roots are in both the working class and the class that exploits them & we should have learned to never tolerate turning a blind eye & when ugliness rears its head we can be invisible and feel sick about it for weeks & we take hate-crimes, military solutions, and McCarthyism personally & "Gypsies," homosexuals, and intellectuals were targeted, too

& because other people try to define what it is to be us, WE ARE JEWS UNITED FOR JUSTICE.

The text is now used on an appealing JUFJ poster. The JUFJ text packs its message, asserting a "natural" affinity between Jewishness and left politics, and acknowledging the dangers of anti-semitism and the alienation of many progressive Jews from the Jewish mainstream.

Between Jewish history and Jewish morals, our job as Jews is pretty clear.

These groups do not, for the most part, focus on anti-semitism, though they all acknowledge and confront it as it blocks alliances or scapegoats Jews. In part this reflects a (mostly unarticulated) sense that anti-semitism gets plenty of attention from more mainstream Jewish groups, albeit in an isolated hysteria-generating or competitive fashion. Nor do these groups focus on Jewish poverty, which today afflicts a sizeable minority of the Jewish community—especially seniors, immigrants, and Orthodox Jews—though Jewish poverty is included in the range of poverty they expose and challenge. These groups may implement their values differently, with varying emphases on technical assistance, community empowerment, local electoral politics, and street solidarity; and different key issues, such as housing, labor, police brutality, health care, immigrant rights. But none of these groups sees itself as doing social work or "helping"; this is not Christian charity, which marks the giver's goodness. They speak the language of political radicals—partnering, coalition, transformation—which also reflects a Jewish expectation: to be human is to seek justice.

Often these groups get asked, "Why are you helping *them*? What's Jewish about that?" JCUA's Jane Ramsay responds,

> That goes to consistently connecting the dots for people, but I think it also goes deeper to a lack of leadership within our community that is teaching and passing on the values. Among those reasons is why we felt it was so important for us to start creating environments to nurture the leadership—young leadership, old leadership, rabbinic leadership—to remember Jewish values for justice, and teach them and hold them central to who we are as Jews.[3]

All these groups emphasize local, as opposed to national and especially international, arenas.[4] The most contentious issue in "the" Jewish community generally—the morass we call in shorthand Israel/Palestine—is carefully defined as outside the purview of most of these groups. JFREJ is unique in taking a position on Israel/Palestine, though insisting simultaneously on limiting the organization's focus, a compromise reached after a protracted struggle, and a promise not to deal with the issue again for some long (unspecified) period of time. Even so, JFREJ lost some members over this decision, in disagreement not so much with the politics as with the organization going anywhere near this potentially divisive and resource-consuming issue. JFREJ's statement reads as follows:

> JFREJ will begin to take positions on foreign affairs in limited situations only: when the issue relates directly to our local work and taking a position facilitates that work, or when there is a clear and compelling need to present an alternative Jewish voice that is not being presented by other visible Jewish groups.
>
> Specifically at this time, on the issues of the Israel/Palestine conflict . . . , we take the following positions: JFREJ opposes the Israeli occupation of the West Bank, Gaza Strip and East Jerusalem and supports a negotiated, just and secure peace for Israelis and Palestinians. JFREJ opposes collective punishment and attacks on civilians. We take these positions while reaffirming that JFREJ is a community of Jews with diverse political and ideological relationships to this situation—JFREJ members are Zionists and post-Zionists, non-Zionists, anti-Zionists and those with no identification with these framings.
>
> At the same time, we reiterate our belief in the Bundist tradition of *doikayt* ("hereness")—the idea that Jews, in coalition with — others, should focus their struggle for universal equality and justice in the place where they live. In this spirit, JFREJ rejects the notion that as a Jewish American organization we are required to take a position on the Israel/Palestine conflict, nor do we believe that our identity or priorities as a Jewish organization should be determined by the actions of Jews in another country. We do believe that, in these instances, as residents of the United States, we have cause to speak out on matters related to our own government's foreign policies.[5]

Two strong arguments for the New York-based JFREJ taking such positions is that New York politicians, especially, presume Jewish obsession with, and uncritical support for, Israel, and play accordingly. The mainstream Jewish groups have been attentive to anti-Arab and anti-Muslim bashing in the wake of 9/11, and many have been outspoken in condemning this racism. Yet the racism itself continues to permeate Jewish communities, as it permeates the larger society, and permits the systematic dehumanization of the Palestinian people under the auspices of U.S. tax dollars. Anti-Arab, anti-Muslim racism inside and outside Jewish community in the United States makes possible not only the targeting at home of Arabs, Muslims, and those who might be either, but also the continued occupation of the West Bank and Gaza Strip. Racism and immigrant rights are squarely within JFREJ's mission.

JCUA's stance, while rock solid on fighting anti-Arab racism, is more typical of the local Jewish social justice organizations. Jane Ramsey explains:

> We don't deal with Middle East issues. We're very clear straight out that it's not the work we do. Our work has always been domestic social justice, very local, and that keeps us from diverting our attention. Once Israel comes into the equation, that's the focus and you lose the ability to move forward. . . . Our partners in the Muslim community want to reach out locally, too. They want to build working relationships and they can't do it either if they get into the Israel/Palestine question.[6]

Similarly, JCA steers clear of foreign policy, but connects with relevant local ramifications. Vic Rosenthal spells it out:

> We work hard to keep foreign policy issues from having an impact on our work. There are a handful of people, particularly on the left, who are discouraged by the fact that we're unwilling to take on the issues of war or terrorism or Israel. The one way we've gotten involved with these issues is through their impact on local civil liberties.[7]

All of these groups have raised explicitly Jewish voices in opposition to mainstream Jewish community wrongs, bringing identified Jews out to the picket lines at Jewish-owned or Jewish-managed institutions where workers are trying to organize: delis, factories, restaurants, old age homes. At moments when bosses or political figures or members of the mainstream Jewish community have attempted to use spurious charges of anti-semitism to evade issues of economic justice, a visible Jewish presence with a strong message about Jewish ethics has deflected these charges and kept the issue focused.

Summer 1993: a union organizer for SEIU/1199, the hospital and health care workers, phones the JFREJ office. It seems that the mostly immigrant, mostly women, Latina and

Caribbean workers at a nursing home are trying to organize. The nursing home's owners are Hasidim, and they are
charging the union with anti-semitism. The union wants
JFREJ to send a speaker to the rally.

We check out the anti-semitism charge—we wouldn't
just ignore the possibility—and it's baseless. So I arrive at the
rally in the street outside the Brooklyn nursing home. I am
one of perhaps three white people in the crowd. When it's
my turn to speak, two men have to help me step up onto the
sound truck. I say who I am and a few general statements. No
one is listening all that much. Then I define *shande* for the
crowd (Yiddish for something shameful). And I yell through
the megaphone at the Yiddish-speaking owners of this business, this is a *shande. Shande.* The word resonates with the
workers. *Shande* echoes back from the crowd: *Shande.*

FIGHTING SLUMLORDS, BUILDING COALITIONS: JEWISH COUNCIL ON URBAN AFFAIRS (CHICAGO)

JANE RAMSEY

Jane Ramsey is one of the most respected
people in the world of progressive Jewish
activism, and one of the most sensible. Her
work with JCUA began in 1979. When the
great unifier Harold Washington was elected
Mayor of Chicago, as part of a powerful multiracial coalition, Jane worked as coordinator
for the Jewish Committee for Washington, in
both the '83 and '87 campaigns. She served
in the Washington administration as Director
of Community Relations from 1986 until his
death in 1987. She also served in her own words as "the house Jew." She
returned in 1988 to lead JCUA.[8]

JANE RAMSEY: JCUA is more than forty years old. It was established
with a threefold mission coming out of the civil rights movement
in the 1960s. One, to help people in grassroots, disenfranchised
communities to help themselves, communities that were impacted
by racism and/or poverty. Part of our work has been community

organizing in grassroots communities and working in partnership with African American and Latino and other communities to address social justice issues such as housing, jobs, schools, inequities, police, slumlords. We were involved in early years in neighborhoods where the [white] Jewish community was moving out and the African American community was moving in and there were some bad slumlord incidents. Some black families bought homes on contract from Jewish families because of redlining by mortgage and insurance companies. There were some unscrupulous sellers that took advantage and there was a lawsuit filed called the Contract Buyers League. JCUA worked with the African American families, first to try and negotiate some settlements and then joining the lawsuit. The *Atlantic Monthly* did a story that said because there were Jews on both sides it kept it from being a black–Jewish confrontation. That was in the late sixties–early seventies.

We are the oldest local Jewish social justice organization in the country by far and, to my knowledge, the largest. My sense is that there are things we can test here, in terms of how broad and deep, how far can we move this Jewish community to be progressive, that we can't test out in any other place in the country. Our interest is not just local, but in testing models and in developing ways of reaching the Jewish community and then sharing it with others across the country. I think we do have an opportunity and we've reached a level where we can try and start to see how far we can reach our mission, which says we're going to involve the Jewish community in making social change.

In the early days there were minority communities that were completely disenfranchised from government, and to get any equity out of government, whether it was sewers or access to any city services, to schools, it took a lot of fighting and organizing. JCUA worked in partnership, from the earliest days and through to the present, with the community organizations to address equity issues. Housing has been a major issue for us over the years, both confronting slumlords as we did and in partnerships helping to develop housing for very low-income singles and families as well.

Community organizations approach JCUA and ask for our assistance. We never go into a neighborhood unless we're invited in. These are often communities where they've never seen another Jewish person. JCUA partnerships address social issues coming out of our Judaic, prophetic commitment. From the standpoint of the

Jewish community, it also builds relationships and addresses issues of anti-semitism that you cannot begin to address if you're strangers. Over time, in some instances for forty years, we've had consistent relationships. We believe that's how you address the stereotypes, anti-semitism, and racism.

We provide technical assistance to grassroots community groups on the issues they choose, whether it's housing, jobs, living wage, police brutality, or schools. JCUA will work with an organization for two, three years at a time. They come to us with the issue. We'll decide whether it fits our criteria—is this a vulnerable community, are there other resources available to the organization. . . . We don't give out cans of food or coats or shelter. Our work is to help communities become able to feed their people and provide shelter. We're not a social service agency. Nothing against social service agencies, but that's not what we do. We do social justice work.

Another piece of our work is coalition building, where we bring people together from the Jewish, African American, Latino, and multiple communities where issues cross to work together. JCUA participates in many coalitions and in coalition-building around social justice matters in Chicago, state-wide, and even nationally where appropriate.

The third thing we do is educate and mobilize the Jewish community. We have a curriculum that we have taught for the past twenty years with Jewish synagogue youth. We reach about one thousand a year, teaching them issues of poverty and justice and how to work in our community and in other communities, and what we as a community can do to bring about systemic change. That's done in about thirty synagogues each year. Our membership is about seven thousand. We're trying to get a handle on "What does that mean?" We've been around a long time and we've worked with a very limited set of resources, but JCUA has always been on the cutting edge of issues, not just on the edge in Jewish communities. We're one of the few organizations that stand with public housing residents and is willing to take on the mayor. We're independent, so we go out far. That, by definition, has made the fundraising piece difficult, but we've gotten a lot better at the fundraising and membership development.

We don't want to just get young Jews who want to dabble in social justice, we want them to understand what happens when public housing residents are moved out and why we care about that and why we need to be in partnership with the public housing residents to ensure that they have justice and housing and that their kids aren't yanked out of school six times to be moved all over the city.

The educational component and the involvement of the membership is something we're looking at. That is a major responsibility we have—how to get the message to Jewish families, how can we involve high school youth, how can we reach the college campuses more effectively. We're really looking at all the different components, including synagogues, obviously.

In terms of involving members, the lion's share of day to day organizing work over the forty years has been done by staff, but the direction of policy setting has been led by the board. It's a very gutsy board; for example, the board members were among the people who stood with the people who were evicted from the west side of Chicago with the contract buyers. They physically put people's furniture back in their homes.[9]

In the early years there was major resistance. In the very early years, JCUA was significantly funded by the Federation.[10] When we started getting involved with the Contract Buyers League, some people put pressure on the Federation to renege on the grant and they did. Those kinds of battles were very painful. It is really to the credit of a strong group of lay people who were very gutsy, very courageous, and kept JCUA going. They raised and gave the money and made sure there was a strong Jewish presence on civil rights and all these issues in Chicago.

The Chicago Federation is a very strong Federation, and there was a desire, particularly in the sixties and seventies that if you were going to speak as a Jewish organization on any issues—black/Jewish relations or whatever—that you have to be speaking from headquarters, from the central Jewish community. Our position as an independent organization was that the Jewish community is multifaceted, and that we represent a part of the Jewish community. We're not speaking on behalf of all of the Jewish community, but a strong portion of it. So, if it's pro-affirmative action—we had a strong affirmative action coalition, for example—at a time when there were Jewish organizations that weren't for affirmative action. There was a struggle in terms of the legitimacy of an independent Jewish voice. I'm very happy to say that's not the case anymore. We have good relationships with the Jewish Federation, which has given JCUA modest annual support since the early eighties. We have good relationships with other Jewish organizations too, and we are seen as a significant Jewish organization in town.

JCUA's successes are all tied up in the successes of the organizations we work with. Twenty-five years ago we were working in the Mexican community in Pilsen, a Chicago neighborhood. They were very concerned about gentrification, it was close to downtown, a hot spot for developers who would have liked this Mexican community to disappear so they could take over their property. A lot of our work with that community was and continues to be working with them to organize for their survival.

One developer wanted to take over an industrial area and turn it into little boutiques. We worked in partnerships with one of the organizations and were able to build a coalition with the industrialists and to fight off the wholesale turning over of that industrial property, which would have been a loss of jobs, as well as to prevent an enormous spur of gentrification.

There was a plan by Mayor Byrne to build a 1992 World's Fair, and we found out they were going to take Pilsen and Chinatown and turn them into parking lots for the World's Fair. One of our staff members and early founders was a historian and researcher and dug up all this information that people had no idea about at the time. People didn't know there was going to be a World's Fair in Chicago and they certainly didn't know that Pilsen was supposed to be a parking lot.

Part of our job was digging up information and sharing it with the right people to blow the lid off it. A big portion of the black community on the west side was going to be a golf course for Mayor Daley (the first Mayor Daley) and we helped dig up that information and get it to the right people. When JCUA and its coalition partners got the information to the media, the plan was abandoned by City Hall. Lawndale remained a community of houses and people as opposed to a golf course. Pilsen and Chinatown remained neighborhoods too.

JCUA has partnered over the last ten years with community development corporations to get technical assistance and seed money from some of our members to develop low income housing for single people and for families. We've helped to build over two thousand units of housing in Chicago. We've done some economic development and job creation work, all in partnership with local community groups. A lot of our work has been in the African American community, and in the Latino communities, both Mexican and Puerto Rican. We've also done work with the Orthodox Jewish community on housing.

Recently we've been very active in the Justice Coalition of Greater Chicago which JCUA helped to convene several years, a large coalition of eighty organizations involving many different groups focused on police and prosecutorial misconduct and the death penalty and other issues that heavily impact the minority communities in particular. We got a city councilman to introduce an ordinance to make some major changes in how the police department operates. If that ordinance is enacted it will help to stem police misconduct.

Other kinds of work we've done in the past include helping organize a community to get a high school in a Puerto Rican neighborhood. On the west side of Chicago I've already mentioned the Contract Buyers League, but there was also a lot of work to build community infrastructure and organization—create industrial property, commercial property, establish a bank for the black community, and housing developments. Our concern is to strengthen local grassroots community groups so that the communities themselves can fight for housing and schools. We help do the organizing, but much more important is to help strengthen the groups so they can be empowered to address these issues themselves.

After September 11, it was very clear to us what was going to happen in terms of backlash to the Muslim community, and we immediately reached out to them and held some solidarity actions and started working with them. We were part of a coalition that organized to get a resolution passed in Chicago that calls for the repeal of major sections of the Patriot Act. In fact, JCUA wrote the resolution and it was submitted by a group of city councilmen, and we helped with the Muslim Civil Rights Center, to organize the hearings. A big new piece is that the Nathan Cummings Foundation funded us to work on Jewish–Muslim relations. So we have a series of programs we are enabled to initiate and relationships we have been able to give time to over the last year and a half after the initial 9/11 attack to start building relationships.

We don't deal with Middle East issues, which is not to say it's not tricky. We can't be in a place where someone's going to stand up and make anti-semitic statements. Our work has to be very clear and the organizations we're working with have to be very clear on what we are all about. We also have to be respectful of each other, both as Jews and Muslims. So far we've been able to. We are planning a program for Jewish and Muslim girls who will participate in a poetry class together and tell their life stories. It's finding the ways, both to talk about who we are as people, and also what are our common agendas.

As a mostly Caucasian group, we've thought a lot about inclusion of Jews of color. A number of years ago we initiated a committee we named Shalem to explore how to strengthen relationships between Caucasian and minority Jews. Chicago has a relatively large number of African American Jews, and it's ironic, JCUA has a huge history with the African American community, but not with African American Jews. Shalem created a series of programs. Capers Funnye, who is African American and an Orthodox Jew, who was on staff at JCUA as the office manager, became quite a well-known rabbi; he works with Gary Tobin on studying multiracial Jews.[11]

There's a seminary in New York dating back to the 1920s that has ordained many African American rabbis, including several Chicago rabbis. Aaron Freeman, a well known African American Jewish comedian, was involved with Shalem and JCUA. We had meetings and social gathering, a wide range of people, including Hebrew Israelites and more traditional practice. A couple of years ago some rabbis did a presentation and their practice included some elements of Christianity, and that was a dilemma. And slowed the efforts of Shalem. We've worked at insuring representation by African American Jews on our board, such as Dr. Lily Golden, Rabbi Funnye, and Aaron Freeman.

Besides the dialogue, we had some successes; for example, Capers hadn't been invited to join the Chicago Board of Rabbis, and there was nothing unconventional about his practice, he's totally Orthodox. We challenged the Board of Rabbis and they finally invited him. There were large differences in the movement, from Capers who was traditional and others who identified as Jews but with some Christian beliefs. We tried some outreach with Latino Jews also, but there is a lot more work to be done. The numbers are small, and this makes it hard to sustain. But it's important to actively reach out—an opportunity, really, to recognize the diversity within our community, and to reach out to Jews of color who the mainstream Jewish community, and even antiracist Jewish organizers, don't ordinarily communicate with and who are often not wholly welcomed.

Update:

As noted above, in April, 2005, JCUA organized a National Conference on Judaism and social justice as the start of an effort to strengthen a national Jewish voice on social justice issues. The conference, *Tzedek Yalin Bah/Justice Shall Dwell There*, was intended as the first step in launching a national Jewish social justice movement, bringing together Jewish social justice professionals, lay leaders from social justice organizations, schools, synagogues, Hillels, and other communal groups.

Out of the conference came an e-newsletter which has mobilized a collective voice on several occasions, and a follow-up training conference, also in Chicago, in December 2005, in collaboration with Minneapolis-St. Paul's Jewish Community Action, attended by sixty organizers.

CONFRONTING POWER IN THE JEWISH COMMUNITY: JEWS UNITED FOR JUSTICE (ST. LOUIS)

Linda Holtzman is Associate Professor of Communications at Webster University where she served as Chair of the Multicultural Studies Committee for ten years and designed and coordinated curriculum and a program in Media and Cultural Diversity. Linda is the author of the book *Media Messages* which examines how popular media, personal experience and education shape how we see race, gender, class and sexual orientation. She is a regular commentator on the local NBC affiliate on a segment called "Media Messages." Linda works as a consultant to Jews United for Justice, and has served as a diversity/anti-oppression trainer, facilitator, speaker, and consultant to many groups.[12]

LINDA HOLTZMAN: Jews United for Justice was brought into being by a group of people, some of whom had been involved with New Jewish Agenda,[13] and what they were missing was an organized progressive Jewish presence in St. Louis, an organization that would be a Jewish presence in the progressive community, and a progressive presence in the Jewish community. They came up with ten or twelve criteria and a mission by which to choose issues and projects that had to do with transformation and social justice, and it had to have a component of addressing racism because that is such a major issue here.

We've been around less than five years. We started out being a relatively small group, maybe twenty, twenty-five people, liberal to left. One of our issues was union busting in the Jewish nursing home in St. Louis. We worked with a local rabbi, Andrea Goldstein, who helped us write a working paper about Jewish tradition and teachings around labor, and also connecting the care of Jewish elders towards the end of their lives with the care for the largely African American women workers who take care of them.

So we were working with the local union and did research and dug up horrible stuff. The nursing home board had been building this 50 million dollar home, and although all of their 276 beds had been Medicaid-eligible, they suddenly they announced they were cutting eligible beds down to 100. So the shit hit the fan in the community, and we were there ready to organize. It became a huge issue that brought in an amazing blend of the Jewish community. We went from twenty-five members to a hundred and fifty in the last year—some of whom share all of our values and some of whom just really care about this issue and feel like this nursing home really sold out the Jewish community and the Jewish character of the home and poor and middle-income old Jews.

We're working our way back to workers' issue being more central. We have some members who don't see things that way, but we've got a process in place to discuss moving in that direction. I know we're going to lose some of our members when we return to the workers' rights issue, but we're also going to gain members.

The nursing home campaign is the first time that we know of in St. Louis that Reform, Orthodox, Conservative, and unaffiliated Jews worked together on something this big, and confronted the power brokers in the Jewish community. When the Federation did their fundraising, people were telling them, "Well, we're not gonna give you any money until this thing with the nursing home gets settled." So they formed a panel and they've been in communication with us. The work we did really made a difference.

We've worked a lot with Jobs with Justice as a kind of a model group that was pulling together work around health care. We were in the process of forming a strong partnership with SEIU [hospital and health care workers] in St. Louis and they had to back off organizing in this particular nursing home for political reasons, but there was no breakdown in that relationship; we just went in different directions.

Right now we have two issue-based task forces, one on health care and workers' rights, and one on educational equity emphasizing the academic achievement gap. We have partnerships with other organizations around the education work, more African American groups. Task forces are where the decisions get made on the ground. I'm only a part-time staff person for JUJ, and I'm the only staff person.

When something is bigger, like when we decided we were going to challenge the Jewish nursing home, we called a membership meeting and made a proposal so that the whole membership had the opportunity to vote on it. It's a different kind of model, not without problems, but there's a freshness about it, not a traditional board of directors, so we have to be really clear about the lines of accountability. One of the reasons we were so careful about making sure our membership was completely on board with challenging a Jewish institution, was that we predicted a whole lot of backlash towards us. And we got some of that. There was an article up front in the daily newspaper (*The Post Dispatch*) that featured what we were doing. Even people who were our friends would say "You don't air your dirty laundry. This should be within the Jewish community."

Originally some of the people on the board of Jewish Center for Aged said that we were ensuring bankruptcy of the Center and that the only reason they had temporarily cut back on Medicaid was because of money. Then people would visit the home and it was ridiculously extravagant. There were letters, front-page articles in the *Jewish Light*. One time I was invited to go to the Social Action Network meeting with someone from the Center board. I challenged him and he wasn't too pleased. They had hired an expensive PR firm, but our members were always at the meetings challenging them because we had the facts.

One important piece where we stayed really committed to and kept the Orthodox members involved, was to push the Center to keep being a kosher facility. Because for observant Jews who kept kosher that was really the only place they could go to where there weren't Christmas trees and Easter bunnies, and especially where they could get kosher food. It was amazing how coalitional that issue was. In some parts of the community people were saying "Why should we cater to the Orthodox?"—some real Orthodox bashing. We have probably eight to ten Orthodox members who are active, and then a whole bunch who are members but not that active. But a lot of our members are family members of residents of the Center and they may be Reform but their parents or aunts and uncles are Orthodox, and the only place they wanted to be at was the Center. So JUJ was really fighting for the needs of our old people.

We've been able to recruit a lot of rabbis to work with us, even a few Orthodox rabbis. I don't expect that the partnership will continue past the nursing home issue, but we've formed incredible relationships with some of them. I didn't even know what a *rebbitsn*[14] was. Now I have an incredible relationship with the *rebbitsn* and she is a member of JUJ. We've placed ads in the *Jewish Light* to challenge the plans of this nursing home. We've raised a lot of money around that and tried to get prominent rabbis and other Jews to sign these ads; even the head rabbi signed these ads.

We're at that point now where we've got a full-time agenda. We've got a website, we've got publications, we've got partnerships, we've got two active task forces. Luckily, we've got great, reliable volunteers, but we're really at that stretch point where we have to make a decision to have a full-time staff along with our full time organization. You know how things can really shift—in a good way—but then they become more institutionalized and harden.

We talk about racism overtly. We wrote a draft of a piece on the Jewish context of the academic achievement gap, and did a trial run presentation at Central Reform Congregation, about forty–fifty people. CRC is the most liberal congregation in St. Louis, and I was horrified to hear some of the responses. One [white] woman talked about driving her son (who is white and Jewish) and some of his African American friends to school and there was something on National Public Radio about a country in Africa. None of the kids except her son was familiar with the situation. So her solution was, if black families would only have their kids listen to NPR there wouldn't be an achievement gap. That level of misinformation and misunderstanding. But also real confusion between anti-semitism and racism and how these sit on people in the U.S. in really different ways.

There were a lot of comments like "If they would only do what we've done as Jews, then there wouldn't be a problem. So maybe we can teach them to do what we do." That particular task force then began to recognize that this is a long-range project, that we can't just start with the academic achievement gap. We needed to back up and do more work on the parallels and intersections of racism and anti-semitism, which will be the focus of our next publication.

So that's kind of where we are now, and we will be doing more congregational presentations and workshops to recruit members. We're developing a menu of things that people can do, from tutoring or mentoring to joining the effort to close the city-wide gap. There is an adult institute sponsored by the rabbis in St. Louis, and we're going to offer a six-week course on Jewish activism around racism. We're going to recruit people as we go to different congregations and organizations, especially people from what in St. Louis is called the Social Action Network—all the congregations that have social action or social justice committees send representatives to this group that meets several times a year. The tricky part is to figure out the self-interest for the Jews. The Jewish nursing home had self-interest out the wahzoo because those were people's loved ones. But the academic achievement gap feels more distant from people in the Jewish community. So it's a slow process. We've got an amazing core of volunteers on both issues. Any given month, we have twenty–thirty volunteers working on different issues. When we have a big event, like one of our public forums, we've had a hundred fifty–two hundred people show up. In St. Louis that's real big.

There are a lot of us in JUJ doing this work. We've got people in their thirties that are a part of JUJ, but a lot of people are in their fifties and older. Many of us have worked in communities of color, particularly with the African American community in St. Louis, for many years, and have solid relationships with people who are in leadership of black organizations. We have a strong relationship with the Black Leadership Roundtable, the main organization we've worked with around the academic achievement gap. The relationship with SEIU was the most challenging because we were starting from scratch, but our relationship with Jobs with Justice really helped us build. It's a formative relationship, a lot of getting-to-know-you-type stuff.

Are Jews of color involved? Yavilah [McCoy] is marginally involved, but she is the only one I can think of. The Jews of color I know are at the Central Reform Congregation, some other congregations, but it's a relatively small number in St. Louis, and we haven't specifically recruited Jews of color. We haven't really talked about it because historically it's been such a small number. And also because we've been recruiting around issues rather than around particular groups. Yavilah and I did a one-day workshop last year at CRC for multiracial families and families of color. Some leadership in the congregation—the rabbis, some board members—were there the whole day, which was amazing. There were some religious school teachers, and a few others, and seven or eight multi-racial families, and a couple of people who are single and African American. Part of what we deal with is how—and this is the piece Yavilah has done so much work on—our internalized oppression as Jews, our internalized anti-semitism, and our history of oppression really get in the way of our ability to think clearly and to feel positive about ourselves in a way that allows us to understand racism and to form partnerships with people of color. I emphasize how our confusion about racism and anti-semitism keeps us from working effectively in coalition with groups of color.

Susan [Rabbi Susan Talve] brings to this work a real concern about the children of color, whose parents are of color, or who are adopted by white Jews, children who are primarily Asian, African American, and mixed race. She's really concerned about the messages they get about not looking Jewish, questioning how can you be Jewish, that kind of thing. Susan did a sermon at Yom Kippur specifically about racism and got a lot of response from it and donations to work on it. We're going to kick off this summer with a day-and-a-half retreat with the families. That group would meet before the High Holidays to help map out a year of addressing this issue. Susan will do a major kick off at the holidays.[15]

What would the Jewish community look like if it were truly inclusive? I haven't really thought about it. I have been so used to thinking about the Jewish community in St. Louis as being predominantly white, and that's still true, even though there are certainly more people of color who are Jews in St. Louis. For it to be truly inclusive, there would have to be more diversity in the community. It's hard for me to fantasize about that without thinking we're going to go out and start converting people.

One thing that was really powerful in one of the workshops Yavilah and I did is that her mother came. We talked with the families in the morning and then we split up—the adults were together and the young people were together and Yavilah's mother worked with the young people. Also Yavilah has a twin brother and sister who are sixteen and they are all Orthodox. Some of the Jews by choice who are African American talked about how much they love the Jewish liturgy and how connected they felt to being Jewish, but that they missed the music from their churches. There was a gospel-sounding Jewish song that Yavilah's grandfather had taught all of them that they sang and it was so powerful. People were crying, especially those who had converted, and it was part of feeling like home to have that richness there. I guess if I were to fantasize about how inclusion would feel, it would be that everybody would feel like that when they participated in the Jewish community, that it felt like home.

TRYING TO CHANGE CONGREGATIONAL LIFE:
JEWISH COMMUNITY ACTION (MINNEAPOLIS)

VIC ROSENTHAL

Vic Rosenthal is a founding organizing committee member and past board president of Jewish Community Action, on JCA staff since 1998, and Executive Director since 2000. Before that he spent more than nine years as executive director of the Minnesota Senior Federation and more than twenty-five years organizing around issues such as affordable health care. Having received a Bush Fellowship, he spent seven months studying and working with a variety of organizing efforts, including JCA. Vic earned his Master of Public Administration at Rutgers University and a B.A. at the State University of New York at Binghamton. He is co-chair of the Temple of Aaron Social Action Committee (Conservative). In 2004, Vic was awarded on behalf of JCA a Ford Foundation's Leadership for a Changing World Grant.[16]

VIC ROSENTHAL: JCA was started in 1995 by a few people in the Jewish community who looked around at other faith groups that were involved in social justice work in the Twin Cities and saw a real lack of Jewish involvement. Not a lot of people at the table who would claim that they were there because of their Jewish connection. One of the most important things that JCA did at the beginning was to use a community organizing model and start within reach. We went into synagogues and also reached out to Jews unaffiliated with any congregation, to talk and especially to listen to people about what was most important to them. What did they care about? What were their social justice priorities? A number of issues emerged and we began to work on those, to do some traditional organizing efforts, developing criteria to assess what issues would make the most sense for JCA to get involved in as well as what would help to build JCA as an organization. The issues that emerged were affordable housing —and there's been a lot of work around that—community reinvestment, and racial justice, which was partly an internal education process. And since that point, we've also done work around immigrant rights, that emerged from our racial justice work.

Our constituency consists of anyone from the Jewish community with an interest in social–economic justice. I think we have spent more time in the last several years focused on affiliated Jews, who are members of congregations, because they are easier to identify. To help people understand the connection between their participation in a congregation and how that relates to social–economic justice. But in some ways our constituency is much broader, in that many of the issues we work on have little direct relationship to Jews. The immigrant rights work we've done has been primarily about Latinos, Somalis, other immigrants whose civil liberties have been at risk, especially since September 11. The work we do on affordable housing often has nothing directly to do with Jews—Jews in the Twin Cities are probably underrepresented among people who are lacking quality housing.

I think the biggest difference between us and [groups like JCUA or JFREJ] is the tremendous congregational effort, the fact that we're trying very hard to change congregational life and increase its focus on justice. And our belief that synagogues are places that have power, and if used correctly, that power can really make a difference in working on social and economic justice. We participated alongside the NAACP in an effort to preserve funding for the human rights department in the city of St. Paul; we brought some Jews to the table. We testified at the state capital on issues of racial profiling. Our immigrant rights work has provided opportunities for people to be effective. We have a working group on racial justice.

Being a minority in Minneapolis pushes us to be more focused on alliance building, because the Jewish community is too small to have sufficient power all by itself to get things done. So I think there's an understanding that we have to build alliances with other groups in order to succeed.

Jews of color in JCA? There are a couple, and we've made efforts to cultivate relationships with people who are of color and Jewish, but I wouldn't say it's been entirely successful. A truly inclusive Jewish community, from the standpoint of what JCA is trying to do, would include Jews from all the different parts of the community, unaffiliated, Reform, Reconstructionist, Orthodox, Conservative, that would really be working together to be accomplishing social justice work in the community.

One of our strongest projects is the Gateway Interfaith Table for Affordable Housing. It's made up of synagogues and churches in one neighborhood in St. Paul, and it came about as a way of responding to housing and commercial redevelopment plans. The initial plan called for the demolition of a bunch of houses that were largely affordable to be replaced by largely commercial development and very little housing. We built a coalition to fight the plan. After several years the group has developed a presence in the community, some real influence. The project is almost completed, and we expect ground will be broken this fall on over five hundred units of housing. Like any other group effort, it's not like it happened only because of us. But we played a significant role in making sure housing was seriously on the table.

I also think that our work around the immigrant issue has been important. The larger Jewish community should have been involved with this issue, and wasn't. At a time when civil liberties were truly being threatened, we were able to raise the question of what happens when the state begins to brand people for who they are, not for anything they've done. We were able to raise connections about how Holocaust victims were treated and what led to the Holocaust, and even arranged for a Holocaust survivor to testify at a hearing.

One of the best pieces of work we're doing and will continue to do is around community reinvestment, getting institutions to invest assets in banks that do economic development. We still have a long way to go to build our presence, but we're a name that's known in broader circles. If you want Jews at the table on any issue that has a left-wing or progressive connection to it, we're the place to go.

We work with the NAACP, with specific churches, with other faith-based organizing groups that deal with housing and other issues. We've done some work with the Urban League, then there's just a variety of other nonprofits especially around housing. We've done a lot of work with unions, especially around the immigrant work. We're doing "Labor on the Bima" in five synagogues where JCA members and/or rabbis will speak.[17] We did work with the Russian Jewish community, we had a bilingual staff person through the Americorps Vista program, but her term ended and we don't have the funds to hire someone. The point was to try to connect Russian-speaking Jews to a community that largely wasn't paying attention to them, but it was also about leadership development, and trying to give people a sense of their power in order to do work on justice.

Our volunteers are probably from mid-thirties to fifties; gender, maybe more women than men, that's true generally. Having done social justice work for a *loooong* time, I think there are always more women involved than men, even truer in the Jewish community. Largely the people involved are middle class. Part of being able to do this work is having the time to do it. More of our newer members come from congregations, though we still have many people involved who are unaffiliated.

I don't think JCA is monocultural, but it's not as diverse as it probably could be. But we have different viewpoints and different people in terms of their level of Jewish observance.

I continue to believe that one of the big avenues that all progressive Jewish organizations need to look at are the congregations. Because that still is where it's easiest to find Jews. Maybe it's different in New York, because the Jewish population is as large as it is. But in most other parts of the country it's not. I think congregations remain these sleeping giants. If mobilized and organized the right way, they can be powerful institutions around justice.

Update:

JCA perhaps demonstrates the most growth, with some spectacular achievements. When I asked Vic what he felt proudest of in the last couple of years, he pointed to a coalition of churches and synagogues JCA had helped emerge, thus creating support for more than five hundred units of housing in St. Paul. JCA helped get ordinances passed in both of the Twin Cities to protect immigrant rights. They mobilized some $3 million in community-based banks with a commitment to inner-city communities. In addition, JCA was instrumental in designing the curriculum for the December 2005 training conference for organizers. They have not developed a focus on racial diversity. Though there is a racial justice working group, Jews of color is not a big topic.

BRINGING OUR BODIES TO THE PICKET LINE: JEWS FOR RACIAL AND ECONOMIC JUSTICE (NEW YORK)

Esther Kaplan is a Brooklyn-based journalist and a community activist, and the author of *With God on their Side*. A former editor at *The Nation*, *POZ*, and *The Village Voice*, she is now a radio producer for WNYE and co-host on WBAI/Pacifica Radio of *Beyond the Pale*, a program on Jewish culture and politics. She is a former director of Jews for Racial and Economic Justice, and served as the co-chair of the JFREJ board of directors through 2004; as a member of the workers rights board of New York Jobs with Justice

ESTHER KAPLAN
Courtesy Cindra Feuer

NAOMI BRAINE

and of the advisory board of the Center for Immigrant Families. She currently works as the Communications Director of Communication Workers of America, Local 1180.

Naomi Braine is a sociologist and long-time social justice activist. She has been involved in feminist, queer and antimilitary organizing, and was a member of ACTUP in both Chicago and NYC. She has written and spoken extensively on women and HIV, and on community-based public health interventions as both a professional and an activist. In the last few years, her activist work has focused more on organizing within Jewish communities, to support progressive Jewish voices in relation to both domestic politics and around the struggle for justice in Israel/Palestine. She served as co-chair of the board of directors of JFREJ through 2005.[18]

ESTHER KAPLAN: We started early on feeling that here were all these liberals and leftists and radicals and socially committed Jews in New York City who were not speaking with one voice, and the only ones who were speaking as Jews were on the liberal-to-far-right edge of the spectrum. JFREJ—legitimately, I think—spent a long time kind of ingathering people who were already activists, advocates, and giving them a Jewish voice, a Jewish base of operations. For several years now we've talked about trying to expand our reach and we've tried various ways, all of which have had promising beginnings and haven't had the level of follow-through that was needed. For example, trying to reach Russian Jews and do antiracist work in that community, trying to reach out to working- and middle-class Jews who have their kids in the public schools, and to Jewish teachers—that was a big part of our public education campaign. Bringing youth theater project performances[19] to Brooklyn and the Bronx, trying to incite a conversation about resources and race relations in the school with a really broad community. I think we did that with mixed success. We did serious door knocking in the Bronx to organize people against privatization of public schools, we turned out a lot of people, and people won against Edison.[20] There are a lot of different ways in which we're trying to reach out to people we see as part of our constituency; for example, to fixed-income elderly Jews, people we have tried at times to organize, to do outreach sometimes haphazardly and sometimes in more systematic ways. I don't feel we're at the point where we've made the great leap, where our constituency has expanded to include all of those communities.

We've done work specifically around Arab Jews, Jews of color, trying to bring the perspectives of Jews of color into our work—with mixed success. We've had important leaders on our board over the years, but this didn't catapult us into a broader constituency in any permanent sense.

What are our strengths? We've hung in there. Stayed the course politically. Managed with some integrity to keep both economic justice and racial justice at the heart of our mission, finding a way to take a principled stand on the Middle East while still remaining true to our mission. In different ways over the years we've walked the walk. One of my quintessential JFREJ images is showing up every Sunday during a terrible snowy winter to join the picket line at Silver Palace Restaurant in Chinatown and running into—some weeks half a dozen and some weeks a dozen and a half—JFREJ people on the line in that battle for workers' rights. At that point JFREJ was very new, the group organizing that event, Chinese Staff and Workers Association [CWSA], didn't have a reason to know or trust us. But at the end it was just obvious that we were serious, bringing the issue to the Jewish community and bringing our bodies to the picket line. I think we've done that in large and small ways over the years. Sometimes we haven't followed through as much as we would have liked, but on the whole, we're known and respected for delivering what we say we're going to do.

NAOMI BRAINE: One of my favorite images is from Racial Justice Day, focused on police brutality in the year of the police torture of Abner Louima in Brooklyn [1997]. The march was organized by various communities of color, and JFREJ worked very hard to organize a large Jewish contingent. Police brutality is such a key issue for our allies in communities of color. We had just conducted one of our workshops on racism and homophobia at a Long Island Jewish day school, which resulted in the school sending buses of high school students to march in Racial Justice Day. That's JFREJ at its best, community education strengthening the politics. Interesting that the white presence at that march came from three places: Jews, queers, and the Lower East Side (all of which probably overlapped a fair amount).

Another strength of JFREJ—through the coalition work we've been able to sustain some relationships, develop long-term ties like with Chinese Staff and Workers, with Black Radical Congress, with a number of groups around the city. I've worked with other organizations where ties are much more fleeting, where it's very difficult to connect and build and keep that moving, to sustain trust and engagement—particularly true of predominantly white groups working with predominantly people of color organizations.

Internally, whatever our critiques of JFREJ as relatively homogenous —we do manage to get a bigger age spread than most other organizations into one room time after time with some consistency. Especially in the mid-nineties, in a time when relatively few young whites were organized against racism, young [white] Jews were drawn—and continue to be drawn—to JFREJ. It is a cross-generational organization. We also manage some spread among people who wouldn't be caught dead in synagogue and those who are quite religiously observant. JFREJ attracts unaffiliated Jews who see in JFREJ a Jewishness they can relate to, and also deeply identified Jews who want to strengthen a gutsy progressive Jewish voice. We manage to bridge some gaps that aren't easily or commonly bridged. We're so critical of the limits of our internal diversity that we sometimes don't recognize what we've achieved.

EK: One thing I really value in JFREJ is that we still have that generation of 1930s radicals in our midst; they are an incredible resource. I think also we take it for granted with JFREJ—but it's not to be taken for granted in the organized Jewish world—we've always had strong gay lesbian bisexual leadership even though that's not our agenda, our agenda is racial and economic justice. But we've managed to create a culture and a constituency that implicitly values women and gay people.

Here's an example of a unique kind of role JFREJ plays in New York. We began a campaign against anti-Arab racism before September 11, 2001, in spring and summer of 2001, a decision we made that this was important for us organizationally, and we did it in small steps. We planned a public forum in collaboration with allies from the Arab American community, and we held a teach-in on anti-Arab racism. So we'd already begun to develop some relationships and to discuss the issues when September 11 happened. In the wake of that, obviously we thought there was a very important role for a left-wing Jewish organization to play, and we were reaching out to our Arab American and Muslim contacts, and trying to expand our contacts, and to support the organizations.

What we found—there were Arab groups we were working with that mainstream Jewish organizations wouldn't speak with because they [the Jewish organizations] had a litmus test around [Arab] groups' position on the Middle East and whether they had sufficiently condemned terrorism or Hamas. JFREJ got all these phone calls from mainstream Jewish groups who felt like they should be doing something as this wave of anti-Arab and anti-Muslim violence was erupting, but they couldn't talk to any of these organizations directly. So they were phoning JFREJ to secretly find out what these groups were saying and planning. That moment clarified for me a role that JFREJ is able to play with Jewish groups who are so bound by intensely pro-Israel ideology that it blocks them from being able to confront some of the major issues of our time, like anti-Arab racism, the Patriot Act, the crackdown on immigrants, all the stuff we've made the center of our campaign work.

NB: Another place where JFREJ played a role no one else could have [was] the conference on Jews and the Radical Right back in 1995. That was really important, and put something publicly out on the agenda. The level of hysteria that got generated around it certainly confirmed for me—this is exactly the right thing for us to be doing.

EK: That coincided with the Jewish Theological Seminary actually honoring Newt Gingrich at their annual banquet, and JFREJ organized a protest outside the JTS banquet, which was also very controversial. These events mark the distance between where we're at and where the big moneyed Jewish institutions in the city are.

NB: I think the Radical Right conference and the JTS–Gingrich protest, similar to the story you were telling about post-9/11, was JFREJ creating a venue, a network for other people to tie into. The Jews and the Radical Right event was packed. Not just JFREJ stalwarts—people came from all over, from Boston and Chicago. Tapping something that was a lot bigger than us. Creating a space for people to say—not the hysterical response of *we want to squash this, you can't say these things out loud*—but *thank god someone is saying this.*

131

EK: If you think back to our founding steering committee, we had people who had been major policy staffers at the American Jewish Committee, and who were truly urban justice/racial justice people. We actually worked on the Jews and the Radical Right conference with Ken Stern of the American Jewish Committee.[21] That's a breed that barely exists any more, powerful committed progressives inside the mainstream Jewish institutions. Most of those people have retired, they're gone. Although I know there are some young progressives picking up the banner.

NB: It's a general institutional trend, not just Jewish. Spaces for dissent are shrinking. Dissenters in those institutions are feeling squeezed and silenced.

EK: On the issue of racial and ethnic diversity, we brought leadership on to the board, asked people we've worked with on various projects to join the leadership with an eye to make our membership more diverse, or to bring guidance to our political campaigns. And to send a signal. We've done projects: when we began working on anti-Arab racism we brought in Arabs, including Arab Jews, as part of the planning. Also around our public education campaign, we built a youth theater project that was for a couple of years one of our central organizing tools. We worked with young people to create a critical theater piece about the public schools and inequities in funding between suburban and urban schools, and that piece went around to try to excite interest in the campaign. The students were a mix of public and private school students, Jews and non-Jews. It was a multiracial effort, and there were several biracial Jews who were part of that effort.

A couple of years ago we developed a working group to look at how we might revise our antiracism workshop—which has always had Jews of color as participants—but how we might revise it to make it speak more effectively to Jews of color, and how to integrate Jews of color into more of our work. What kinds of campaigns we might embark on, which might include direct challenges to Jewish institutions, that would attract Jews of color to our ranks. We also brought together a group of people within JFREJ, including Mizrahi and Sephardi and biracial Jews. This group conducted one-on-one interviews with folks with varying degrees of connection to JFREJ, people who were Jews of color, Mizrahi Jews, [white] parents of children of color. We asked them about their attitude toward the organized Jewish community in general, JFREJ in particular, the animating social justice issues, and we compiled the answers. The idea was to be systematic and thoughtful, so we weren't just bringing people on to the board or on to committees, but we'd really engage in some deeper thinking. We got derailed by some internal crises, but there is organizational commitment to that process.

Also we do a weekly radio show on WBAI—*Beyond the Pale*—and we've pretty consistently covered the full diversity of the Jewish community on the show: Russian Jewish electoral politics, hunger among elderly, major conference of Bukharian Jews, Sephardic film festival, Ethiopian Jewish advocacy efforts in Israel, gay parenting, cross-racial adoption, literature by biracial Jews, forced adoption of Mizrahi Jews in Israel. The radio show has been a major place where we've projected a comprehensive view of the Jewish community, though it hasn't always been realizable in organizing campaigns.

NB: JFREJ has tension—like many organizations—between campaign work and internal work. With our limited resources we're kind of pulled between them. At this stage, the Jews of color work requires some internal focus, and that's hard for JFREJ to sustain. We're more of an action group.

EK: Also, it's hard for us to figure out who to partner with on this. Ivri-NASAWI we partnered with on a number of projects—we cosponsored events with them, we planned segments of our radio show with them. One of their leaders [Ella Shohat] came on our board. We did some collaborative work with the Jewish Multiracial Network, including a hugely successful Hanukkah bash with lots of kids.[22] Both these institutions are in flux. Other institutions in the city, like Sephardic House, our politics don't match, they're very conservative. There's some potential to do cultural events with them. We cover their events on the radio show, film festivals and so on. But JFREJ's model for collaboration, relationship building, has to do with working with another organization as equals.

I've felt for some years now, a really interesting future for JFREJ could be in providing radical education for kids. We have a ton of parents, secular left-wing Jews, struggling to find that for their kids. We have a lot of people in our organization who are in mixed-race partnerships, who have kids of color; that's an arena where we could do really important work that would be incredibly loved by our members in multiracial families and others, who want to provide some radical education for their kids that doesn't give a monolithic picture of who a Jew is.

NB: If JFREJ were more fully integrated, it would really change our relationship with communities of color. We have such a public and private identity as a white ally organization. If we became more of a home for a substantial number of Jews of color, that relationship would be changed because we wouldn't be an all-white group. I'm not sure how but it would put us in a different relationship—not next to but overlapping.

EK: Some relationships I don't think it would affect, like Chinese Staff and Workers, Latino Workers Center. They're people-of-color groups but they're focused on labor issues. I think some of the highly politicized coalitions of specifically people of color groups that have a kind of pan-people of color or brown coalition analysis, I think those are the groups where it might influence the relationship. I also think our antiracist community education work would shift. It would be really interesting to have multiracial teams leading the workshop. We've occasionally had that, but more typically we've had Ashkenazi pairs. It would shift things in a salutary way.

Update:

As we go to press, JFREJ is running two campaigns; one organizing immigrant Jews, particularly Bukharian Jews from Uzbekistan who confront anti-semitism in immigrant communities and racism in Jewish communities; they experience a lot of pressure from Hasidim to give up their traditional religious practice and assimilate to Ashkenazi practice. The other campaign, in support of domestic workers, offers massive education and pressure in the organized Jewish communities on fair employment practices, Jewish tradition, and the history and present-day situation for Jewish domestic workers.

The current director, Dara Silverman, has mobilized and provided training opportunities for a new generation of JFREJ activists, and JFREJ is about to undertake strategic planning. In the arena of Jewish racial diversity, JFREJ has regularly partnered with Ayecha, Beta Israel of North America (BINA), and other Jews or Color and mixed-race Jews, as well as working in partnership with new immigrant Jews of color around the city.

THE PLACE TO GO FOR A PROGRESSIVE JEWISH VOICE

These groups and others like them have proudly reclaimed a tradition of radical Jews. They have forged educational and political campaigns in their local communities on a wide range of issues including workers' rights, affordable housing and health care, against police brutality, for equitable public education. They have mobilized Jews to stand on picket lines, to turn out in the streets, to engage in nonviolent civil disobedience in coalition with communities of color. They have organized political, sometimes secular holiday rituals, like a radical *tashlekh* for Rosh Hashonah to rid society of such excrescences as poverty and racism, or to free ourselves from the obstacles that block us from making change. They have written liberation seders for Passover; mobilized Purim protests in front of Disney stores with CEO Michael Eisner cast as Purim's arch-villain Haman.[23]

And yet: as I originally conceived of this book, I assumed that the connections between activist work and increasing Jewish racial and ethnic diversity would be obvious. I had imagined drawing links between acknowledging the racial and ethnic diversity of Jews and doing stronger, more effective antiracist work, more connected with communities of color, in part through our bi- and multi-identitied constituencies. This seemed to me a no-brainer. After all, in JFREJ it had seemed to work naturally with queers and feminists; the large-scale participation of both constituencies had made connections with queer and feminist groups easy and strong.

What I discovered is that among activist groups doing fabulous organizing and community education, groups which have achieved some extraordinary victories, the relevance of building Jewish diversity and multiculturalism inside their organizations and inside Jewish community was not always self-evident.

Race in the Jewish world is complicated. JCUA and JFREJ, bigger, older, located in larger and more diverse Jewish communities, have devoted substantial energy to issues of Jewish racial and cultural diversity. Considering that New York houses perhaps the world's largest Jewish community with a pool of Jews of color much larger than in most other cities; and considering that Chicago has a large African American Jewish population, these two groups might, more readily than organizations in smaller cities, achieve critical mass. JCUA has invested some thought and organizing around African American Jews. JFREJ has conceptualized attention to multicultural identity as a strategy, and has made "integrating JFREJ" a priority with some targeted outreach, but with mixed results. As this book goes to press, it seems that JFREJ is expanding its Immigrant Rights Campaign deeply into Jewish immigrant communities. The most successful work on racial diversity has come through co-sponsorship of Jewish multiracial events.

In JCA (Minneapolis) and JUJ (St. Louis), connections between Jewish racial and ethnic diversity and antiracist activities have not been widely discussed or manifested in political practice. Instead, it seems that Jews of color are seen as a small community, attention to which has uncertain purpose or ramifications. Jewish diversity is not a secret, but is not seen as broadly relevant, perhaps in part because these groups focus on neither culture nor identity. As Linda Holtzman of JUJ said, "We're focused on issues."

There remains the dilemma of numbers. Much thinking about diversity derives from a more explicitly politicized discourse about oppression by race, gender, and class, and, as such, is premised on actual majority status. *Do the arithmetic.* We call on this discourse all the time when we look at the world. Globally, people of color are the majority. Most people are workers. Women hold up half the sky. We stake a claim, explicit or implicit, for justice based on numbers.

But Jews in the United States will continue to reflect a large majority of Ashkenazim and visually white people. This is a demographic fact, not the end of the discussion. Jews—ourselves a tiny minority—should be brilliant on the issue of justice for minorities. But it seems that many Jews think Jewish racial and ethnic diversity is too small an issue to matter, seem simply not to grasp the strategic importance of acknowledging and mobilizing around Jewish racial and ethnic diversity. Yet the more we think and talk and just look around, we find that there's enough Jewish diversity to blow away presumptions of the "normative" Jew; way more Jewish diversity than is normally recognized by the mainstream. And growing.

What none of these groups has developed—yet?—is a full-blown political practice that in some way reflects, incorporates, and resonates with Jewish diversity. At base level, what is most missing is a sense of why one might do this work. Nor do any of these groups seem to address proactively issues of Ashkenazi dominance, or tease out the tangle of Sephardi–Mizrahi history.[24] People are clear that immigrant rights work connects deeply to racism, and especially since September 11, to repression against Arabs, Muslims, and South Asians. Jewish social justice groups have risen to the occasion in providing Jewish support for targeted communities, and venues for Jewish–Arab connection. JCUA drafted a resolution and helped get it passed by the Chicago City Council, calling for the repeal of the Patriot

Act. JFREJ, even prior to September 11, invested considerable resources in raising issues of anti-Arab racism in the Jewish community. JCA invoked the Holocaust to warn of the dangers of racial profiling of immigrants, and brought a Holocaust survivor to testify at a hearing.

But while Jewish history and common humanity are invoked, for the most part these activist groups have not grasped that educating the Jewish community about common Judeo-Arabic culture, or about the content, history, and culture of Sephardi and Mizrahi Jews might be a positive strategy. Why isn't the connection being made, or made more strongly, by the antiracist organizations?

In part I think this is because while the issues are not new, talking about them is. There is definitely a new buzz on multiracial identity, including Jewish, but the discourse is young. Educational and cultural work is needed to expand the Jewish community's understanding of our multiplicity. In the academy, in Jewish studies, and in progressive communities the impact and ramifications have not yet been absorbed.

Even where evident in theory, there's tension between acting in the world—which is how all the explicitly social justice organizations conceive of their mission—and internal education.[25] I know what it is like to work on staff or sit on the board of groups like these. I am aware that these groups that do so much with such limited resources can barely do *more*.

And yet they/we must.

[5] JUDAISM IS THE COLOR OF THIS ROOM

Looking at a room packed with many Jews of color come to participate in a Jews of Color Speak Out, African American Jew Robin Washington declared, "Judaism is the color of this room."[1]

A number of innovative organizations and projects have emerged that are focused front and center on Jewish racial and ethnic diversity. The discourse of these groups is not primarily about battling racism—though all do battle with racism in a variety of ways. All call attention to the invisibility of Jews of color in the mainstream Jewish community, to the presumption that Jewish means white or Ashkenazi, and to the exclusion of Jewish racial and ethnic minorities from intellectual, cultural, artistic, and political events and decisions. They tend to use language that stresses empowering Jews of color; challenging Ashkenazism; creating venues for Sephardi and Mizrahi culture; and educating "the" Jewish community about its own multiracial multiethnic character. They are not seeking to replace a monad Ashkenaz with a binary Sephardi-Ashkenazi; all these groups in distinct ways are trying to explode the binary.

I interviewed leaders of seven such groups: Ayecha, Jewish Diversity Resources (national in scope, based in St. Louis and New York); New Association of Sephardi/Mizrahi Artists & Writers, International (Ivri-NASAWI); Beth Shalom B'nai Zaken Ethiopian Hebrew Congregation (Chicago); Beta Israel of North America Cultural Foundation (BINA; New York); Congregation Nahalat Shalom (Albuquerque); the Afro-Jewish Studies Center/Temple University (Philadelphia), and Central Reform Congregation (St. Louis).

These groups have never been yoked by a connection like the Jewish Social Justice Network. They don't have common funders,[2] nor could I pull from their materials a set of common principles. What they share is a commitment to widen the Jewish landscape to include not only their own communities and other Jews of color, but also other excluded groups. Yavilah McCoy of Ayecha wants "to bring together the full experience of diversity as it exists in the Jewish community, not just around color—around age, gender, class, sexual orientation. . . . Sometimes it's fine to work on issues of race, but it's not necessarily fine to work on issues of heterosexual privilege in the Orthodox community; it's liable to isolate you in a very deep way."[3] Beejhy Barhany of BINA remarked, "Some of the Jewish communities . . . need to understand that Judaism is not only European, Judaism has different dimensions and different colors. If you're Reform they might not consider you a Jew as well."[4] Rabbi Capers Funnye talks of the welcome place his shul aspires to be for all Jews: "When you come to Beth Shalom we want it to be a house of peace, and not only a house of peace, but a house where all are welcome."[5] Generous in their analyses and practices, these groups are interested in empowering their community, and in educating others.

All of these groups acknowledge Arab/Muslim–Jewish relations as crucial, and some take positions against the Israeli Occupation. BINA does not take a position, but, as Barhany remarks, "Of course we want to see peace and stability in the region. Our families are all back there."[6] Rabbi Lynn Gottlieb, of Nahalot Shalom, stands publicly against the Occupation, and builds bridges with Muslim communities, while Ivri-NASAWI undergoes internal struggles about the sometimes competing demands of culture and politics. Still, Jordan Elgrably of Ivri-NASAWI comments that Mizrahim "have a different relationship to the Middle East, one that's more organic and historical."[7] Ivri-NASAWI and Ayecha both produce cultural and intellectual programming to nurture their primary communities and to educate those—including Ashkenazi and non-Jews—who want to learn. Ivri-NASAWI promotes Mizrahi and Sephardi culture, as well as a much wider understanding of the historical and cultural intimacy between Jews and Arabs. Knowledge of this intimacy should undermine, as Jordan Elgrably points out, a sense of inevitable conflict, of unbridgeable cultural difference between the peoples: "ignorance reinforces the idea that Arabs and Jews are two really separate peoples and helps them be enemies."[8]

Nahalat Shalom remembers to welcome the stranger, a strategy and a goal that primes them for coalition and bridge building. As a congregation, Nahalat Shalom does some work with other congregations, but their outreach is not primarily to other synagogues; instead the rabbi prides the congregation on reaching beyond the edges, breaking new ground, carrying Jewishness into new places. Similarly Rabbi Funnye sees interfaith work as critical, especially in the African American community, Muslim and Christian. For Ayecha and BINA, the synagogue is a primary place of outreach, while Ivri-NASAWI is explicit about their secularism; their constituency is progressive Sephardim and Mizrachim, not the religious or traditional Sephardic community. The Center for Afro-Jewish Studies at Temple University, founded in 2004, has created and occupies a unique space in the academy; it is a space for research to transform both Jewish and African studies. Imagine what such a space would have meant for Yavilah McCoy as she negotiated her complex identity during her college years:

> While I was in college, I never felt that I had to hide my Jewish identity among my African American friends. In fact, it was almost a non-issue; just another interesting aspect of who I was. In my second year I served as a programming coordinator for the Jewish Student Council and during my third year I was elected as president of the college chapter of the NAACP. It seemed fairly easy, at that point, to manage to keep my feet planted in both communities, but this feeling came to an end as tensions arose on campus following a well attended talk by Kwame Ture that equated Zionism with Racism. In the heated debate that followed his talk and the continually escalating tensions in the weeks that followed, a petition to the president was circulated among the organizations of color on campus to get the Religious Zionist Alternative kicked off of campus for their public posting of a number of Meir Kahane's quotes in the Campus Center lobby. During this escalation, it was very hard to even get Jewish and African American groups to talk with one another regarding the issue of Zionism. Because of my relationships in both communities I felt obligated to try and bring leaders together for the purpose of our mutual education on the topic. Unfortunately, most of my efforts in this direction were perceived by other African American leaders on campus as a lack of solidarity with "the cause." Despite support I received from many of the professors and senior administration on campus, the backlash that I experienced that year caused me to rethink what it meant to have a "black-Jewish" identity. I had always thought that if racism caused me to be an outsider among Jews who associated being Jewish with being White, I would always be welcomed by the black community where I could be a run-of-the-mill black girl who just happened to be Jewish. What I found out that year, was that if my being Jewish meant that my philosophy or politics ran counter to what my African American peers judged to be the black "cause" I could still be outed for thinking like a "Jew." Thus began my journey to create space where I could bring my whole self, and the unique mix of thinking and being that my heritage afforded me, to whatever groups I joined, and I made a commitment, that year, to be willing to stand in what could often be very hot water in order to be able to do just that.[9]

THE TEMPLE OF MY FAMILIAR: AYECHA (NATIONAL)

Yavilah McCoy is a teacher, writer, editor and diversity consultant. Her parents converted to Orthodox Judaism, and raised her and her five siblings as Orthodox Jews in the Flatbush and Crown Heights areas of Brooklyn. She attended Hasidic elementary school, Yeshiva University Modern Orthodox High School, the State University of New York at Albany, and the Hebrew University in Jerusalem, and has taught in Reform, Conservative, Modern Orthodox, and Hasidic day schools. She is a trained facilitator for the Anti-Defamation League's A World of Difference Institute and board member for the St. Louis Anti-Defamation League. Her most recent project is Ayecha, Jewish Diversity Resources.[10]

YAVILAH McCOY: Jewish tradition teaches that the existential question "*Ayecha*/Where do you stand?" was first posed by God to Adam in the Garden of Eden, to facilitate his introspection on the unique role and purpose he had within the universe. Ayecha started in St. Louis, with relationships I'd been developing with synagogues. My husband and I had made connections to a myriad of different synagogues in the area since we'd moved to St. Louis in 1997, and after much "shul-hopping" and many synagogue speaking engagements on the topic of "Jewish Diversity," I began piloting Ayecha's training model in the day schools and yeshivas of our area. It continues to amaze me how much resonance there was to our subject in each of the places we brought our work, regardless of religious affiliation. As word spread, it was not long before I had made presentations at the majority of the synagogues in our area. In our first program, I worked with young people to explore Jewish identity by examining a huge display I had created of Jewish faces from around the world. The exercises and discussions that followed the viewing of the display helped students to explore perceptions and misconceptions around what "Jewish" looked like and helped to broaden their understanding of the great cultural diversity that exists among Jews.

That exercise was the first of many that later came to be included in the educational resources that Ayecha currently offers through the Jewish Diversity Initiative. One major goal that I have in leading Ayecha is to help the community to organize its resources around supporting Jewish Diversity education. "One-shot-deal" events where people can come and be exposed to the diversity of the community lays good groundwork, but in order for the structure of our community to change and reflect the diversity that is a part of our people, more intentional education will have to take place to give individuals and organizations practical tools for building an understanding of the spectrum of our similarities and differences as Jews into how we build and reach out to our communities.

Ayecha's training for Jewish communal leaders, staff, and boards of directors is about helping the Jewish community to build better community around diversity over the next ten years. Over the last seven years, I've sat on the board of directors for Hadassah, Anti-Defamation League, Jewish Family and Children's Services, Jewish Community Relations Council, the St. Louis Jewish Light, and other Jewish agencies where I have had the opportunity to see the need for diversity, in our community leadership, both on local and national levels. Fortunately or unfortunately, the major policy decisions that are made by the leading agencies of our communities reflect the age, social, cultural, racial, gender and even class make-up of the decision makers that are gathered around the table. The aging of our leadership across the nation continues to be the impetus for building new initiatives to inspire young Jewish professionals to make their careers in the Jewish community, but there are more layers of diversity that can and should be included to enrich the perspectives from which our organizations are led. Many of the boards that I have sat on have been most heavily populated by affluent men, of Ashkenazi heritage, in their late fifties or above. Despite the deep love and respect that I have for many of these pioneering leaders, the question that I, and many other young Jewish professionals that I know, have is how can these organizations help our community to work toward a meaningful future that includes our dreams and desires if the experience around the table is rooted in the past and not the future? I believe that the work of our Jewish communal agencies is motivated by a deep love for the Jewish community and humanity in general, and it is my hope that this love and vision will inspire our current leadership to begin taking steps to diversify our community from the top down *and* from the bottom up, so that we meet somewhere in the middle. Ayecha, in its work to gather resources for the community around Jewish Diversity and in its support and advocacy for Jews of Color and other diverse Jews in the United States, would like to play a role in helping to galvanize this process. If we are going to seize the challenge and opportunity that is before us in "the changing face of

Jewish identity," our communal leadership will have to think about looking to grassroots organizations for input so that some of their thinking can inform the way our "business" is accomplished. We will also have to think about making room at the table for leaders with different perspectives and experiences so that the diversity of our community has a chance to impact the direction that we take toward our future.

Reaching for the diversity that is within our people will give us a broader sense of our Judaism, that feels more like a work in progress than a collection of frozen fragments and pieces that have been salvaged despite our historical oppression. When we find ways to make room for ourselves and other Jews to be authentic with each other we enrich and broaden the margins of our community.

Ayecha's primary mission, at this point, is to educate. I feel like the journey toward making change has to happen in stages. There's a cognitive dissonance that I think people can get stuck in, when it comes to seeing Jews as historically and presently diverse, that I feel is connected to the way in which we are educated about Jewish identity, history, and culture in the U.S. The Euro-centered perspective of much of what we learn about the Jewish people is a lens that is often invisible to us until we are introduced to knowledge and experiences that help us to shift that center. Many of us do not notice when we pick up a Jewish history book and 75 percent of the information is on one-quarter of Jewry. We don't notice that we're missing the others. We don't notice when we're sitting in our synagogues and we look around and see all white faces, that this is not the way it is around the world. The diversity of our people, as a practical reality, is invisible to us in so many ways that it is easy to assume that what we see before us is the way it is.

So the first thing is to raise awareness that there are various types of Jews who have lived and developed across the world, and they're all valuable and essential to our understanding of what it means to be a Jew.

Ayecha's mission is to provide Jewish Diversity education and advocacy and support for diverse Jews in the United States. We have a training model that assists participants in utilizing a diversity lens to reaffirm Jewish spirituality, reexamine Jewish identity, and reinterpret Jewish community. In Hebrew, we've named these sections of our training *Tzelem Elokim* (the image of God), *Tzelem Yehudi* (the image of a Jew), and *Tzelem Kehillah* (the image of community). Our current projects reflect this three pronged focus through our work with rabbis and spiritual leaders, educators, outreach professionals, and Jews of Color.

What does building inclusion look like? One step toward inclusion is reaching out to people who are different and creating spaces where people of different cultures and backgrounds might enjoy "community" with each other. Inclusion might mean a concerted effort by leaders to teach and model diversity as an integral part of Jewish identity. Inclusion might also be about giving people a chance to interact with difference and explore what they know and don't know about other Jews. For me working on inclusion in the Jewish community is about teaching people to look around and appreciate who is and who is not in the room when we consider contemporary and historical Jewish life, and then creating enough hope and safety for people to feel comfortable reaching for each other.

Inclusion also involves letting the experience of the "other" inform our work to build more inclusive environments. There are many places around the country where individuals and small groups of diverse Jews attend communal programs or services and experience being "other," most recognizably through well-intentioned questions like "Are you Jewish?" The experience of integrating racially or culturally homogenous environments creates a sensitivity to "difference" that can be informative to a process to include and enrich a community's understanding of what their house looks like from the outside. Without placing the sole burden for being "creative" about inclusion on the shoulders of the "other," inclusion could also mean inviting people from the margins to the center to deepen understanding of what it means to experience exclusion.

Twenty years ago, when women were struggling to take their place as leaders in the Jewish community, some of the learning curve for our community was in noticing that 1) women could be powerful Jewish leaders, and 2) it was okay to try something different. Working toward meaningful inclusion is not always comfortable. Often it involves risk taking. Often, the beginning of Ayecha's work toward inclusion of individuals and organizations is about assessing the climate for change in an environment and gauging the willingness to risk being uncomfortable in the short term for the long-term reward of creating relationships and environments that individuals join willingly and enjoy being a part of.

In St. Louis, Ayecha is working with Jews United for Justice with Linda [Holtzman], and Rabbi Susan Talve [of the Central Reform Congregation]. Susan is a fabulous rabbi; she's very committed to ending racism, to making sure that her synagogue is not a place where racism can abide, making it a place that's welcoming to Jews of color. She brought us in to do a full-day training with the administrators of her synagogue, with her staff, with the faculty and with the families of Jews of color that were there. We started off looking at Jewish multiculturalism, and we did some exercises on the messages that we received growing up around Jewish identity, and then we moved into racism itself: what does it look like, what do you know, what have you learned, what do your relationships look like? And then coming out of racism we look back into: What does it mean to claim a Jewish identity that's divorced from oppression? What does it mean to live or have a Jewish identity that is not associated with the messages we've received on anti-semitism? At the end of the day we came back together, and the young people's focus group came back talking about, how can we empower young people to have their visions be validated and valued and appreciated and integrated into what we do in the future? It was beautiful to see the young people. They did not see barriers and saw everything as possible. A lot of the work we do around building allied relationships between young people and adults involves teaching adults to make room for young people's visions so that walls don't grow in the spaces where young people place their faith and hope in our future. A job for those of us who are maturing into "elders" is to stay clear about the difference between maintaining power and control and sharing power and control so that there is enough room for young people to keep dreaming and being an integral part of moving our community forward.

We did the training with Susan and it went so well that funding was soon raised to do a year-long training with members of the full congregation. Susan is committed to providing every member of her congregation with an opportunity to develop a deeper understanding of racism and apply this understanding to how they build community at CRC.

As a facilitator, I love working with synagogues, because I have always seen them as a place where Jews have the potential to experience a real sense of community. Over the years, the format of what is done in synagogues has changed, and the number of people that attend services has changed as well, yet, the fact that after all these years, Jews in places around the world still build synagogues and gather in them for the purposes of worship and spirituality, gives me faith in "the synagogue" as a tool for building community. My dream is that through Ayecha's work on *Tzelem Elokim,* the image of spirituality, we can help people to increase awareness of the many ways that Jews relate to spirituality, so that the "shul" can re-emerge as a gathering place that all Jews can call their own.

At the "Jews of Color Speak Out" at one point, I remember saying to the audience, "This is the temple of my familiar," and that was true, because when I looked out and saw the diversity of people in the room, I thought, imagine if this were my synagogue. Imagine if when I gathered with other Jews to pray and be "a member of the tribe" all these faces were a part of that experience. Twenty years ago, the landscape for Jewish diversity was very different, but the numbers have grown, and families are changing. The audience that gathered for the speak out inspired me, and when Michael Saxe-Taller [of the JCC] asked about next steps, it was easy to come up with a proposal for the December celebration of African Jewry. With little marketing outside of our sponsor circles, close to three hundred people showed up. This event cemented my conviction that the work we do is a service that the community would like to support.

Is there a danger of voyeurism? Well, that's why I did a listening partnership as part of the intro to the event. As a facilitator, I often try to encourage people to get the most out of workshops by endeavoring to go beneath the surface, and that evening I tried to get people to begin conversations with each other, as well. I think that the Celebration of African Jewry was a wonderful opportunity to get a variety of people in the same room with the chance to interact with each other as they experienced the educational offerings around the room. In the coming months as Ayecha opens its New York office and begins concentrated programming in the New York area, I hope that there will always be some element of one-on-one, person-to-person interaction involved so that our events assist people in going a little deeper than their initial assumptions and this growth goes both ways between Jews who never had to second-guess their identity and those that experience Jewish identity as a question. At the Hanukkah event, people of color were in the majority, and one of the people on our committee commented: "In all of my experiences with Jewish events, I've never been to an event, outside of this one, where so many people with white skin worked so hard in the background to serve and make happy so many people of color. This is what I'm going to take from this evening."

Update:

As noted above, Ayecha has opened an office in New York City with a Bikkurim residency. Ayecha continues to organize and sponsor multicultural Jewish events, including a Jewish Soul Celebration concert.[11] Yevilah wrote in January 2006: "Ayecha's board recently agreed to shift our mission and vision to focus our programs and resources more precisely on our constituency of Jewish educators, communal professionals, and Jews of Color. Our official name is now Ayecha Jewish Diversity Resources and our dual mission is to provide a) resources for Jewish Diversity Education and b) advocacy and support for Jews of Color and multi-racial families in the United States. We want communal professionals to know that they could come to us for awareness, commitment, and change-making resources in regard to Jewish Diversity, and we wanted Jews of Color to know that they could come to us for programs and resources that would support and advocate for their inclusion and graceful participation in Jewish institutions and environments."

CROSSING MANY BORDERS:
IVRI-NASAWI/LEVANTINE CENTER (INTERNATIONAL)

I interviewed Jordan Elgrably in Los Angeles, Joyce Maio in New York, and integrated their remarks into a single document, while retaining their distinct voices.[12] Ivri-NASAWI has since morphed into the Levantine Center in Los Angeles.

JORDAN ELGRABLY

Jordan Elgrably, a writer, editor, and producer of Moroccan origin, founded Ivri-NASAWI in 1996, Open Tent Middle East Coalition in 1999, and co-founded the Levantine Cultural Center in 2001. A frequent speaker on the history and identity of Sephardic/Middle Eastern Jews, and the Israeli–Palestinian conflict, among his innovations are several versions of the Sephardic Arts Festival produced at the Skirball Cultural Center in Los Angeles; the Poetry of Peace series in the 1999 World Festival of Sacred Music; and Open Tent's 1999 and 2000 Middle East Film Festivals at the University of California—Los Angeles. He also spearheaded a large educational conference, "The Israeli-Palestinian Crisis:

New Conversations for a Pluralist Future." Jordan's essays, articles, and stories have appeared widely, including in *Salmagundi, The Paris Review,* the *Los Angeles Times,* the *Washington Post, Le Monde, El Paíís, Sephardic American Voices, The Burning Library,* and *The Best of Writers at Work.*

JOYCE MAIO

Joyce Allegra Maio was born and raised in Paris; she is of Egyptian Jewish heritage. She studied Spanish literature at the University of Mexico and translation at the Monterey Institute of International Studies in California. She has produced and cast docudramas, short films, music videos, and national commercials, specializing in multilingual and "real-people" casting, and has also produced and written experimental and multimedia theatrical performances. Since its foundation in 1996, Joyce Allegra Maio was the New York contributing editor of Ivri-NASAWI. She opened its New York chapter, producing and hosting regular salon series as well as coordinating cultural/education programs with other institutions. With Jordan Elgrably in 1998, she produced "Sephardic Voices," a tribute to the winners of the National Sephardi Literary Contest. She has worked as a consultant on many arts projects, including as a cultural group leader to visit the Cuban art community for the 92nd Street Y in New York City.

JORDAN ELGRABLY: Our official statement explains that Ivri-NASAWI was founded by "Sephardi/ Mizrahi writers who felt that Sephardic and Middle Eastern Jewish culture needed representation in the United States, and who have long argued for Arab-Jewish coexistence, modeled along historical examples from the Levant and the Iberian Peninsula (Al-Andalus)."

Ivri-NASAWI started as a conversation between Victor Perera and myself. In '95 Victor published a seminal book on Sephardic culture, *The Cross and the Pear Tree: A Sephardic Journey,* and the *Washington Post* gave me an assignment to write a feature story about him and the book. Victor came to Los Angeles and we met and there was a meeting of minds. He was like an older brother figure to me, and he reawakened my interest in my own Sephardic background. Some of the stories in his memoir resonated, and we remarked that we knew a number of Jews who were artists and writers of Sephardic or Middle Eastern Jewish–Mizrahi background, and we thought that we could band together and try to create more awareness in the Jewish culture and mainstream American culture. Our first impulse was to try to create a magazine and call it *ivri*, because *ivri* means border-crosser.

JOYCE MAIO: Of course, being Sephardic Jews, we have crossed many borders. We've moved and moved from so many countries because of history—I think more than the Ashkenaz have. And all this moving, crossing has contributed to our identity and to the richness of our culture. Sephardic Jews come from many different countries and speak many languages. So there was a need for a voice.

JE: Quickly we realized we wanted an association, so we came up with NASAWI—New Association of Sephardi Artists and Writers—International at the end to justify that we were from Israel, Europe, Canada, the U.S., and South America. So it was Victor, Ammiel Alcalay, anthropologist Ruth Behar in Michigan, and Ella Shohat in New York, and we began to do some outreach to Jewish organizations and other cultural institutions, museums, and so on. One of the first things we did was create the National Sephardi Literary Contest. It was open to everybody who was either of a Sephardic or Mizrahi background or interested in writing on themes that touch on Sephardi or Mizrahi culture or history.

Ivri-NASAWI became more political with the coming of the second Intifada, because as Jews, this is one of the big issues, and Middle Eastern Jews—just like everyone else—have a range of opinions and experiences. But they also have a different relationship to the Middle East, one that's more organic and historical. Some people were more progressive and left wing in their responses, and others—fewer in number—more to the right, taking the Israel-my-country-right-or-wrong stance (even if they never lived there). That created a bit of a schism. Actually, I think all five of the founders had the same perspective, critical of the occupation, and it was difficult for us to remain silent.

JM: The political is very difficult and it became more difficult as the years went on. I find it hard to distinguish what is politics and what is not. I am not a political person, I believe much more in culture and in art. I always felt that culture offers a stronger voice than politics, which tend to divide. But we had conflicts about how much to be cultural, how much political, and about issues, especially Israel/ Palestine. You know, there are some countries where it's very difficult to separate culture and politics; Palestine and Israel is one. Cuba is another. It always comes up. And I find myself forced to defend how I feel, backed into a corner because someone says, you're being political here.

JE: As we went forward, we knew the official Jewish community was largely going to toe the line and not be outraged by things we found objectionable. So we became less interested in the mainstream, and I think they were less interested in us. Some of us have ended up on this ridiculous "self-hating" shit list.[13] Seven thousand names, I guess we're all self-hating.

The association was very active for a couple of years; we had many programs going on in L.A. and some in New York and the Bay Area. Our work was largely funded with small contributions from memberships, and only a couple of grants that I wrote. I went to see a lot of potential donors, wealthy Sephardic Jews, and found that mostly they were interested in giving their money to established [Ashkenazi] Jewish institutions to do Sephardic programming, rather than to us. This makes us feel like we're good for an exotic festival, but in terms of looking at us as important intellectuals and planners, it's not happening. With some donors I think it was difficult because we didn't just talk about Sephardi culture. We talked about Arab Jews. We used the term *Mizrahi*, which is what most [Arab] Jews in Israel prefer to call themselves. Some Sephardim seemed to bristle at that. So our main obstacles were financial.

JM: We tended to be very proud of our Arab origins, and there were some Sephardic Jews who were not comfortable with that. Yet the difference between Sephardic and Mizrahi is real. A lot has to do with economic and social background. In the past everybody used to be a Sephardic, and then the Mizrahi started saying, you know, the Mizrahi is a little different. We felt like, okay, we need to say Mizrahi *and* Sephardic. The key division is historical and linguistic. So a Sephardic might not speak Arabic; he would speak Ladino. And a Mizrahi would not necessarily speak Ladino, he would speak Arabic. There is a difference. But a lot of Sephardi went from Spain to the Arab countries, so then they were both. In my family [from Egypt], Ladino was not really spoken among themselves, it was more Arabic. But if you go a few generations back, you find Ladino.

JE: We met a lot of people along the way who were enthusiastic and there were a lot of articles in various publications. We did *NASAWI News*, mostly paid for out of our pockets. We created a lot of programs.

None of us was paid. Right now Ivri-NASAWI is in hibernation, but Joyce and I are going to put the website back on line and refurbish it. There's a lot of information, a lot of archival stories. We intend to write a new proposal and see if we can get some support.

JM: There's not much attention [in or out of the Jewish world] to Sephardic or Mizrahi culture. There's the Sephardic House, the American Sephardic Federation, but they appeal to a pretty conservative base. I would like to bring in a voice that is fresh and not afraid to say what they want to say. A spectrum. Now, obviously, we're more progressive but I would hope we don't get too political because I have seen the cultural piece lose focus. And for me Ivri-NASAWI still means the arts and artistic expression. We're a secular group, and a lot of Sephardic Jews tend to be more religious, so many didn't care about what we were doing. Some who were progressive did. But religion was not a main focus for us. Our constituents really are young people, or progressives. People who respect tradition, who respect their heritage, but also who are open-minded. Intellectuals.

JE: I guess what makes Ivri-NASAWI stand out from other Sephardic organizations—the few that there are—is we are the artsy and progressive wing. So it's important and I'd love to see it continue. I went on with some other people to found the Levantine Cultural Center in Los Angeles because I wanted to see something that was more inclusive of the cultures of the region.

JM: The review was quite good in bringing different stories from different perspectives, giving an array of the whole richness of Sephardic and Mizrahi writing and new voices. And the salons were a place where our beliefs and stories could be shared. But then the salons started becoming places where people were taking out their frustrations, Sephardic vs. Ashkenazi, defending one's point of view. All the divisions are not healthy. They can create isolation or self-righteousness. But in terms of the Ashkenaz, there's a definite difference, and that's what Ivri-NASAWI is supposed to speak out for. Eastern Europe is quite different from the Levantine.

JE: We did the Sephardic Arts Festival at the Skirball Museum in 1997; four thousand people showed up. We did it again in 1998 and 1999, and then we split away. We also did some events with the Getty Research Center, called *Arabs and Jews: Beyond Boundaries, Culture,*

Community, and Identity. We had several panels, showed films, and had discussions. A lot of Arab Americans don't even realize that their countries had significant Jewish populations, and American Jews don't know it either. So this ignorance reinforces the idea that Arabs and Jews are two really separate peoples and helps them be enemies. When we would create programs that involved Israeli culture, which our programs often did, we would seek support from the Israeli consulate, and they would usually be happy to give support. But they didn't like it when it became too political.

We created strong excitement and curiosity among people of that cultural background who'd been away from it because they weren't really attached to traditional Sephardic observance and they almost never saw themselves represented within Jewish culture. So now they were able to come to our events and meet people they could connect with. A lot of new relationships were started; we also were able to introduce artists to collectors and museums who hadn't been noticed by them before. We were able to create community where there had been a vacuum.

Originally working with Arabs was not difficult at all—they don't have a problem with American Jews, so, as a rule, you go to an Arab community and say we want to bond with you. They are like, fine, I don't have a problem with you. But just because you and I sit down to listen to some music together has no effect on our feelings about the injustices that the Palestinians are suffering. Then the Jewish response is often defensive. When we stay away from politics we've had a fair amount of success in presenting a program that would be of some interest to the Arab American community—for example, Yair Dalal, an Iraqi musician. The Arab community identifies with his music too, it's the same music. But if you don't come out as a Jew and say you don't agree with the occupation; if you don't show the same degree of humanism and fairness toward what happens to Palestinians as you would to, say, the blacks in South Africa, then you lose credibility.

These days because of 9/11, the Arab–Muslim community has a lot of their own problems. We had a Muslim–Jewish group here that was meeting on a regular basis and that fell apart around 9/11. I started another organization in 1999 called Open Tent: Middle East Coalition, just so I could take the politics out of Ivri-NASAWI and be able to talk about these issues in an educational format. Open Tent was really strong until 2001. Again relations because of political differences became really strident and I reverted to feeling the only way we're going to get anywhere is if we celebrate our cultural differences and similarities, within the context of the arts.

So the Levantine Cultural Center was designed to be nonpolitical. We had a pretty strong year in 2002–2003, and now we're back to the same questions: there are human needs in Iraq and Afghanistan and other places; the Palestinian issue hasn't died. There's still a lot of unemployment. So the Arab American community is less interested in donating money and time to cultural stuff because they know people are hurting and they want to be effective. But that said, there are artists, especially musical artists, who are beyond politics. You have Jews and Arabs who play music together and that's nothing new for them.

What's very much on our minds is fighting racism within the Jewish community. We were outspoken about what we saw as Ashkenazi cultural hegemony in the institutions; for example, the big show that the Jewish Museum put together called "Too Jewish." The show was interesting but we were entirely absent. There was a little note in the introduction to the catalogue by the curator, about how he had looked for Sephardic Jews and just couldn't' find any. We just thought it was totally ridiculous. The Jewish museum is planning a show that includes more diverse perspectives and they did try to reach out more to non-Eastern European Jewish creators.

Ivri-NASAWI was very in your face. We wrote letters to UCLA when they'd come up with programs—the Jewish Studies department would create conferences and leave out anything Sephardic or Mizrahi. As a result in more recent years I've noticed a change. They even invited Ammiel [Alcalay] finally, after many years, to come out and talk. They had Jacques Derrida and other Sephardic Jews. They invited Sami Shalom Chetrit who's a real Mizrahi rabble rouser from Israel to come and show his film *Israeli Black Panthers*.[14] But we're still very much on the edge. There's no Sephardic museum or cultural center or magazine.

So I've been working on the Levantine Center, which is Middle Eastern, Arab, Persian, Jewish, etc. The concept is to have a large building with several smaller offices for several different organizations. So that these Persian and Armenian Arab and Sephardi groups can produce programs in a shared space. We've created a business plan and a lot of programs, we have a diverse board of directors, but we're looking for funding. There is a major Arab cultural institute in Paris; it took them thirteen years of fund raising.

JM: Levantine Center has much more of an Arab emphasis. I keep telling Jordan, I don't see much Jewish Sephardi here. It's all Arab and Persian. There are some Jews on the board, but the voices are not coming out.

JE: We've gotten criticized for not having enough Jewish presence or programming. We've done a number of things that are Sephardic or Israeli culture. The other Sephardic Jew who founded it with me, Elio Zarmat, he was born in Egypt—we both felt if we're going to be legitimate as an inclusive Middle Eastern cultural central, we can't have a predominance of Jewish culture. Because the Arab community will say this isn't for us. So we didn't try to do much Sephardic culture in the first year. We did programming that was more multicultural, or Arab or Persian or Turkish. But at the end of the first year we started to have Israeli writers or a Palestinian-Israeli cultural evening. We had some Sephardic music. The model is to create the center and have Ivri-NASAWI as a member, and they would produce the Jewish programming. But we're not there yet.

If the Jewish community were truly inclusive . . . it would perhaps also be less afraid of self-criticism. Because of the Israeli problem and right-wing organizations like AIPAC,[15] it isn't inclusive, it's divisive. If it were going to be inclusive, it would look like Levantine Center. It would include Jews from different countries and different religious orientations. Everybody would accept everyone as legitimate. But in the Jewish community if you're anti-occupation you're not legitimate because you're self-hating. And if you're a Mizrahi Jew dealing with the National Foundation for Jewish culture, you're not equal to someone doing traditional Ashkenazi scholarship, and if you're a Sephardic you're a nice piece of folk art, come and play your Sephardic music, but we're not really interested in the way you practice Judaism. It's quaint, it's something for the window display.

A truly diverse and integrated Jewish community would be a new world order for us as Jews. In order to be an honest intellectual I don't think you can really adhere to a national identity. For a lot of Jews, Jewish identity is kind of nationalist, because it's Israel and Jewish community and marrying another Jew. I don't have anything against that but sometimes it delegitimizes your humanism because you have a bias. You see anti-semitism everywhere and you see Jewish suffering as more important than other suffering.

Today there's a big debate about whether anti-semitism today is worse than in the thirties. Recently in the *L.A. Times* there were two contrasting articles. One was saying yes, anti-semitism is something to be really afraid of, and the other writer was suggesting that, yes, what Israel is doing to Palestinians is affecting people's disenchantment with Jews, but anti-semitism isn't really worse than 10–20–30 years ago; if anything, Jews are better off. I don't think about anti-semitism as much because I see the Arab and Muslim community is suffering more. But it is happening outside the U.S., like in France, where there are 600,000–700,000 Jews and close to four million Muslims. Twenty years ago when I lived in France, being a Sephardic Jew was a good thing, cultural, highly respected. Today because of disgust with Israel the younger Muslims are being taught to dislike Jews.

Update:

Ivri-NASAWI no longer exists; in its place is the Levantine Cultural Center, a project that bears a great deal of resemblance to its Ivri-NASAWI roots, but is far more inclusive of all the cultures of North Africa and the Middle East, from Morocco in the west to Afghanistan in the east.

A MIXED MULTITUDE:
BETH SHALOM B'NAI ZAKEN ETHIOPIAN
HEBREW CONGREGATION (CHICAGO)

Rabbi Capers C. Funnye, Jr., was born in South Carolina in the African Methodist Episcopalian Church and grew up in Chicago, where he is rabbi and spiritual leader of Beth Shalom B'nai Zaken Ethiopian Hebrew Congregation. He also serves as a Senior Research Associate for the Institute of Jewish and Community Research in San Francisco. He earned a B.A. in Hebrew Literature and rabbinic ordination from the Israelite Board of Rabbis, Inc. (Queens, NY), and a B.A. in Jewish Studies and M.S. in Human Service Administration from Spertus Institute of Jewish Studies (Chicago). Rabbi Funnye has served as a consultant to such institutions as the Du Sable Museum of African American History, the Chicago Historical Society, the Spertus Museum of Judaica (all in Chicago); the Black Holocaust Museum (Milwaukee), and the Afro-American Museum (Los Angeles). He has lectured at numerous universities, synagogues, churches, and community organizations throughout the United States, and has appeared on national and local television and radio programs. He sits on a number of boards in the Jewish community: the Chicago Board of Rabbis, the Jewish Council on Urban Affairs, Akiba Schechter Jewish Day School; and he is vice president of the Israelite Board of Rabbis. He celebrated his twentieth year as a rabbi in 2005.[16]

RABBI CAPERS FUNNYE: Beth Shalom is the synthesis of three distinct groups. The oldest—Ethiopian Hebrew Congregation—was founded in 1915, and formally chartered by the state in 1921–22. Beth Shalom merged with Ethiopian Hebrews in 1984. And B'nai Zaken approached us in 1993 about merging with their congregation's remnants. We have congregants who were part of the original Ethiopian Hebrew Congregation, some of those families are third and fourth generation. More recently families that come in go through the regular prerequisites for becoming Jewish, studying and going through a Bet Din, a *mikveh* and, in the case of men, establishing the covenant of circumcision. So the processes in our community are the exact processes laid out in *halakhah*.

As part of the Chicago Board of Rabbis, I do congregational visits and pulpit exchanges with Reform and Conservative congregations. We've also assisted Orthodox congregations. One synagogue was trying to get repaired. We took some thirty people up there to help with repairs, and shared a lunch with them. We try to be as a congregation and myself personally involved with the entire Jewish community, every stream of it.

My congregation is primarily people of color. But every time we've purchased a synagogue we've invited the congregants to join us, to still consider the synagogue as their home. So in the case of a synagogue we purchased twelve years ago in South Chicago, of the eight remaining families, three joined. Of those three, only one family still belongs, due to illness and death. In the old synagogue people would come and say, "Rabbi, can I sit here? This is where I used to sit with my grandfather when I was eight." We had a man come, in his seventies, and he had been bar mitzvahed in the synagogue.

Others who haven't joined officially said, "Rabbi, can I come for Rosh Hashonah and Yom Kippur?" and I said, absolutely.[17] Rosh Hashonah and Yom Kippur we might have anywhere from twenty-five through thirty guests; one year we had upwards of forty guests, all from the Ashkenazi community.

Our house is open to all Jews. We have young adults now, Jewish kids I taught in religious school and they say, "You were always my favorite teacher in religious school. We don't do much with synagogue now, but when we think about synagogue we think about coming here and worshiping with you." Our shul is made up of newborns to late eighties, several generations of families, a lot of diversity. More often than not when our young people meet someone who is not Jewish I would say 90 percent of the time they become part of our community as opposed to our young people going out. Maybe because our community isn't overwhelmingly large. It's welcoming. And our music has been created by our members over the years, so we add music to our tradition.

When you come to Beth Shalom we want it to be a house of peace, a house where all are welcome. Mechanisms of exclusion in the mainstream Jewish community don't apply. The mainstream excludes us by acting like we don't exist. A genuinely inclusive Jewish community would have within it every color of the rainbow of humanity. Every Jewish historian knows that there were Jewish communities all over the world, and wherever those Jews were they looked like the people of those communities where they lived.

So why the utter amazement: "When did you convert?"

Well, when did *you* convert?

Like WE—the mainstream Jewish community—we keep the door, and you can't come in unless we say so. As if Judaism is not broad enough; as if the table is not big enough to accept all of us.

When you come to Beth Shalom, if you come in the door and you have a tallit and you know how to hold the prayer book and you sit down and you start davening and you're reading in Hebrew, after the service, none of our members is going to come up to you and ask are you Jewish. Unfortunately I can go to a synagogue and after the service, that's the question I'll get asked. Like I don't have a right to be Jewish. What amazes me is Jewish *halakhah* says you don't ask that question.

Whenever my wife says she's Jewish, her husband's a rabbi, people say, "Oh, you're married to a white guy?" And she says "No, he's a black guy." You see the mindset. I think in the case of America particularly, the Jewish community has long wanted to see itself and be seen as white. So you don't even see many pictures of Sephardic congregations when the media covers stories on Passover or Hanukkah. It's an Ashkenazi group. It's as if the Ashkenazi community wants to push Ashkenazi Jewry as quote unquote this is the face of Jewry; this is the *only* face of Jewry.

So what happens in the African American community: you say "Jew"—it's white. That's why when I teach at various synagogues, I have to remind my coreligionists, "Listen. Jews became a people on the continent of Africa. The Torah was given on the continent of Africa. Sinai is a part of Africa, not Asia. When the children of Israel went to buy Jacob back in the land of Canaan, the Canaanites said, this is a burying place of the Egyptians. The Egyptians were an African people. If we examine the Bible itself, the location of all the biblical stories—Ethiopia is mentioned in the Bible more than forty times. Yet there's this amazement that African people, black people, could be Jews.

Why isn't this known? Because, unfortunately, the history—particularly from the Jewish perspective of reconnecting people to Judaism on the continent of Africa or in the case of the Black Jews of Cochin, India. . . . It's like we don't want anyone else in the club. But the truth of the matter is others *are* in the club. Judaism has never been a race; it has always been an admixture of a variety of ethnicities.

The Book of Exodus tells us twice very profoundly that a mixed multitude went up with them. Also in the Book of Exodus you have the prohibition of "Thou shalt not feed the kid in its mother's milk." That's said two or three times, and we have a whole system of *kashrut* that evolves out of the mother's milk.[18] But what of the times we're told *a mixed multitude went up with them*? There's no synthesis or understanding of Judaism including all types of people. Of Judaism being a mix. That's not been stressed and developed the way the two or three times we're told not to feed a kid in its mother's milk has grown into this elaborate system.

Interfaith work is very much at the heart of what I do and who I am. Fighting racism for our synagogue manifests in the interfaith work. I tell Jews, go there, be that face. Don't make Jews a faceless people. Jewish visibility helps to temper and to enlighten others in what they perceive to be the Jewish community. I do pulpit exchanges. I believe in interfaith dialogue with Christians and Muslims. We've just passed Ramadan. We opened our social hall, and from the Orthodox Muslim community two sheikhs came, and several imams, both Arab and African American. During this time of crisis, the fast of Ramadan offers people prayer and they broke the fast and we shared a meal together (*iftar*). I talked to them about Judaism, and they talked about Ramadan. I believe in having a working relationship and understanding with various faith communities.

We are a growing congregation. One of our challenges is how do we grow? We advertise in the newspaper, but do we have spiritual conversations? Do we invite them to Torah study or *shabat* service or to the Hanukkah party, so that people can begin the process of engaging, questioning, and learning? Currently our congregation is about 180 people. We want to grow the congregation; broaden the understanding of Judaism in the African American community, both Christian and Muslim. We want to work to increase the connections and reconnections with those individuals and groups on the continent of Africa that want to officially reconnect, make *t'shuvah*, return to Judaism.

My wife and I are leaving for Africa shortly to work for three weeks with the Ibo community in Nigeria.[19] There are already some twenty congregations that have formed and they need assistance. We're going to do a needs assessment. This is a real connection. For years it was a dream but now it's happening.

Update:

"The trip was wonderful. I met with representatives from thirty congregations in Nigeria and they have all agreed to join the Pan African Jewish Alliance."[20]

RESPECT AND KNOWLEDGE:
BETA ISRAEL OF NORTH AMERICA (INTERNATIONAL)

Beejhy Barhany is of Ethiopian descent and Jewish heritage, a speaker of five languages. Her family immigrated to Israel when she was seven. Her life in Israel included army service and four years on a kibbutz. After this, she took a year-long trip throughout South America where she encountered peoples of various ethnic backgrounds. She soon migrated to New York, where she utilized her organizational skills to create BINA. Her global perspective and experiences have proved fruitful in founding this organization and in developing her linguistic capabilities. She is BINA's Executive Director.[21]

BEEJHY BARHANY: I was born in 1976 in Ethiopia. My family immigrated to Israel when I was seven years old. We left Ethiopia when I was four and we walked in the desert for a couple of months to get to the Sudan. Then we stayed in Sudan for three years because the Israeli government didn't recognize Ethiopians as Jews. That's why it took us a few years. There was a struggle in the Israeli parliament.

Living in Sudan wasn't bad; the Sudanese never bothered us with anti-semitism. But Ethiopian Jews have been dreaming for thousands of years of going back to the holy land. It was the time for us to go.

Coming to Israel was—kind of a disappointment, to put it mildly. As people who had waited so long and suffered so much in order to arrive in Israel, to be welcomed by racism, discrimination, prejudice. . . . Disappointment. Schools not accepting Ethiopian Jews. Poverty, unemployment: statistics show Ethiopian Jews are in a bad situation.

As a child I remember a lot of Israelis used to call me *kushi* (like *nigger*). In some way you don't feel part of the society. You are there but Ethiopian Jews are not part of the parliament, there is no representation. No Ethiopians in high positions, no good jobs. Discrimination in housing, segregation but a new type of segregation.

There were two waves of immigration, 1983/Operation Moses, and 1994/Operation Solomon, when the Israelis sent airplanes and brought Ethiopians to Israel.

A few years ago there was a big scandal about the blood. Whenever Ethiopians had donated blood, the Israelis threw it in the garbage. Like Ethiopians are not good enough to donate blood. Blood is life. It was like killing them.

It's very sad that when Ethiopian Jews immigrated to Israel they had to prove themselves as Jews. We Ethiopian Jews have been practicing Judaism for thousands of years. Ethiopia is the only country mentioned so many times in the Bible. Abraham—I don't think he was Ashkenazi. I think he was a black man. Ethiopia is close to Egypt. We have the same Blue Nile. Moses was a king in Ethiopia for forty years. In the Bible it says Moses had a black wife, *isha kushi*, which means black woman. Rashi [Ashkenazi scholar in France, 1040–1105] said black doesn't really mean black; it means she was beautiful.

The legacy of Ethiopian Jews has a lot to offer, a lot we can teach the rest of the Jewish diaspora. Judaism had a huge impact on the Orthodox Church of Ethiopia. They keep *shabat* from sunset on Friday. They perform circumcision on the boy babies on the eighth day. They don't eat pork.

I came to New York six years ago. It seemed so interesting, all the different cultures. I thought I'd stay a year. I go to CCNY. I was studying African American history and I said to myself, how come we Ethiopian Jews have no representation here in the U.S.? There are organizations talking for Ethiopian Jews. But the most accurate and proper thing is for we Ethiopian Jews to speak for ourselves and educate about our culture and heritage.

I talked to a few friends of mine and they were skeptical. But I had the idea and in 2002 I managed to found BINA. It's incorporated with 501c(3) status. Our aim and mission is to promote our proud Ethiopian Jewish culture and heritage, and empower Ethiopian Jews so they can speak up for themselves. We want to serve as the official voice of the Beta Israel community. We want to provide legal aid, advice, and advocacy to the Beta Israel community in Ethiopia, Israel and the U.S. BINA creates and promotes cultural and artistic events, to contribute to the growth of the greater Judaic culture and provide a multicultural view of Judaism through joint programs with other Jewish groups. Also BINA is dedicated to the harmonization of relations between the peoples of the Jewish diaspora and those of the African diaspora. I think there are similarities in experience, tribulation the two groups have endured. As Ethiopian Jews we can understand the two groups and be kind of a bridge. Our constituency is all Ethiopian Jews in the U.S. And if there are other Jews who want to be part of this, everybody is welcome. Jews of color, like African American Jews of course we would encourage working with them. Any human being working to help BINA grow.

We want to educate so people won't be racist, but it's not only about racism. We want justice just like anyone else. We want to open people's minds about Ethiopian Jews. We're tired of hearing, "oh the poor Ethiopian Jews, they're starving." Like we're a franchise everyone wants a part of. We Ethiopian Jews can talk for ourselves. Big donors, people "helping" Ethiopian Jews always look at us like, oh, our poor black brothers. Why don't they say something positive about Ethiopian Jews, our history, our accomplishments? I'd like to see a different understanding of Ethiopian Jews: you guys have so much history to offer. I'd like to see some respect and knowledge.

We organized an annual heritage festival at the Center for Jewish History [in New York]. We had the Ethiopian ambassador, a professor. It was a fundraiser for the famine in Ethiopia. We also assist newcomers, try to provide them with apartments, help finding jobs. We do public speaking, like at the 92nd Street Y, at churches, mosques. We speak to Jewish groups, to African American churches. People in the churches are willing to learn, especially when I say I'm a black Jew. There's a lot of people in the churches who know about black Jews, and a lot of people who have no idea, they thought all Jews were white. So we want to let people know: there are different kinds of Jews. The foundation of this ignorance starts in Israel, none of the kids learn about Ethiopian Jews including the Ethiopian Jewish kids. So they know nothing about their own history and culture to be proud of. Israel is like a small U.S. back in the thirties or forties. It's an oppression nobody sees. If people learn who they are it will encourage them to have a positive role in society.

In summer 2004 we organized the Sheba Film Festival, the first Ethiopian Jewish Film festival in North America. It took place at the Faison Firehouse Theater in Harlem. It was very good; the audience was very diverse, and we got some good media attention. We had a lecture by noted Yemenite Jewish academic and lecturer, Dr. Ephraim Isaacs. A great number of Ethiopians attended, not just Jewish Ethiopians; African Americans, people from the Caribbean. Now it's an annual event. We're working on an Ethiopian Hanukkah party.

Funding is really hard. We're new and funders want to give money to organizations they already know. It's hard to get started. My long-term goal is to have an office and a small center, like a museum, where we can display some art and crafts, educate people, maybe teach some Hebrew, some Amharic.

I just came back from Cleveland—the General Assembly of the Federation. I didn't see hardly any Jews of color. Like 99 percent white. Maybe ten of us out of three thousand.

The issue of Israel and Palestine—it needs to be solved, the Israeli government needs to compromise. BINA doesn't take a position on this, we're trying to stay focused on our mission. But of course we want to see peace and stability in the region. Our families are all back there.

Some African Americans think that Ethiopian Jews going to Israel was basically like the Israeli government kidnapped their brothers, taking them from Africa to enslave them in Israel. They think Ethiopian Jews are like slaves down in Israel. And in some ways it's true. The non-Jewish Ethiopians say, why would you leave your country and go to Israel where you suffer from discrimination? Some Ethiopian Jews are trying to return to Ethiopia. But I say that's why I'm here right now, and I'm hoping to go back and make some changes. I intend to return to Israel. I'd like to have an office in Israel and an office in Ethiopia. For now I'd like to have an office in New York!

Basically we want to create a different world with better understanding between ethnic groups, not only about Ethiopian Jews.

Update:

BINA, like Ayecha, has been awarded a residency at Bikkurim, "an incubator for Jewish ideas, which is part of JESNA at the UJC (see note 2 this chapter). BINA is planning a Passover Dinner and developing the upcoming Sheba Film festival.

HOSPITALITY IS THE FIRST PRINCIPLE: CONGREGATION NAHALAT SHALOM (ALBUQUERQUE)

Rabbi Lynn Gottlieb is one of the first ten women to become rabbis. She is an internationally known storyteller and kabbalist, percussionist and klezmer dancer, author, and ritual artist, and human rights activist. For the past several years she has co-led peace-building delegations sponsored by the Fellowship of Reconciliation to Israel and Palestine. Locally, Lynn co-founded the Jewish Arab Dialogue of New Mexico. In the fall of 2003, Lynn and Abdul Rauf Campos Marquetti co-founded the Jewish–Muslim Peace Walk to build a national movement of Muslims and Jews committed to the work of bearing witness to the Wall of Separation, and creating spiritual bridges of understanding between Muslims and Jews. She has received human rights awards from the Albuquerque Chapter of the UN and the City of Albuquerque.[22]

RABBI LYNN GOTTLIEB

LYNN GOTTLIEB: Nahalat Shalom, this congregation, is something I co-founded in 1983 with people who were interested in creating an alternative, grassroots Jewish community through the arts, love of learning, and soulful celebration. There are four dimensions that we focus on: spiritual life, learning community, visual/performing arts, and *tikkun olam*. A special aspect includes Sephardic heritage. Our constituency is quite diverse— Jews involved in creative expression, Jews and their non-Jewish partners, single households, gays/lesbians, activists, feminists—a lot of people who are usually outside traditional Jewish community. Seekers of Jewish learning, people who are alienated from traditional Jewish learning. Jews by choice, college students, Sephardic, Ashkenazi, and Middle Eastern Jews. Visual/performing artists, ecologists, healers. Multi-identitied people. Lots of different professions, though very few accountants! Couldn't find one accountant in our congregation to do our books.

For *tikkun olam* we emphasize especially Jewish–Arab dialogue, Jewish–Muslim outreach. Also we've had an ongoing participation, along with other congregations, in Project Share, where you bring the food and serve the homeless. Also we do outreach to Albuquerque Holocaust survivors, which has been really wonderful over the years. We've tried to extend our outreach beyond yearly events into ongoing kinds of relationships.

There is a remnant community of Sephardi *conversos* here in New Mexico. We've always had Sephardic heritage programming. But five years ago we started doing monthly Sephardic services. It's a remnant, but people come, and we have services in Ladino. The band plays Sephardic music, and the Ashkenazi cantor, Beth Cohen, is very familiar with Balkan, Sephardic, and Middle Eastern music. This happened because I wanted to respond to people who were coming to me, *Hi, I'm Sephardic, and I'm Jewish.* Often they're not clear about their Jewish roots, both Ashkenazi and Sephardi. Unfortunately, the Sephardic cantor of our congregation just committed suicide, so we're in kind of a mourning period, over the loss of him.

Ever since I've become a [congregational] rabbi, I'm aware that there are so many people who don't fit in any definition. They're multi-identitied. Therefore I try to relate to the spiritual needs of people and get a feel for what's important to them, where they've emerged from, where they're located. The Sephardic Jews of New Mexico—many are still connected to their Catholic heritage, and they want a place to come sometimes to be Jewish. Even though they might still go to church.[23] This is something the Jewish community always says "Nooo!! You have to decide, you have to stand squarely in one place." And that's never a helpful approach in dealing with people's spiritual needs. You have to give people time to find their base without pushing them. And I really like the idea that there's no compulsion in Judaism, in the sense that we're not conversion-oriented. So I think that we should apply that to our own folks.

Most people here are okay with innovation. Some people are inflexible. What's new? Flexibility is a spiritual issue. Get over it. I know that's harsh. In a post-Holocaust era, in particular, we have to be a lot more flexible and a lot more generous, and the main spiritual principle of my congregation has always been hospitality.

Also it's not just that we have Sephardic services once a month. Sephardic music, poems, stories are part of every major holy day. It's not like there's normal and there's Sephardic. Sephardic is integrated. Like feminism is integrated. On occasion, I'd say there's a focus. But we also have a thirty-person community klezmer band. We play all our own music, it's intergenerational, we've had over the years about seventy people playing in the band. Some have graduated and gone to college. Some people continue to play. There's a core of about fifteen–twenty people who continue to play.

What principles have allowed us to flourish? An emphasis on the arts. I believe people should make their own culture. So the training that we do for bar/bat mitzvah, for leadership development, is to make people draw on their strengths, to put them in a context where they're doing something. Most congregations might have people read from the Torah or be involved in a trillion meetings, you know how that goes—there's a social action committee and a this/that committee. Some people enjoy that sort of activity. We focus on cultural activity. I think that's where Jewish culture will survive.

I want to enable people to make music, to create artifacts, carving a *dreydl,* making a *tzedakah* box. We work with artists. We have mentors who are real artists whether in paper cutting or dance, music, whatever. We have a klezmer dance project, which is, I think highly unusual. This congregation knows ten klezmer dances really well—not Israeli dancing—the old, Eastern European dances, the *Romanian hora, freylekh, bulgar, honga,* and others. You can go to a klez concert or weekend and dance, but who remembers, who takes it back to communities? Well, our kids know these dances. And that's because we've video-ed them, we have a teacher come out every year, we learn them, I'm a main dancer; I've trained leaders. So when you come to a holiday like Passover, there's theater, music, band, dancing, poetry, traditional recitation of parts of the *Haggadah:* the seas part. It's extremely interactive. It's potluck, very participatory. That's how culture is created. People have to do it themselves.

How do we fight racism? A lot of folks in the community work on these issues in their other lives. Individual members have different kinds of commitments. Gay/lesbian rights, work in solidarity with the African American community. But because we emphasize the arts, our focus has been more on creating an atmosphere where lots of people come and feel welcome and participate.

We had a program in response to 9/11 which we called "Creating a Peace Culture." We invited folks from Southwest Organizing Project, Sage Council, a Native American organization that's trying to prevent a road through their sacred ground. Some folks who work on nuke issues spoke. When we do the peace walks we always start with a Native American blessing. Native people walk with us. I guess we don't so much "fight racism" as put ourselves in solidarity with communities that are directly impacted by racism. Racism manifests itself here a lot through environmental racism. So Southwest Organizing Project organized around the location of certain industries in Chicano communities. It was very successful. They had a dialogue with Kirkland Airforce Base. We participated in a bus tour of contaminated areas. We might legislate, join in solidarity with groups working on specific issues.

The first Jewish–Muslim peace walk had 350 people in five days of organizing. Our congregation is about 110 households. Not real large. Then there's a small group in the community that meets regularly these past two years to study text and to plan events together. The walk came into being because New Mexico is a land of pilgrimage. Our congregation is asked to participate in many pilgrimages. Three years ago someone called me up and said are you a radical rabbi? One Native American group was walking across the country with 100 eagle feathers for sobriety. They stayed at one of the Native American universities in town. They had a conference there and they invited me to come and share a Passover ceremony with them. And they came later with 100 eagle feathers for us, and tobacco, and we put tobacco in the ring while we were playing the Romanian *Hora* as a procession around the feathers with Indian drums. It was pretty wild. We've been on a lot of walks against drugs. Chimayo, a little sacred town in New Mexico, has the highest percentage of drug overdose in the country.

So we walked ten miles to Chimayo. That was the first time in four hundred years that the Penitentes[24] had come out in public, and they wanted it to be interfaith. We participated in the Hiroshima flame pilgrimage, which is run by the Nihoji Buddhist order. Their whole thing is peace walk. I met them in 1982 as part of the U.N.

167

Disarmament Session that brought a million people to New York City. So they called me and they were looking for a place to stay in Albuquerque and I said, come to the shul, and it happened to be *shabat*, so a bunch of us walked with them from Bernolillo to the synagogue, and we had three hundred people for *shabes* dinner, Native Americans, Christians and Buddhists. They had their altar, the Hiroshima flame, and the native people who came said they felt so comfortable in our shul. It's like a long house; you walk in and you're in it, there's no hallway really, just a vestibule. You're in a big room that has no fixed seating. People feel really comfortable because it's extremely unpretentious.

After that walk, Operation Defensive Shield started, and about fifteen of us who've been doing Palestinian–Jewish reconciliation work in the congregation got together and said, what are we going to do now? We said, let's walk to the mosque. We had this peace walk, and it was almost like an insight. We hadn't managed—through the Arab–Jewish dialogue which I co-founded with Mahasin Shukri—to extend the participation of more than five or six members of the mosque. Even though many of them had come to the congregation on different occasions when I'd had Palestinian speakers. So with the walk, they were just amazed. Three hundred people! "Hi, want to go on a peace walk?" "Yes." It was like that. So then we had another one where we started at the mosque on September 11. And the mosque opened up, it was the first time they had an interfaith service, the first time men and women sat together. It was 6:30 a.m., pouring rain, and 250 people showed up.

Since that time, Abdul and I also went to Israel together and we've been speaking, trying to merge our Jewish–Palestinian work with Jewish–Muslim work. My experience has been that activists are usually secular, Jewish ones, and yet the potential for organizing a real opposition is in the Muslim community, who have extremely strong feelings about what's going on. So making inroads and creating dialogues and relationships, and figuring out how to walk the balance between partnership and dealing with the anti-Jewishness has been an incredibly effective tool. It's amazing to me how many mosques are willing to have this peace walk. We did one in New York City this past September 11; we actually walked the entire island.

The Hiroshima flame pilgrimage was so stunning that people were ready for a next step. And right after September 11 we invited ten of our closest Muslim friends to come to the synagogue and to speak about what Islam means to them. Two hundred people at services, a lot for us. That was interesting too because people got to see the diversity of the Muslim community just like people say, *the Jews, the Muslims*—it's all very diverse. Walking to the mosque wasn't such a big thing because there have been so many Muslims at the synagogue over the years. We had a little Muslim–Jewish youth group that my son was part of and helped establish, where we'd get the Muslim and Jewish kids together. They'd come together and talk about how they felt about Israel, their favorite holidays, what's it like to be Jewish and Muslim. It ended up being a very solidarity-building kind of event. We met ten times over two years. It wasn't a lot, but of course it had a huge impact. We've gone over to the mosque, I have field trips every year, usually around Ramadan. So I think it worked because we created familiarity. Built relationships.

All of this work, fighting racism, fighting prejudice, and so forth is a matter of building relationships that last over decades. Because the work is work of decades. It requires extremely strong personal relationships, especially in the leadership of people who are friends and who can take the heat that you're gonna get!

Both of us take heat, myself and Abdul. *Why are you talking to them, they hate us? The Jews wanna kill us, the Palestinians, the Muslims wanna kill us.* All these polarized concepts of the other, which of course is basic, grounded in unfamiliarity. Then you have the liberal dynamic, where if you do an interfaith service once a month and you have a Muslim come talk on your pulpit, you've done it. So when you start pushing for structural change, people go berserk. Then of course there's Israel. I've written about torture and home demolition, and it was syndicated in ten papers around the country. There was a national campaign against me. It drove the Reform and Conservative rabbi crazy, and it's taken a long time to repair those bridges. I don't think they're completely repaired. This year as a sign of the progress, the Taste of Honey, which is a Federation-run event in its second year is having a panel of voices on Israel—including the left, which is kind of remarkable. There's still a lot of "she's on this panel, I won't be on it," and that kind of crap. But we've definitely made inroads.

One has to have seven skins. Some people in my congregation have left. Not a lot, but at least three. You have to endure all kinds of bullshit rumors. Like when I went to Israel—you know I lead a delegation every year with the Fellowship of Reconciliation—so people were passing the rumor that Hamas was paying for my ticket. People would come up to members of my congregation and literally say to them, "Do you know Hamas is paying for your rabbi's ticket?" And they say, "Well, no, it's not Hamas, it's the Fellowship of Reconciliation."

New Mexico is kind of an unusual place, a little different from the rest of the world. When our Sephardic cantor died, for instance, I went to visit the family, and they're all Catholic. I'm listening to them try to figure out where to have a rosary. They're now on their fourth Catholic Church. I'm in the living room, I'm listening to Lorenzo's sister and she's saying, "No he's Jewish, but the rest of the family's Catholic; no, he's not a member, no we're not a member." Finally she hangs up the phone and rolls her eyes and all the *abuelitas* [grand-mothers] are sitting around the table, and I said, "You know what— just have the rosary at the synagogue." They all fell off their chairs. They were like, *we can have the rosary at the synagogue?* So we have the rosary at the synagogue, and the funeral the next day, also at the shul. And people were so moved.

Now what was really hard for us personally was, his sister put together this twenty-minute video of him with nothing about his Jewishness. He was a rock star, that's pretty much what killed him, he got addicted to alcohol. That's when he came back to Judaism. And there was nothing Jewish in the video. So that was very painful. What I find really hard is Chicanos and African Americans and Native Americans who have a Jewish connection, whether they're married to Jews or they become Jewish, who have a very hard time with their own communities accepting their Jewishness or their relationship to Judaism.

So the way we've tried to bridge that is, we have a day of interfaith prayer at the shul where everybody has a half hour to pray their thing. We started with a bunch of Chicano ladies. They set up the whole deal, little Jesus, the rosary, the whole thing. That was hard for me, but on the other hand, it's also remarkable. That we can be a place of welcome. That we can say, we have our religion, this is who we are.

What does this require of me? Being with it, as open and vulner-able and honest and clear and nonrevengeful, and very forgiving, and process-oriented as I can possibly be, with whoever I'm with. And trying to teach my community that. I've learned that when you approach these issues, here in New Mexico, first you have to eat. And I've learned over the years from Chicano and Native work—with Buddhists too—to begin with ceremony. Even at a meeting. And to create some kind of hospitable common ground. People too often start with what divides us, not what unites us.

Walking to the mosque and creating the peace walk, wanting to create a national day of peace walk, which we're building up to next year, to have in many cities Muslims and Jews walking to each others' places. That has been the main impact on my work, to create pilgrimage. I'm really interested in creating a peace-walk spiritual order. An interfaith order. Because what I see happening is this creation of a culture of hatred between Palestinians and Jewish Israelis. And of course that's extending out into American Jews, this culture of hatred. My main interest is how to break that down. It's also very clear that people live in denial. They cannot tolerate what's happening. They refuse to see it. There's such a wall of resistance that very few people pass through that wall, that fire. How do you break the cycle? That's the question that has been the center of my life since I was fourteen years old.

My own methodology has been much more spiritual/cultural than political. I'm not for living room dialogue that never goes anywhere. There has to be programmatic outcome. Because people are suffering. But sometimes you can't even get people to talk to each other. So I think, they won't talk; maybe they'll walk. I haven't tested it out yet enough. But that's what I'm doing these next few years, testing it out.

The other thing that I learned: when I got my training as a feminist, and the first time that I went into a congregation I gave a talk about feminism and a lot of people were hostile—to the concept, the word, the notion. Then I would tell stories, and it was like night and day. I could tell a story, any story, endless stories, and people would be laughing and crying and enjoying themselves and moved and open and responsive and vulnerable, and then material would sink in. I created a theater piece about a Palestinian woman, a very simple piece about a mother who lost three children, killed. She's sitting on a concrete block, and her house has been destroyed. She's sitting there in the ruins of her life, telling her story, and people who were completely anti-Palestinian would cry. I think that methodology is important in fighting against racism and fighting all of these institutional entrenched hatreds, entrenched disparities.

One year we brought a fellow, he was Incan, from Peru; he was part of the Fellowship of Reconciliation. It was during Passover, he came to the Seder and he was completely blown away. At the very end of the Seder, I gave him a shofar, I blew it—even though it's not a *sederdik* [Seder-like, suitable for seder] thing to do—I thought that would be meaningful to him in terms of his own cultural appreciation. And I said, "You know, this is our freedom horn. We blow this horn and we remember the creation of the world and the possibility of transformation and liberation and so forth." He wept in front of all of us and said, "The only way to resist oppression"—and we're among indigenous people, people who have had five hundred years worth of resisting oppression, it didn't happen yesterday . . . he said, "The only way is through cultural survival. That is the only way to resist." The way his people fight is by remaining who they are. Using the wisdoms you can garner from your tradition to move you forward.

Update:

Rabbi Lynn Gottlieb has moved to California to do specifically interfaith, intercultural work with Interfaith Inventions, to educate and enrich the lives of children and adults through programs that promote respect and understanding between people of diverse faiths, and provide a life-changing experience in which children can learn firsthand about each other's customs and lifestyles. This work includes a national network of summer camps, and education of parents and teachers.[25] She reports that "Nahalat Shalom is thriving, and has hired a new rabbi, Rabbi Deborah Brin. The work continues, absolutely. Among a host of programs and alliances, NS works with Jewish Community Relations Board, Jewish Family Service, Peace Now, the Jewish Historical Society, the Anne Frank Exhibit, the Anti-Defamation League, the Arab Jewish Alliance, Women in Black, Hadassah, the Jewish Community Center, and the Jewish War Veteran's League."

JEWS WERE ALL PEOPLE OF COLOR: CENTER FOR AFRO-JEWISH STUDIES (PHILADELPHIA)

Lewis R. Gordon is a Laura H. Carnell Professor of Philosophy and Director of the Institute for the Study of Race and Social Thought and the Center for Afro-Jewish Studies at Temple University, as well as president of the Caribbean Philosophical Association. Gordon is the author of several influential books, including the award-winning *Her Majesty's Other Children,* and most recently, with his wife Jane Anna Gordon, the anthology *A Companion to African American Studies.* Professor Gordon has lectured internationally, and for the past several years, he has been very active in work on Jewish diversity. Born on the island of Jamaica to an Afro-Jewish mother and Afro-Asian father, he came to the United States when he was nine years old to live with his mother and his siblings in the Bronx. His work with the Center for Afro-Jewish Studies involves developing research on Afro-Jewish communities worldwide and on Jewish and African diasporic peoples. He is currently working on a book on philosophical and historical questions posed by the existence of Afro-Jews.[26]

LEWIS GORDON

LEWIS GORDON: I had a unique relationship to the issue, being Jewish, black, and from the island of Jamaica. In my childhood the only people I knew who were Jews were either dark-skinned brown or beige—in other words, all people of color. So there was this whole world of Judaism I knew about, that I grew up in, that was in no way reflected by the presentation of Judaism in Judaic Studies.

I didn't go to graduate school in Judaic Studies. It's the difference between being a scholar of Judaism and being a Jew. But research in Africana Studies, especially on the African diaspora, invariably brings one in contact with African Judaism. As a scholar I knew about African Judaism. But the problem is, all the scholarly activity that dominated Judaic Studies had already centered itself without recognizing its limitations.

When I looked at Judaic Studies programs across the country, they seemed to be exclusively about Ashkenazi Jews. That for me was very disconcerting. When I was teaching at Brown it became clear to me that there was a large lower-middle class black Jewish community as well, that's under the radar because of the class construction of Jews in the U.S. Russian Jews, too, are excluded in this way—I knew this from my teenage years–early twenties in the Bronx. I tended to be around Russian Jews, because I was working class. Around fellow black Jews—except for my family it was very rare. It struck me at that moment that Brown University was not the right place to do what I wanted to do because an institution like that would only attract the upper strata.

So I decided to start bringing together scholars who do work on Judaism. But while I put the word out about organizing it, a good friend, an African American Jew who was in rabbinic training contacted me and said I must go meet Gary and Diane Tobin who were creating the Institute for Jewish Research and Community in San Francisco. So I flew out and they had organized a think tank of nearly one hundred Jews of color. Some I already knew but it's one thing to have three or four names and another to have a data base of nearly one hundred. I was invited to participate in that Jewish think tank, and ultimately I wrote the forward for Gary and Diane Tobin's *In Every Tongue*.[27]

At that time I was rethinking my relationship to those institutions anyway. It was important to me to be in a place conducive to this research. So it had to be a large public university with a large black population so that's where Temple came into the picture. I decided when I got to Temple I would negotiate some start-up money to create this center, and that's what I did. I took my discretionary funds— money usually spent for travel and research—to use for the Center.

To create the Center I talked with many of my colleagues in Judaic Studies who at Temple are far ahead of many other programs in terms of how progressive they are intellectually. One of them is a rabbi—Rebecca Alpert—who had helped found women's studies and she helped found the Center. She's extraordinary. Rebecca and Laura Levitt [currently director of Jewish Studies at Temple] were excited about what I was doing. So this made the Center unique partly because my relationship with it began not with individuals who were obsessed with ancient philology. It began with feminists.

What Rebecca did was invite me out with the entire department of religion. We spent so many hours talking about ideas, so the relationship was a very coherent and committed one. It wasn't perfunctory. Laura is very concerned, as am I, with the question of secular Judaism. There are concerns with gender and Judaism. We began to think through our ideas, and Rebecca offered me three rooms with which to build that center, and also an institute for race and social thought in the religious studies dept. Together we sent a proposal to the university that created a race and religion line, and that brought two new faculty. From there, we created the Center for Afro-Jewish Studies.

And by then I continued my work with the Institute for Jewish Research and Community in San Francisco. But as happens when the word gets out—I became more informed by founding the Center than eight or nine years ago when I was thinking through these issues at Brown.

The Center for Afro-Jewish Studies at Temple University is a research and learning institution dedicated to scholarship on Afro-Jewish peoples and developing awareness of the historical, political, religious, and philosophical issues that arise from the convergence of the African and Jewish diasporas. These issues include the study of black Jewish religious practices; the role of black Jews in the fight against anti-black racism and anti-semitism; the demography of black Jews; the archeological and historical study of Afro-Hebrew people in antiquity, the Middle Ages, and early Modern ages; the development of resources for the study of Afro-Jewish people; the cultural diversity of Afro-Jewish people; the political plight of Afro-Jews; the unique problems faced by the Israelite and related New World Afro-Jewish communities; and the invisibility of secular Afro-Jews. The Center also aims to offer the largest archive of materials on Afro-Jews worldwide, open to anyone interested in their study.

The Center itself is primarily research in nature because right now as we know there hasn't been any organized assemblage of research on Afro-Jewish Diasporic Communities. A book, an article appears here and there but it struck me that there should be a central place where people could get informed data. There's been a proliferation of materials on Internet wesbites but they're not necessarily reliable. What we need first is a journal that is peer review so experts can check the claims that are being asserted. We're going to link up with demographic projects so we can actually answer questions like how many of us are there. Complicated when you ask how many Afro-Jews are there, because of a host of problems in formulating the response. What definition of Jews are you using? What is your position on rabbinic vs. priestly Judaism? Priestly Judaism is older. Interestingly, a lot of the African Jewish communities come out of priestly Judaism which is a sign that they may come from the Hebraic people who migrated to those regions much earlier than some would imagine.

Then there's the complicated questions about converts. About individuals born from Jewish mothers. In a lot of the older communities they practice patrilineal descent, not matrilineal, which surprises a lot of people. If we look at China where as we know ancient Hebraic people were following trade routes for more than two millennia—well, in China there are Kaifeng Jews and they practice patrilineality.[28] So what happens is they live as Jews all their lives and they decide to do aliyah and they discover in Israel they don't meet the criteria so they have to go through conversion. And many of them do.

But that is a big issue around the corner. Of course it doesn't raise much of an issue if both parents are Jewish anyway. But in cases where the father may marry out, a child might be raised Jewish and then discover that things are different elsewhere. I take the position that if anyone has a Jewish parent and is Jewish identified my interactions with them would recognize them as Jews. But I do understand the complications.

Back to the Center. In addition to developing this journal, we're starting up a newsletter to bring the word out into community. We also organized a meeting—in collaboration with the Institute for Jewish Research and Community—of rabbis of color, a roundtable discussing fiscal issues in developing new synagogues. We're just beginning the liaison thing, we're going to different synagogues, finding out what they're trying to do. We also linked up with Shari Rothfarb Mekonen and Avishai Yeganyahu Mekonen, documentary film makers co-producing with Be'chol Lashon *Judaism and Race.*[29] We've created fellowships for graduate students who are interested in doing work on Afro-Judaism. We don't really have much money yet, but this is an issue that's so dear to the community that they come out and volunteer. I use my own funds to help the students travel, help with their research. We have room for undergrad internships. We hope to organize a group of faculty who will devote part or all of their research to questions of Afro-Judaism.

We plan to create a booklet series. More grandly, if we were to receive the funding we hope for I'd like to support archaeological work in west and central Africa. Looking at Hebraic populations moving throughout Africa raises important questions not only about how we understand Judaism but also how we understand African history. There's a tendency in African history to look at African populations as sedentary. But in fact a lot of Africa is dominated by trade. Much of the ancient world was dominated by trade. And as we know, outside periods of pogroms, and other forms of persecution, a lot of Jewish history is also dominated by trade. It makes absolute sense that a community whose life is dominated by trade would find its way along African trade routes. One of my dreams is to have serious archaeological research on those trade routes to bring out the complexity of ancient medieval and recent Jewish populations.

I just came back from Brazil, where I began to see not only the presence of Moroccan and Ethiopian Jewish communities there but also some of the lay rituals. I've seen people on the street who reflect the West African Jewish community who may have come over through slavery. But no one is asking those questions so the research hasn't developed yet. It's just me going through the streets, meeting people in the market.

This will give some idea of the complexity. In the way in which I've formulated the list of Jews right now, when I say Ashkenazi Jews, for a long time I—and most people—really just think of white Europeans. But an increased number of Ashkenazi women are marrying men of color. But the children are being raised in Ashkenazi Judaism. Not to mention most converts. Increasingly when we say an Ashkenazi Jew we have to understand that we don't know the racial makeup of the individual so described. I, a person whose active academic and political practice is linked to understanding this diversity, I am actually working at this. I'm not an Ashkenazi Jew, but my children are half Ashkenazi Jews, and the only Judaism they know when they go to synagogue is Ashkenazi. But now, when I travel I take my children with me, they're seeing the diversity of Jews, everything from Israelite to Sephardic, to Yemenite. In my children's consciousness, they just think of Jews as a very diverse community. But there will be people who want to be very formalistic and they will look at the children, whose mother is an Ashkenazi Jew, as Ashkenazi.

The other thing we're doing in our research is processing some creolization. What my children, when we are at a Seder, the elements that come into our practice from the Caribbean—many U.S. born Jews of European descent wouldn't think about the way Jews in other parts of the world do things. For instance if one grows up in the Caribbean there's regular access to goat. Ancient ritual uses goat. Most people don't realize there weren't any chickens in Europe. No reference to chickens in the Bible. Along the trade routes chickens were brought in. Tells us something very interesting. Today of course in terms of Jewish authenticity, many people take Yiddish culture and chicken for granted, but the chicken is a very recent phenomenon.

It's great working with Rebecca [Alpert] because Rebecca would point out all kinds of things associated with authenticity that are really very recent efforts to assimilate with non-Jewish communities. Things like wearing the *kipah* was not originally a Jewish thing, it came out of a medieval practice of Christians. One thing we look at in our research is to what extent some confusions emerge through the adoption of various Christian practices as if they were authentic Jewish ones. For instance one would find correlates from the Christian communities, like a lot of Lutheranism in Reform Judaism. Not something many want to hear. But one could find similar correlates in Orthodox Greek Christianity and so on. We notice that many African Jews, same as Ethiopian Jews, when they visit the U.S. and visit a synagogue they're very quiet about it because they should have felt like guests but what they see around them are Christian communities. So while those communities are busy looking at the black-Jewish communities, thinking of them as them Christian, they don't realize that the black Jewish communities are looking at them as Christian in practices.

For instance, for many Ethiopian Jews a temple is supposed to be very simple and very plain. Take your shoes off. Not supposed to be ornate and covered with gold Torah scrolls, things like that. The thing in the end is not to say that one is more authentically Jewish than the other. What the migration issue tells us is just as today where because Ashkenazi Jews in Europe where they moved to another country where the population is, say, a majority of color, it's highly likely the children will not only be of color,, but also will adopt many of their local practices.

I went to a wonderful wedding the other day of a couple who is in Conservative Judaism and it was a blast because the bride was Argentinian. Even though they were Eastern European Jews who had moved to Argentina, in the end they speak Spanish and the band was a wonderful salsa Jewish band which had everybody dancing from the moment they played the first song at 8 pm and nobody would leave the floor, didn't stop until two in the morning. Even though the bride and groom were lifted up in the chairs and all the things that are familiar from Conservative Jewish weddings, the point is there so many things that were creolized, wonderful mixtures with Latin America. This was a wedding of a former student of mine, the man was from Texas, and in the process in many ways his children are going to be speaking Spanish and bringing all kinds of wonderful things to their understanding of Judaism, what his descendants will be as Jews.

One other—very ambitious—area we'd like to address. Something that would prepare rabbis to deal with diverse Jewish populations. I've been speaking with the dean of the School of Social Administration at Temple in preliminary conversation about creating some form of rabbinical training agency to create a special joint degree, where the individual would come out as a trained rabbi but also with special training that would lead to creative work on social dynamics of community, especially those that are connected through management of nonprofit organizations. And this would be crucial because as the African Jewish community that wants to aid Africa becomes more visible—as we know the economic realities of Africa are such it will be very important for individuals who have that commitment to be trained as well in the financial management.

We've also experienced some of the ugly side of what happens when the community becomes visible. A colleague was trying to get a grant to do research that would bring out even more accurately the question of diverse Jewish populations, looking in Africa. The head of the foundation who was being asked to give the grant went to consult some rabbis in Israel. They advised him not to give the grant because that research would attract too many poor people to Israel.

Generally I've not encountered negativity around my own way of being in the world as Jewish—Primarily because if you're well known or successful many communities will happily claim you. So I don't delude myself that the way I'm treated is how everybody else will be treated. Second, because I'm married to a Jewish woman.

I'm black and Jewish. The U.S.A. is constantly reminding me that I'm black. And I'm very happy to be a black person. The thing I hadn't thought about is that my wife was white and what reminds me is a context with individuals who are hostile to an interracial relationship. The unfortunate thing at the moment is that the only time I've come across negativity was in the context of black colleagues who are hostile to the idea of my wife being white. In other words they wouldn't mind if we were both black Jews.

There's still social anxiety about race mixing. At Brown there were many Jewish students of color, in the Ivies generally, but not much opportunity to make themselves known. At Brown also there are so many white Jewish students. There was a brief period at Brown when a group of black female undergrads organized a boycott of my classes because my wife is white. At the same time I have all of these white Jewish students because they discovered I was Jewish. None of the Jewish students, black or white, boycotted my classes. At Temple the Africana studies program is very Afrocentric, and it is anti-interracial relationships. Complicated because if one works within the framework of Judaism where one's children are born Jewish through the mother. . . . If you're a man of color and you want to be with someone with whom you talk about Judaism it's not the race or complexion of the person. What you find connecting is this aspect of yourself that it's difficult to share with other people. It struck me that before my wife and I got married we would talk about all kinds of things. She was happy she could speak critically about the Jewish community. She was very concerned with the anti-black racism she saw in many white Jewish communities. She was concerned about the obsession with assimilation while at the same time the representation of itself as different. She was also concerned about Jews who constantly bring up anti-semitism—she grew up in Hyde Park—where all around her was poverty in the black community while the Jewish community she knew was fairly affluent.

At the Center we see our work as fighting racism but we see anti-semitism as linked in with fighting anti-black racism. One of the arguments we make about the importance of Afro-Jewish communities in the struggle is we bring out the complexity. I'm concerned, with the ongoing construction for instance, of black communities as anti-semitic. Related to the construction of Jews as exclusively white. I know this because I have rarely come across genuine anti-semitism toward me from a black person when they find out I'm Jewish. The only times were ironically from very close colleagues, academics, who tried to be cool but were clearly uncomfortable. I create a problem for them. Because these are the individuals who want you to make everything absolutely black first. Because they've constructed being Jewish as white, if you're trying to assert you're Jewish they assume you're trying distance yourself from being black. I was part of the Radical Philosophical Association. The language presumed a white Jewish population. For an African American Jew at Seder—not only thinking of Egypt, thinking about today too. I create a real confusion for them because of how positively black identified I am. I create discomfort for someone who refuses to *see* a black Jew. It's not the anti-semitism in the form of "we're not going to let you in our home" but you can tell the person is uncomfortable.

For the most I haven't experienced anti-black racism from white Jews. Where I have experienced anti-black racism is from those who are clearly committed to white Jewish assimilationism. They are interested in Jews being white. So blacks represent a kind of problem of unassimilability.

I can see where racism or anti-semitism occur. People ask: why are you so positively Jewish identified? Why are you associating with poor communities? People actually say to me, I don't understand how any progressive individual can identify as a Jew; or, you must not be religious. I don't have to play these authenticity cards. If I stress my identity as a born Jew—while a white Jew with no Jewish content is accepted at face value, a black Jew who is devout might be rejected. Communities can better work for social justice if they really admit who they are. I'm not going to say I'm Jewish only when it's easy.

We work cooperatively with other Jews of color: we do projects together, we *daven* together. Rabbi Capers Funnye and I are planning some projects together. I just met with Rigoberto (Manny) Vinas, founder of El Centro de Estudios Judios-Torat Emet. He is a master Torah scribe as well as a social worker and herbalist. He's a Cuban rabbi in Yonkers. His view is everybody in the community, it doesn't matter if you're a born Jew or not, should go through a conversion practice, not only an act of return but also to get rid of some of the authentification issues. A rabbi in Tijuana, Carlos Salas Diaz, focuses on *converso* communities, on bringing them back to Judaism.

My children are black and Jewish. We decided to raise them Jewishly in a substantial way and began to practice our rituals, to develop an inner understanding of what they're about. We've come to love these through our decision of how central they are to who we are.

I PROMISED THEM IT WASN'T GOING TO HAPPEN AGAIN: CENTRAL REFORM SYNAGOGUE (ST. LOUIS)

Rabbi Susan Talve is the founding rabbi of Central Reform Congregation, the only Jewish congregation in the City of St. Louis. The rabbi is of mixed Sephardic–Ashkenazic heritage. She performs life-cycle events, leads worship services for the seven hundred plus households that comprise the congregation, and is actively involved in the teaching of young and adult members. A past president of the St. Louis Rabbinical Association, she was ordained by Hebrew Union College in Cincinnati in 1981, where she earned a master's degree in Hebrew Letters. Her many honors include the college's Stephen Levinson Award for Community Service; the Jewish Federation of St. Louis's first Woman of Valor award; the Trumpet of Justice Award by the Institute of Peace and Justice; the Brotherhood and Sisterhood Award of the National Conference of

RABBI SUSAN TALVE

Community and Justice; and many others. Rabbi Talve has led her congregation in promoting inclusivity by developing ongoing relationships with African American and Muslim congregations, and by fostering civil liberties for the LGBT community.[30]

SUSAN TALVE: One reason to do this dismantling racism work, we have kids of color growing up here; two generations ago we had kids of color growing up and they told us—I spoke to all the five I knew, kids of color who grew up in Jewish homes in St. Louis. I sat down and really talked to them, and their response was once they hit third grade they saw that they were different. Once they hit middle school they knew they had to choose between being black and being Jewish, and they couldn't choose not to be black so they stopped being Jewish in their own hearts.

So that was a real challenge for me. These were kids I know, adult children of people in the congregation. Connected to our congregation. And I promised them it wasn't going to happen again to the next generation of children.

It was one thing to say it but how would we put that into action? What we saw over many many years is people came—they came, but then they didn't come back. So our goal was figuring out how to make it more welcoming so that people would belong. It's what we did with the lesbian and gay community at the beginning. It wasn't enough to say "welcome." We had to really put our money where our mouth was. We had to change the curriculum. We had to change the imagery. We had to change the role models. So that people feel not just welcome but celebrated. Valued.

The other commitment we have: being the only Jewish congregation in the city, and one of the reasons we're in the city is because of the segregation of our city; we wanted to be part of the solution, part of the integration; to have a Jewish presence in the primarily black city of St. Louis. So that was also a motivation for us to do this work.

Yavilah [McCoy] was amazingly helpful, setting us on the path, inspiring us with a sense of possibility. Now, after a little more than a year of consciously doing dismantling racism programming within the congregation. . . . We had two retreats, one on site, one offsite.[31] The congregation read a book together. Every circle [committee] went through some dismantling racism exercise. We spoke about it for the holidays. We put it into every bit of our programming for over a year. When Passover came we had a Seder focused on, using the imagery of, American slavery. And at that Seder we had as many Jews of color as we did white Jews. It was very powerful.

There are two other antiracism projects going on in the community. One of them is this ADL project for teens going through dismantling racism work together. That came from Rick Recht; he's a Jewish rock star. He just did a huge concert here to kick off this Tear down the Walls project.[32] He did the Dr. King event in Memphis at the Civil Rights Museum this year.

The other is a program called Cultural Leadership which we've been very involved in. One of our members, Karen Kalish, put together some twenty-plus kids, half of them black, half Jewish; a couple of the kids of color were Jewish. They spent a year doing very serious work, looking into each other's hearts and souls and then traveling three weeks through the South and to the Holocaust Museum. Now a second group has started up, and three of those kids are CRC kids. Because I think they're getting how important it is to do this work.

Some of people on that retreat ended up getting involved with Cultural Leadership We're benefiting now from those kids, from that work. Because those kids come back here—and they see differently. It's about opening up to possibilities. About welcoming someone and assuming they belong here so they'll come back.

Here is our indicator: We really hoped that after doing the internal work, our indicator would be that we would start to be integrated. So—two weeks in a row—one because we had a Dr. King service and the other because we had a Hebrew Israelite speak—many people of color came, including many Jews of color. It's happened that more and more people are seeking us out because they are Jews of color. We're finding that we have many more people of color become interested in converting; or just checking us out, feeling comfortable coming here. Two Fridays ago we had as many Jews of color in the congregation as white Jews. There isn't a *shabes* service without people of color, including many Jews, showing up. People bring their kids. I just did a biracial marriage, a couple who decided to raise their kids to be Jewish because of us, because they have a place to do this. That too is an indicator.

Just this past Saturday morning we had a double b'nai mitzvah, a brother and sister who are five months apart. The parents are white Jews who adopted a biracial girl and then found out they were pregnant. So the sister and brother decided to have their b'nai mitz-vot together, to go through this process together. And this beautiful young woman, she never felt like she belonged. She looks different. So I'm sitting next to her while her brother gives his speech, she's getting ready to give her speech, and she says, "Rabbi, can I say I'm proud to be a Jew?" And this kid got up at the end of her speech and without notes she said, "I want everyone to know I'm proud to be Jew." Her mother totally lost it. Because it meant she was part of the family. It wasn't just about being Jewish. It was about belonging. She belonged.

That was my proof that we can do this work, even in St. Louis, which is so racist and so segregated, if we're intentional about it. The first weekend in February [2006] on Friday afternoon we have Ephraim Isaac who is our scholar in residence.[33] The Ethiopian com-munity is cooking for us. Sunday afternoon we have Joshua Nelson the kosher gospel singer. It's a big financial commitment for us. And Rabbi Capers [Funnye] is coming. For the big Sunday concert, I expect to see a lot of our friends in the African American commu-nity, a lot of Jews of all colors. It's been a real bridge.

The other thing that's happening—we have befriended the Hebrew Israelite community. They are wonderful people. It feels like the bridge—a place where it's safe in a segregated racist society. . . . But it's very controversial for Orthodox Jews, because according to them, the Hebrew Israelites are not Jewish. Even though most of them have converted as Conservative. We're inviting them to sing at that Sunday concert. It's wonderful to connect with a group that is really getting what Torah is, they love Judaism, they love Israel. They're so interested in learning. It's very complicated, but there is a comfort level between us. We get it; as Reform Jews; we also experi-ence prejudice from Orthodox Jews. We've found a real *shidukh,* a match with them. They love our services. They love coming. Some people might think, well, that's a cheap shot way to integrate your congregation, but I don't feel that way. It's real. And I think they're going to bring their children here, which will be great for us because it's hard to look different when you're a kid. The more diversity we have—It's bridged a lot of worlds. It's doing exactly what we want to do for our core values as a community. I got the distinguished clergy award from the Martin Luther King celebration community and this last Saturday I got the King Leader Award from the whole state. I'm a honorary AME [African Methodist Episcopalian]. All of this is because I show up. Because the African American community trusts us. Because we're doing this work. And because we're here. I'm included in the work of health care, of economic injustice; of police brutality.

It's been amazing. Just the visuals of it. I look out now and we are integrated. We can do it. And if we can do it here in St. Louis we can do it anywhere.

JEWS OF COLOR SPEAK OUT

In Fall 2003 in New York City, an event organized by Ayecha in collaboration with the Jewish Community Center of the Upper West Side (JCC) startles everyone with its electric energy and overflowing audience—as if in response to those who see Jews of color as a small insignificant category.[34] The palpable excitement marks a breakthrough experience.[35] Laughter. Tears. Heads nodding.

The panel's dominant theme is clearing away assumptions. For some it's about not assuming whiteness, Europeanness. For some it's cultural, not racial at all. For some it's the skin thing. For someone else it's race and faith; or ethnicity and nonfaith. For many, the constant assumption from every corner of Jewish life that these very real articulate folks up there on the stage—and all over the auditorium—don't exist.

Rabbi/Cantor Angela Warnick Buchdahl's Korean Buddhist mother never converted—said she didn't think she could be 100 percent Jewish—though she was active in the sisterhood, the choir, and even learned Hebrew. Angela's Reform Ashkenazi father said Angela surpassed his Jewish education when she was in third grade. Angela came to the U.S. from Korea at age five with no English, and learned that she couldn't assume anything; that her mixed background has led to a very examined life. "Every Jewish memory I created along the way was a privilege." Her mother's Korean-Buddhist tradition informs who she is as a Jew. "Always I felt like a Jew by choice." As an adolescent, when Jews would tell her "you're not Jewish, you don't have a Jewish mother"; it was a "stab in my heart." In college, leading services for Hillel, "I would be chanting in Hebrew and wearing a *tallit*, and afterwards people would still say 'Are you Jewish?' . . . I would feel like saying ''Are you blind?' All the clues were there but they couldn't suspend their stereotypes enough to see me."[36] In response to Jews who denied her Jewishness, she once cried to her mother, "I want to stop being Jewish." "Is that possible?" her mother replied. Instead, Angela chose to undergo a Reform conversion as a young adult.[37]

This theme of Jewish authenticity or visibility resonates from every corner of the room. Who is Jewish enough? Who is more Jewish? Even white Reform Jews with two Jewish parents wonder about their authenticity. For Jews of color, Jews who don't look Ashkenazi, the pressure is much greater. A young African American woman in the audience speaks with evident pain: "People in my family say anti-semitic things; in a black group I say I'm Jewish and people act like it's inconceivable." Another young African American woman remarks, laughing, "So I took the easy way out, and moved to Israel. So then it became, *and I'm not Ethiopian*."

The audience roars with laughter.

Another theme that reappears is the strong connection people feel both to Jews and to their other communal ties. Jeremy Burton's Mexican American mother converted in college and married an Ashkenazi Jew. Jeremy is close to his mother's extended family, and is very clear about the depth of his Mexican American ethnicity. While he feels connected to Israel spiritually, he couldn't make Israel his home because he couldn't be Mexican American there.

Others speak of having to forge their own relationship to people of color. Jessica Radom, born in Thailand and adopted into a U.S. Jewish family, is a high school teacher who also works with interracial international adopting families. Her home culture is not here. She says her dual identity informed her sense of social justice, and the idea that you could cross boundaries. As an adult she has located her birth family and is building a relationship. "Authenticity is something I've struggled with; the challenge of forming my identity as a person of color."

Racism with its supposedly reassuring tag, exceptionalism, was also cited. Yavilah McCoy, an Orthodox African American Jew, pieces of whose story appear above, spoke of constantly encountering racism among Jews, followed by: *We don't mean you. You're not like the others.* For Jeremy Burton, a gay man, Latino identity meant Mexican American; Puerto Rican and Dominican were not familiar. But when he was in Jewish day school in New York, in Washington Heights,[38] his classmates would say negative words about Latinos. "So I said, I'm Latino too. If you say it about them you're saying it about me"—for which he got beat up, thereby "learning to be in your face, and that there were consequences."

What particular strengths have (particular) Jews of color derived from their—at least—double identity?

Yavilah McCoy responds:

> I learned how to dream by being a black Jew. I had to reach hard
> for myself in Judaism, refusing black and Jewish as oxymoron.
> When I heard Jewish students call blacks monkeys, the *n word*,
> *shvartses*, my mother said, "That's what racism does to Judaism.

You are here for god; this is yours." Still I cried when I put my own children in Jewish day school.

Many in the audience are crying.

A young woman identifies herself as the child of an African American father and a Jewish/Holocaust survivor mother—and thanks the panel for making her feel like she can be part of the Jewish community.

"What should we do?" someone asks.

"Don't expect us to do all the work." Heads nodding.

Jeremy tells of serving on the board of a progressive Jewish organization; some people didn't know he was Latino, but as soon as he said it, they began assuming he would be on every committee that dealt with race or color or allies of color, trying to exploit his ethnicity; assuming that this group is where he wants to do that work. "I have other places where I do that work," he said.

More heads nodding.

Angela asks Jews to reclaim our original mixed heritage from both Arabs and Jews, to mark the new waves of Jews of color, how the paradigm is shifting. Pay attention to the pictures in our children's books—include Jews of Tunisia, Syria, Yemen. She talks about "changing our mindset about what makes us Jews."

Jeremy says, instead of hiding, constantly say it. The tradition says if someone converts you don't mention it for ten generations, so as not to embarrass converts, but, he says, we need to talk about our diversity all the time, not be silenced, not pretend.

Yavilah: "Demarginalize this conversation. *Such an interesting experience.* To parents: children need to feel that this is totally their place. Then she adds, "Do this work for *you.* When you walk into a room, if it doesn't look like this, fix it."

The mainstream Jewish community, obsessed with Jewish continuity, has somehow failed to grasp that Jewish diversity *is* a theme of Jewish continuity. As Reena Bernards, a former leader of the Jewish Multiracial Network, has remarked, "Jewish inclusivity is the only reasonable antidote to the shrinking of the Jewish community."[39]

That was fall 2003. Almost a year later, August 2004, I saw basically the same pattern, if smaller, at an event in St. Louis, Yavilah McCoy's city of residence. The event, "Race, Culture and Identity in American Jewish Communities," was organized largely by Ayecha, in co-sponsorship with the Anti-Defamation League, American Jewish Committee, Jews United for Justice, and the National Council of Christians and Jews. Basically every

organization in the vaguely progressive Jew corner was there or supporting it. In New York you can't count on Jewish nostalgia. But what I could
count on—what I saw—was a relatively large number of Jews of color seeing each other for perhaps the first time.

The leaflet read:

> Join national Jewish leaders of color for an evening of dialogue
> and lively discussion as we explore the racial and cultural dynam-
> ics of Jewish diversity in North America.

Panelists included Jennifer Chau, of Ashkenazi and Chinese heritage,
Director of SWIRL, for mixed heritage individuals and families; Beejhy
Barhany, founding director of BINA; Hue Rhodes, an Ashkenazi and
African heritage film writer; Andrea Simckes, an African heritage law-
yer, and the current president of the Ayecha Jewish Diversity Resources;
Dr. Roderick McCoy, of African heritage, molecular biologist and senior
research analyst. I was honored to serve as the moderator. The publicity
named me as an Ashkenazi heritage writer, scholar, and teacher. I am used
to being able to just say *Jew* and feel fairly represented. Not any more.
Lessons are everywhere.

TRANSFORMATION IN PARTNERSHIP

I am seeking not a tokenistic remedy but a shift in paradigm. Attention
to cultural diversity widens the lens, brings in a whole new cluster of folks,
including those who come into Judaism through birth, choice, adoption,
family, partnership/marriage, and discovery of sometimes ancient history.
Jews whose racial and cultural heritage has often meant exclusion; Jews
who want to know more about Jewish diversity; Jews who consider standing
up for justice is their Jewish heritage, and who welcome Jewish opportunities to exercise this heritage.

Organizers and educators should continue to aspire to a room that
looks like the Jews of Color Speak Out. But Jews of color are a minority,
and the project of inclusivity and multicultural education does not, and
should not, require the labor or the presence of Jews of color. Yet looking
back at chapter 4, and considering the two clusters of organizations, one
grouping active against racism but uncertain about how to give priority—or why—to Jewish racial and ethnic diversity; the other grouping with
expertise on this very point; it makes sense to envision partnerships. Co-
sponsorship of events, trainings and other cooperative efforts are already
in motion. Ayecha works with St. Louis's Central Reform Congregation

and with Jews United for Justice, and is prepared for a wide range of training Jewish educators and communal leaders. Loolwa Khazzoom's Jewish Multicultural Project and Ayecha do trainings for a range of Jewish groups. BINA's public education work includes educating Jewish groups about Ethiopian Jewry. Ivri-NASAWI promotes Sephardi and Mizrahi culture in the Jewish and Arab worlds. The Center for Afro-Jewish Studies is a resource for activism and information about Jews of African descent. And Congregation Beth Shalom exists to nourish the Jewishness of a too-neglected population.

Clearly some of the "diversity" groups are equipped to help the more explicitly political organizations strengthen their activism. Jointly created events break new ground, allowing diversity work to flourish at a deeper level intellectually, emotionally, and practically, in the creation of contacts, networks, resources, and just plain great ideas. Educational work informs activists and attracts learners. The explicitly political groups can perhaps contribute venues, audiences, contacts, and resources.

But partnership does not mean that white Jews should lie back and wait for Jews of color to fix them or show up to make the white people feel okay. Tokenism and evasion are not the same as respectfully seeking participation, cooperation, and leadership from Jews of color, especially Jews-of-color organizations. Mostly Ashkenazi, mostly white Jewish institutions need to acknowledge the expertise that is already in play.

On a national and local scale, it is time to challenge the Jewish communal organizations and religious denominations and movements. These institutions exercise vast influence on the communities of Jews, not least through allocation of resources. I think it makes sense to concentrate on Reform, Reconstructionist, and Renewal congregations and institutions, since they are most likely to be responsive on the huge and multifaceted issue of inclusivity.

There will come a time when *Jew* will no longer carry with it an assumed white marker. How can we speed it up?

Activists and educators in mostly Ashkenazi groups need to approach this issue not as a one-shot deal but as a projected transformation. This means gathering resources, books, articles, films, websites; compiling lists of speakers and trainers; examining all the organization's materials, seeking not only to excise bias but also to create opportunities for inclusion. It means planning and organizing series of programs in relationship to this transformational goal. It means always ensuring that programs, workshops, and discussions about racial justice do not posit "Jews" as automatically white or Ashkenazi, explicitly or tacitly. It means declaring zero tolerance for Ashkenazism—while simultaneously encouraging the glorious flowering of Ashkenazi culture *alongside* other Jewish cultures. Nahalat Shalom is a model; Central Reform Congregation is another. There is room for everyone.

Here are a few suggestions drawn from the work of Loolwa Khazzoom's Jewish Multicultural Project. If you organize a black–Jewish dialogue, for example, do the legwork required to include an African American Jew *and* a Jewish speaker from Ethiopia or Uganda. Do not limit your multicultural representation and outreach to events focused on Jewish multiculturalism, or to events directly bearing on a specific community of color. Every Jewish event should reflect multiculturality; a Purim festival, for example, should represent the holiday's multiculturality, in the program, music, and food—and not stingily, with one Persian pastry and the rest business as usual—but lavishly.

A useful rule: one is rarely enough.

As in the larger racism-fighting arena, conscious and determined affirmative action is critical. Depend on familiar networks and criteria and you will get familiar faces. Assume "there aren't any" or "there aren't any who are qualified" and you will find none. Look, ask, poke around, follow threads and hints, use the Internet to explore organizations, resources.

Mostly Ashkenazi groups seeking to transform themselves need to realize that individual Jews of color who join an antiracist, mostly Ashkenazi organization might want a Jewish space where they don't have to explain themselves or play a special role. Like anyone else, some Jews of color might want events that include them without anyone making assumptions about who they are or how they choose to work in the world. They might or might not be political activists; might or might not choose to perform their activism in a Jewish context; might have, as Jeremy Burton said at the Jews of Color Speak Out, other places where they do antiracist work. Valuing participation and insight means not boxing anyone tokenistically into representing a community.

In addition, mostly Ashkenazi organizations need to beware of appropriating the cultures and issues of Jews of color. Grassroots activists who've been around the block a few times know how things sometimes unfold. Those who raise issues and mount struggles on the local level often get overlooked when it comes to material resources like grants, space, inclusion. Meanwhile established people and institutions, perhaps only superficially knowledgeable on these issues, get rewarded with funding and validation, acing out the grassroots. Jordan Elgrably points to ground broken by Ivri-NASAWI, only to be usurped by mostly Ashkenazic organizations receiving funding to offer Sephardic cultural programming. Yavila McCoy of Ayecha has done the grunt work on Jews of color programming, yet Ayecha is severely underresourced. Justice seekers need to address the issues of funding, expertise, and equity.[40]

Organizations focused on Jewish diversity have an essential contribution to make with regard to Israel/Palestine. The mind-blowing information about our centuries of shared largely peaceful experience with the people who exactly at this historical moment are being inscribed within and without the Jewish community as intrinsically our enemies—surely this information might be of use. Think of the power of the slogan from the Palestinian and Israeli women's peace moment, "We Refuse to Be Enemies." Imagine disseminating the information: *For centuries we were neighbors and friends. Now, in the 21st century, we refuse to be enemies.* At the same time, drawing on Joyce Maio's comment above—*Levantine Center has much more of an Arab emphasis. . . . I don't see much Jewish Sephardi here. It's all Arab and Persian. There are some Jews on the board, but the voices are not coming out*[41]—I observe that maintaining equilibrium between programming and concerns for Arabs and Jews, or even Jewish Arabs, is not simple.

Finally, the issue of children and the next generation. A whole generation of Jewish mixed-race, mixed-culture babies is growing up, an increasing part of the next generation of Jews. Jewish cultural and educational institutions need to assign high priority to programs that address interracial families and multiple identities. Ashkenazi mainstream Jews can't expect that Jews of color, Jews with bi- and multiple identities will exactly reflect the same concerns and priorities as a mostly white constituency. This needs to be understood as a plus, challenges offered to the white mainstream to transform. The Jewish community/ies will either radically transform, embrace, nurture and continue to attract these children as they grow to adulthood, or will shrink, alienate, and lose many of the next generation. They/we will lose not only the children being othered and excluded; and all the children whose racial, cultural, and ethnic heritage connects them to more than one home community; but also all the children who themselves are welcomed but who grow up to recognize hypocrisy, bigotry, and fear of difference inside their home community.

What is to be done? What will it look like? Simply put, a teach-in on radical Jewish history will have a Jewish name—or names—that houses all of us, and features more of a cultural range than two Sephardi with everyone and everything else Ashkenazi. Tokenism will shrivel and vanish.

Expectations of racial and ethnic inclusivity will be permanently raised, the way these days many of us are appalled at, for example, an all-male anthology or an all-white panel of experts.

I am not suggesting a hyperactive anxiety. Common sense, memory, history, concern for justice, and a recognition of complexity are our best tools as we build towards collaborative efforts and sturdy alliances. Jews of all races participate in the whole range of Jewish practice and cultures, nor do Jewish categories correspond neatly to racial reality. (Not that racial reality is all that tidy either.) Much of the expansive embrace of Jewish otherness is not racial but cultural, traditional, linguistic, gustatory. Do you eat *latkes* or *sufganiyot* for Hanukkah? Does your *Pesakh* allow rice? Which sweet fruits do you chop for *haroset*?

Remember the *barsa*, the Bene Israel women's ritual for naming a baby girl. Jewish women of whatever culture–ethnicity seeking to create Jewish feminist custom, instead of assuming we have to start from scratch, or that only Ashkenazi culture is sufficiently "advanced" (read *Western*) to include feminist material, might well explore traditions of our non-Ashkenazi Jewish sisters. When I try to find out more about the *barsa*, I locate a wealth of information about baby-girl naming, even though it mostly comes from Jewish websites where Ashkenazi tradition is referred to as "Jewish" and everything else is labeled "other communities." The mainstream Jewish community has a ways to go, but it is not as clueless or monocultural as I had imagined.[42]

As the work of many Jewish antiracist or multicultural groups continues to develop and deepen at the margins, the work will gravitate toward and reshape the center. The Jewish community is not standing still. The Jewish mainstream, for example, has been commendable in its support of lesbian and gay rights: because many understand that *they* are *us*. They/we still need to learn this about Jews of diverse races and cultures. *Do this work for yourself,* Yavilah McCoy challenges us. Because we want to know the full range of Jewishness. Because we know what it is to be a stranger and therefore we value both strangeness and home. Because we want to create a home in which all of us are seen, known, and welcomed.

I am not arguing that Jews are the chosen people in the antiracist struggle, or that all Jews must participate in explicitly Jewish contexts. What is essential is the desire to dismantle whiteness as we know it, and the courage to move forward to create the world we want to live in. By insisting on the multiracial, multicultural nature of Jewish communities in the United States, as well as abroad, we strengthen our best Jewish selves.

[6] TOWARD A NEW DIASPORISM

In the late nineteenth century, in response to a confluence of anti-semitism, European nationalism, and biblical concepts of exile and return, some Jews dreamed of a homeland. Zionism-the-movement sought to normalize Jewish life by creating a Jewish state and ingathering the scattered Jews. Sometimes the projected homeland was biblical, sometimes merely territorial. According to Roi Ottley, Black Abyssinian Jews discussed Buffalo, New York, as a possibility.[1] Even Theodore Herzl, Zionism's putative father, spent the last phase of his life focused on Uganda.[2]

But territorial solutions in general and Zionism in particular were always contested, as Marilyn Kleinberg Neimark's resourceful collection of historical documents demonstrates.[3] Isaac Deutscher, master biographer of Leon Trotsky (or, as I like to think of him, Lev Bronstein) was one of many prophetic voices: "As long as a solution to the problem is sought in nationalist terms both Arab and Jew are condemned to move within a vicious circle of hatred and revenge."[4]

As Jews across the face of the world imagined a wide array of options for how they wanted to live their Jewish—or assimilated—lives, among them were always intellectuals, activists, communal leaders who rejected strictly territorial or nationalist solutions. In the newly reformed Ottoman Empire, Sephardi and Mizrahi Jews, who widely supported the reforms and had high hopes for more, debated: Could you be both an Ottomanist and a Zionist?[5] According to one Sephardic newspaper, the argument raged "bordering on fratricide. . . . [Yet a] defining feature of Ottoman Zionism was this insistence on the fluid merger and reconciliation, rather than [on] the clash or inherent incompatibility, of the aims of Ottomanism and Zionism."[6]

Differences among Ottomanists were muted compared to those between the new Ashkenazi immigrants and the Ottoman Zionists,[7] many of whom had been living in Palestine for years, had neighborly relationships with the Palestinian Arabs, and were somewhat concerned about the incursion of Europeans who spoke no Arabic, lacked experience with the Middle East, and had no respect for the wonders of Ottoman citizenship prized by the Sephardim. Factor in differences in the degree of antisemitism each group had experienced, and their sense of hopefulness or despair about the Jewish future, and there are serious incongruities.

Ottomanist Zionists imagined not so much a national state as "a unique 'Ottoman Zionism' . . . distinct from European Zionism in its support for cultural Hebraism without the corresponding separatist political aims."[8] A "significant component of the Palestinian Sephardim [and Mizrahim] viewed Palestine as a "shared homeland (*moledet meshutefet*) for both Jews and Arabs," reflecting the level of linguistic, cultural, and economic integration the two peoples already shared.[9] Some stressed the importance of learning Arabic and of not "blur[ring] with European culture."[10] Palestinian Sephardim and Mizrahim commonly opposed the concept of "Hebrew labor, the exclusivist call of new immigrants,"[11] a point of view shared by the Palestinian Sephardi press, "because to say that one did not want Arab workers was in contradiction to wanting to bring [Jews and Arabs] closer together."[12]

In return, the Ottoman Jews' "limitless patriotism" about the empire was considered practically pathological by the Ashkenazim.[13] Palestinian Jews were reprimanded as "assimilationists" by "radical elements among the new Russian Zionist immigrants in Palestine." Opposing this view, one of the Sephardi leaders urged, "We the Jews . . . must leave behind our sectarianism; there is now no difference between Jew, Christian, and Muslim,"[14] a call that struck an Ashkenazi Zionist editor as "an inexcusable exaggeration of civic equality."[15]

Among Zionists of all stripes were many who assumed that bringing Jews to Palestine would "lead to the advancement of the Arab community,"[16] "a somewhat [*sic*] paternalistic approach, presenting the Jewish population as more advanced and sophisticated than the Arab population."[17]

Whatever ideology circled the scrap of land, many non- or even anti-Zionists engaged with tasks of "practical Zionism" (e.g., land sales, commerce, construction, law, teaching, medicine, etc.). But Zionist rhetoric initially failed to inspire the Sephardi/Mizrahi community. Instead we hear of incidents such as the one "angrily reported [by the Zionist press] that at one parade in Jaffa, an important Sephardi community leader pulled the Zionist flag out of someone's hands and tore it up."[18] Less dramatic but no less telling, "some of the leaders of the local (Sephardi) Jewish community made formal protests against Zionist plans. In 1920, they signed an anti-Zionist petition organized by Palestinian Arabs. . . ."[19]

Only as the empire disappointed the expectations of Ottoman Jewry did Zionism achieve any traction. History took Europe's side. Between the carving up of the Ottoman Empire and the Balfour Declaration,[20] Palestinian Sephardi and Mizrahi intellectuals were increasingly marginalized, along with their vision of "shared homeland."[21]

IF I FORGET THEE *O DOIKAYT, O HAVIVA OTTOMANIA*

Imagine a history where differences in Jewish experience and aspiration were articulated and pondered;[22] where Sephardi and Mizrahi voices were audible and respected;[23] where Yiddish was neither dead nor kitsch;[24] where masculinist state power was not the only model.

For more than half a century Zionism has typically been represented as the solution to the problem of anti-semitism, and Zion as the authentic seat of Jewish culture. Most Jews in diaspora collude, unwittingly or wittingly, while the rich tradition of dissent around this issue has been almost entirely suppressed. In the United States, the disobeyed imperative to make *aliyah* has resulted in a sort of shamefaced Zionist support industry which sends money and thrives on attack, emergency, and fear. Zionism thus displaces—deforms is not too strong a word—American Jewish identity and experience.

In this way, diaspora—the seat of Jewish identity for some of us, and an intriguing common thread connecting us with so many other cultures with whom we share cities and neighborhoods—from a Zionist perspective diaspora signifies a frail gaping female absence where oppression and assimilation lurk,[25] along with an attenuated identity which owes, but must not criticize, Israel.

Most Jews, including an estimated half-million Israelis, continue to choose to live in diaspora. Yet there is no name for the ideology that backs up the political choice to do so.[26] It's as if the millions of Jews who continue to wrestle with minority status in Buenos Aires, Paris, Istanbul, Minneapolis, Toronto, even Berlin or Warsaw; even, though this hardly counts as minority, New York City: as if all these Jews were accidental or pitifully stuck, a problem to be solved by adequately indoctrinating the next generation about their *real* home.

What if, instead of assuming diaspora is a problem, we identify as a problem the narrowly prescribed options (in the United States) for expressing and nurturing Jewish identity; rarely venturing beyond Zionism; religion; and anti-semitism/the Holocaust. What happens with the many Jews who are not drawn by, or are at odds with, these animating principles?

- Those who are critical of Israeli policy or simply feel disconnected from a nation thousands of miles away

- Those for whom the Holocaust is too distant or too despairing; anti-semitism too negative to place at the center of their identity

- Those who find the cost of membership in a synagogue or Jewish community center too steep (yet are embarrassed even to request a sliding scale because what's wrong with them, aren't Jews supposed to be financially successful?)

- Those who want their identity to be based on proud Jewish histories of struggle

- Those who are secular Jews, atheists, cultural Jews, constantly confronted with the assumption that Secular Judaism is an emptiness identical to assimilation, without its own hearty content

HOME

"Where is home?" asks scholar Avtar Brah, and begins to answer: "On the one hand 'home' is a mythic place of desire in the diasporic imagination. . . . On the other hand, home is also the lived experience of a locality. Its sounds and smells, its heat and dust. . . ."[27] Home in this sense for Jews might not be Jerusalem; home might instead be Baghdad Vilna New Orleans al-Andalus Prague Salonika Chicago Cochin Seville. . . .

Let us begin to imagine a diasporic home.

AURORA LEVINS-MORALES

My mother is Puerto Rican, born and raised in Spanish Harlem and the Bronx. My father is the child of Russian Jews, of Brownsville and Brooklyn. During my childhood we all lived on a long-abandoned coffee farm in the mountains of Puerto Rico. . . . Throughout those years, it was my father who remembered exactly who all the Morales, Moure, and Diaz cousins were and what they did. He spoke high school Latin to people until he learned enough Spanish. He hung out with the farmworkers at the tiny wooden store and found out about the hardships of trying to make a living from small farming. He threw himself into the Puerto Rican independence movement, and fell in love with the whole country. He delighted in all the intricacies of a culture that double conquest, multiple migrations, and prolonged colonialism had made rich and complex. He also loved the food, and it was he who cooked corned beef with raisins, and fried up plantain into crisp garlicky tostones.

While my father cooked tostones, my mother yearned for blintzes and kosher dills, and made latkes for Hanukkah. It was my mother who insisted we light candles, and that my father tell us the story of the Maccabees. She was proud of the Jewish history of radicalism. She took it as a personal gift. She made sure we knew about both the Holocaust and the resistance to it. She encouraged my father to tell stories about his family, and was vigilant against anti-semitism in a place where being unbaptized was oddity enough, and no one was really sure if the Jews were Moors or some kind of pagan moon worshipers. She used Yiddish as if it were a new spice invented just for Puerto Ricans like her, and she would laugh with pleasure and affection, shrugging the way her friends' mother had in New York, whenever she heard Jewish music.

Between them, my parents made a bridge that circumvented the long roads of their respective cultural shame. Each stood proud where the other could not, and they built a bigger place of pride for their children. Because of it, my brothers and I travel like citizens of the world. Even when we're lost, we're eager. Loving someone from a different people, you learn to be a little bit at home everywhere.

—Aurora Levins Morales[28]

RUTH BEHAR

This happens to me often, too often: I am on my way home, driving down familiar streets, only a few blocks to go, and out of nowhere a merciless hand comes and grips my heart and wrings it dry. I tremble. Fog clouds my eyes. I am no longer sure if I am awake or dreaming. If I die, who will find me? All I can do is pray: Let me return home, I am almost there, please . . .

I don't know why this happens. What I know is that, so far, my prayers have been answered. Hardly breathing, I reach my house. And when I open the

197

door, I hear many keys clanging, the keys my ancestors stubbornly took with them to their exile.

—Ruth Behar[29]

I have long stopped looking for home. Home, I have learned, is where we sit down and decide to build it. And of course, this is the most profound lesson of the Diaspora, one that must necessarily change the shape of the identity narrative. Because if we leave open the question of where and what a home is, if we let it remain a question that has to be asked again and again and is never entirely answered, we accept that none of us have only one origin, whether ethnic, geographic, or religious. What we have is a more complicated narrative that intersects and intertwines with other citizens of the world, and remains, ultimately, forever unanswerable and open.

—Kyla Wazana Tompkins[30]

"The Jews were not the only people deported *en masse* by the Assyrians and the Neo-Babylonians," notes sociologist S. Sayyid. "What distinguishes their experience, however, is that they continue to hold on to their 'Jewishness.' The Jewish diaspora is made possible by the development of a proto-nationalism, which prevents its assimilation into other cultural foundations."[31]

Does diaspora, as Sayyid asserts, require a rudimentary nationalism, a homeland to harken back to? Is diaspora "a nation in exile."[32] Sayyid raises an intriguing paradox:

> Diasporas have also been considered as *anti*-national phenomena. Unlike the nation with its homogeneity and boundedness, diaspora suggests heterogeneity and porousness. Nations define "home," whereas diaspora is a condition of homelessness; in the nation the territory and the people are fused, whereas in a diaspora the two are dis-articulated.[33]

What do I mean by home? Not the nation state; not religious worship; not the deepest grief of a people marked by hatred. I mean a commitment to what is and is not mine; to the strangeness of others, to my strangeness to others; to common threads twisted with surprise.

Diasporism takes root in the Jewish Socialist Labor Bund's principle of *doikayt*—hereness—the right to be, and to fight for justice, wherever we are.[34] *Doikayt* means Jews enter coalitions wherever we are, across lines that might divide us, to work together for universal equality and justice. Diasporism also models itself on Ottomanism, which envisioned a loose brilliantly diverse confederation, culturally rich and multilingual, neither nationalist nor assimilationist. Ottoman Jews, about four hundred thousand in number, were citizens of what seemed to be an increasingly benign and progressive Empire. Inspired by the reforms that had already been enacted, Ottoman Jews eagerly anticipated equal rights for everyone, including themselves.[35]

Doikayt and Ottomanism were about wanting to be citizens, to have rights, to not worry about being shipped off at any moment where someone else thinks you do or don't belong.

One step beyond these is valuing the margins; not wanting danger or instability—who would?—but not wanting either to surrender the perspective that diaspora can yield. I name this commitment Diasporism[36] to challenge two related notions. First, that living in diaspora is an unfortunate nameless lapse, unchosen and without value. Second, that true home and safety are to be found in the nation state.

Where Zionism says go home, Diasporism says we make home where we are. The word *Zionism* refers uniquely to Jews; Diasporism deliberately includes the variety of diasporic experience. Zionism premises return (and simultaneously for the Palestinians, dispossession). But as Avtar Brah notes, "not all diasporas sustain an ideology of 'return.'"[37] Zionism is about Hebrew, monolingual, the holy tongue which for centuries only men with time to spend with books knew; Diasporism is about the language of daily life and ordinary working people, and reflects not only communication across cultural lines, but also linguistic invention and absorption: Diasporism's languages include Judeo-Español, Judeo-German, Judeo-Arabic, Judeo-Greek, not to mention Turkish, Polish, Hungarian, Russian, German, French, Spanish, Italian, Portuguese, Farsi, English. . . .

Diasporism is committed to an endless paradoxical dance between cultural integrity and multicultural complexities. Diasporism depends not on dominance but on balance, perpetual back and forth, home and away, community and outside, always slightly on the edge except perhaps at intensely personal moments in the family created by blood or by love, or at moments of transcendent solidarity.

Diasporism is what Meg Barnette and Brad Lander described at the baby naming of their son Marek:

> We hope that you will learn to embrace this gift [your Jewish identity] without thinking that you are better than others, or that your

identity ought to endow you with special privileges. In particular, we are thrilled to pronounce you [as child of a non-Jewish mother] a Jew without the Right of Return. Your name contains our deep hope that you will explore and celebrate your Jewish identity without confusing it with nationalism. . . . We hope you will develop an appreciation of the cultures being handed down to you, along with a willingness to challenge traditions that seem oppressive, even things that we hold dear.[38]

Celebrating dispersion, Diasporism challenges the Edenic premise: once we were gathered in our own land, now we are in exile.[39] What if we conceive of diaspora as the center: an oxymoron, putting the margin at the center of a circle that includes but does not privilege Israelis?[40] "From margin to center" echoes a book title by African American feminist bell hooks.[41] But hooks's constituency—women and people of color—comprises the majority of the world's people, suggesting an inevitable, "natural" centrality: The majority "belongs" at the center.

Jews worldwide number only about 13.3 million, a tiny minority except in Israel. Diasporism means embracing this minority status, leaving us with some tough questions: Does minority inevitably mean feeble? Can we embrace diaspora without accepting oppression? Do we choose to be marginal? Do we choose to transform the meaning of center and margins? Is this possible? Is diaspora egocentric as the Boyarins insist?[42] Is Diasporism inherently transcultural (as I suggest)?

DIASPORISM AND THE HOLOCAUST

From a U.S. perspective, the twenty-first century might be said to have begun in November 1999 in Seattle, with the emergence of huge coalition protests against the World Trade Organization and its brand of globalization; followed by an unprecedented theft of the U.S. Presidency; followed by the terror of September 11, 2001; followed by war—against Afghanistan, against Iraq. Who, what is next? Global warming. The post-Katrina Gulf Coast disaster. As I write, the explosion into public space of millions of immigrants marching for their rights.

In this new century, it is almost time for Jews to absorb and contextualize the Holocaust. Those who survived the Nazi terror are old, and soon we, the living, will be the repositories. There is small danger, I think, of forgetting the Holocaust, as we build memorial after memorial, museum after museum, develop curriculum and courses, bring into classrooms if not living survivors, taped oral histories.[43] What there is, I think, some danger of forgetting, or never learning: Jewish individual and communal relationships with non-Jews were not always genocidal or even always hostile.[44]

There is always the danger of indifference: to know and not care. Danger, too, of not noticing other genocides. The following story, from Jordan Elgrably is typical:

> At a Tisha B'Av celebration in L.A. I was asked to talk, and my focus was "The Holocaust and Other Holocausts"—specifically Rwanda and Bosnia. I made my argument, basically that we should be more proactive and care more about ongoing genocides, and shouldn't always be pointing to ourselves. I say this as someone whose aunt was killed in Auschwitz. People were very upset: "You can't compare, that was *really* a Holocaust."

As we leave behind the first century of world wars, in Muriel Rukeyser's words,[45] as the Holocaust recedes from the massive trauma of personal loss into history, we can perhaps grasp that the Holocaust continues to inflict damage, beyond the deaths, beyond the destruction of culture, beyond the insecurity that often haunts our dreams. The damage includes an existential isolation, a sense that no one will cross the border to stick up for us. Shortly after World War II, Jean-Paul Sartre reported that he received letters from Jews actually thanking him for including Jews on a list of victims of Nazism.

Recently, a woman came up to me after I'd given a talk on a progressive analysis of anti-semitism.

"Whenever I see a non-Jew," she began, "I wonder. I want to ask: 'if I needed to hide, would you take me in?'" She scratched my arm lightly and a shiver went up my spine, my mother's voice echoing through my childhood, *scratch a gentile, find an anti-semite.*

"But there are people today who need to hide," I say, and think (but do not say—why not?) *They might scratch your arm and wonder. Do you take them in?*

This sense of isolation makes us possessive about the Holocaust and our linked status as victims. We cling to the six million, separating ourselves from the other five million, the disabled, the Gypsies, the slave workers, the communists and Jehovah's Witnesses, the Catholics, the queers. What do we imagine would happen if we were to include them in our mourning? We reiterate the uniqueness of the Jewish Holocaust: no other group was slated for extermination. The Communists? Well, that was their politics. The disabled? Well, not because they were born to a certain people. The Gypsies? No one talked about making Europe Gypsy-*rein* (free of Gypsies, by analogy with *Judenrein*). Homosexuals? Catholics?

True, all true. And yet, what is the point? Why is it so important for Jews to claim our position as top victims ever? If we open up the space do we lose some victim-entitlements: Israel's right to exist, reparations, an end to Jew-hating? Does our tragedy diminish its scope, leave us feeling, looking, being "just like the others?" Does an integration of the Holocaust into history instead of holding it aloft, the raw bloody heart of the Jewish world, imply betrayal, the forgetting we swear we will never do?

I am angered and frightened by revisionists and deniers; by those who want to scoot quickly past the Holocaust, who see it as a mere blip on centuries of Jewish power and privilege. But Jews in the United States too often use the fate of Jews under the Nazis as a license to ignore the privilege many unthinkingly enjoy here. In particular, I am sick of contemporary U.S. culture's love affair with the Holocaust. In countless TV sitdramas, an episode sooner or later appears featuring an old person with tattooed numbers and a badly done Yiddish accent. The Holocaust connection is often irrelevant, a touch of local "color," a mask of pathos. "The Nazis took them all," they usually sum up, or, "They died in Auschwitz": a generic history. Beyond the old person-arm-tattoo pathos-trope, the survivor is usually presented as wealthy in the European past, and now, in the U.S. present, wealthy once more (of course, wealthy—after all, they are Jews!), with no context to explain that a disproportionate number of Jews with money survived because they had money to help them do so.

Beyond these caricatures: the constant reinscription of the mythic relationship of the United States to the fate of Europe's Jews. The real story includes massive indifference, determination to keep Jews out, corporate ties to German industry, research by U.S. eugenicists, and—according to Blanche Wiesen Cook's biography of Eleanor Roosevelt—FDR's determination not to speak out about the Jews because he didn't want other nations butting in about U.S. racism.[46]

Of course the Holocaust must be studied, known, absorbed. But it should not isolate Jews from the other victims of the German Reich, or be segregated from the history of the Jewish people or from the history of genocide. Jewish history is part of world history and should be learned in historical context, not as a floating cell that never lit on solid ground until the Zionist State welcomed the homeless wanderer. I would like people to learn about the Holocaust not as filtered through *Schindler's List,* in which Jews are passive victims and the savior/moral agent is a German Aryan.[47] I would like—the Boyarins' critique of masculinism notwithstanding—for people to see *The Partisans of Vilna,* a magnificent, virtually unknown documentary that tells the story of Jewish resistance in the ghetto of Vilna, Poland, an attempted rebellion by young Jews of unimaginable courage. They blew up a German munitions train,[48] and wrestled with whether to save their own families or fight the Germans.[49] A human drama that puts Jews at the center.

Imagining even more boldly, I would like people, including Jews, to learn something about Jewish culture, history, and peoplehood that is *not* reduced to the Holocaust.

Instead, what gets propagated endlessly in the United States is the myth of the eternal good guys against the evil racist empire. A morality play thus takes place around the Holocaust, in which again and again racism is fought, from an historical and geographical distance, safely, far from examining responsibility or privilege: It's over, and we were good, so good. Thus our society, convulsed by race but bent on denying its significance, exports racism onto Germany and imports it safely back as something evil which we—the virtuous "Yankees"—crushed.[50]

Diasporists seek to challenge this false expiation, to teach the salient lesson of the Holocaust, which is: build with allies an urgent and powerful opposition to all hatred. It is frightening to acknowledge that alliance-building is not always possible; painful to remember that the Polish partisans, for example, refused to work with the Jewish partisans. But trying to forge strong coalitions is our best defense. Not Jewish defense leagues. Not an ever more powerful Israeli Defense Force. Not billions of U.S. dollars for the Israeli government to purchase weapons from U.S. arms manufacturers. Not arming first this dictator, then that. Not climbing in bed with the Republicans or imagining that the Democrats can offer salvation.

I think of the rabbis in the state of Oregon who in 1992 united unanimously to oppose a viciously anti-lesbian and gay ballot measure, with the following statement, deeply informed by Jewish history:

> [The Holocaust] began with laws exactly like Ballot Measure 9. Those laws first declared groups of people to be sub-human, then legalized and finally mandated discrimination against them. Comparisons to the Holocaust must be limited. But clearly, this is the start of hatred and persecution that must stop now.

Yes, comparisons to the Holocaust must be limited. But look around. I think we can fairly echo the Oregon rabbis: *This hatred and persecution must stop now.*

Solidarity is the political version of love.

ISRAEL AND DIASPORISM

Trying to tease out Israel from anti-semitism, anti-semitism from anti-Arab racism, the United States from Israel, Israel from the Holocaust, my head begins to swim. I have vertigo. There is no linear progression; instead, it's a fractyl escaping the third dimension. Or an equation, the bottom of which keeps dropping out. If Israel xes then Jews y? If Nazis xed then Israelis y? If Muslims x, then Christians y? Without background and foreground, before and after, how do we move on? Which way is on? Half a million Israelis live in diaspora.

Context is everything, or almost. For two days running, a front-page lead story for New York media told and retold the story of a U.S. Jew who escaped the World Trade Center on 9/11 and was subsequently injured in Israel in the first suicide bombing attributed to a Palestinian woman. A human interest story, yes—but top news?

A couple of nights later the TV news ran coverage of a gathering of Israelis who had lost friends or family to the violence, followed by coverage of masked Palestinians with guns. Yes, Israelis suffer and Palestinians shoot. But given the proportion of Palestinian victims to Israeli victims, the proportion of armed Israelis to armed Palestinians (and armed with what weapons and what state power), it's easy to see that we're being focused through an Israeli lens.

In the dominant culture, as nationalities in struggle for contested turf, as religious others in the Christian world, Israelis and Palestinians, Jews and Muslims in part define each other. Israel is the United States's most-lavished-upon military ally in the region. Arabs/Muslims (merged in the popular imagination) are hypervisible and demonized, while Israelis/Jews (nearly as merged) occupy a more sympathetic space, seen as "Western," and, since 9/11, besieged "like us" by terrorism. Anti-Arab racism goes deep, and in the United States acquires a certain animal persistence in part through constant reinforcement from Israeli society.

Listen to a radical feminist Israeli: Rela Mazali, a co-founder of New Profile, dedicated to the demilitarization and the demasculinization of Israeli society.

> Nineteen percent of Israel's population are Palestinian. But 19 of the 23 communities with the highest unemployment in Israel are Palestinian. Of 14 Israeli communities rated lowest on socio-economic measures, 11 are Palestinian. . . . [T]he state spends

about four times as much on educating a Jewish child [as a Palestinian child]. . . . The current Palestinian population of Israel is six times its size in 1948, but the total size of their lands has been cut by half. In about 80% of Israel, Palestinian citizens are prohibited from buying or leasing land.[51]

Mazali concludes, "Does this sound like democracy?" A recent report from the Israeli Democracy Institute shows "an alarming rise in the percentage of Israelis, now at 53%, that do not believe Arabs should have the same rights as Jewish citizens of Israel."[52] The slightly good if not thrilling more recent news is

a significant rise [11%] in the number of those opposed to the claim that a Jewish majority is required on decisions fateful to the country, such as returning territories (34% in 2005 compared to 23% in 2004); a rise of 9% in the number of respondents opposed to the demand that the government encourage Arab emigration from the country (50% oppose such encouragement in 2005, compared to 41% in the previous year.)[53]

Significant rises aside, the three-tiered racialized structure I suggested earlier could readily apply to Israeli society, construing Palestinians (both inside greenline Israel and in the Occupied Territories) as "blacks" and Sephardi/Mizrahi and other Jews of color as "colored"—those who are not Ashkenazi but at least aren't Arab. So Mizrahi benefit, in the short run, by being Jewish (thus not Arab) and suffer, in the long run, by being Arab (thus not fully Jewish).

If whiteness means the right to not even notice your own ethnicity, you could argue that the only place where (some) Jews have entirely "whitened" is in Israel. According to Ella Shohat, Israeli Ashkenazi resist being identified as such.[54] What Zionism has not done is create a state in which "whiteness" is an empty concept.[55] Instead whiteness/Ashkenazism fills up with privilege; access to power, better housing, education, medical care, jobs: the works. In Israel, Ashkenazi identity divorced Yiddish and morphed into the desert sabra, the paratrooper, tough and macho; speaker of Hebrew; as opposed to the feminized, often Yiddish-speaking, and—most embarrassingly —*victims* of Europe.[56] In this paradigm, Hebrew is the IDF soldier; Yiddish, his semiprotected semidemeaned girlfriend or wife. Meanwhile there are women and children outside the perimeter of his ambiguous protection. It is not even known what language they speak.

Listen to the following true stories.

———————————— In 1942 an official committee of the Zionist movement was charged with naming and designing the Holocaust memorial for the Jews who would be killed, when by far most of the Jews it would memorialize were still alive.[57] Thus Yad Vashem got a headstart. Not a crime, but, as an indication of priorities, a little chilling.

In 1948 Palestine was newly partitioned and as Israel prepared for war, some 330,000 survivors passed through the Displaced Persons (DP) camps. Not all of the 330,000 were eligible for military service; nevertheless this number "constituted a sizeable 'human reserve' for the Zionist movement."[58] A mere 700 DPs enlisted voluntarily in the Israeli Defense Force. In response the Zionists simply made military service mandatory for "every man and woman in the DP camps, age 17 to 35," and announced, "We compel the Jews of the DP camps to enlist."[59]

The DPs were not Israeli citizens. They were devastated Holocaust survivors on European soil. Probably most of them had never been to Palestine, did not know the language, had no friends or family there, and may well have preferred to head somewhere else. Some even had other places to go, and some wanted to stay where they were.[60]

But it didn't matter what they wanted. Conscription was enforced viciously. People who failed to enlist were fined, fired from their jobs, evicted from their apartments, arrested, forced off Camp committees, assaulted, and beaten up. They were denied the supplementary rations distributed by the Joint Distribution Committee that kept the desperately undernourished survivors alive. A few even watched helplessly as these things were done to their aged parents or other loved ones. Archives bulge with official reports of brutality and coercion, "waves of Zionist harassment," in camps all over Germany and Austria.[61] Thus instead of 700 willing volunteers, an additional estimated 7,100 Holocaust survivors were forcibly conscripted into the Israeli army.[62]

Israel as it actually is—a nation state—vs. Israel-in-the-United-States: "the only democracy in the Middle East,"[63] Brooklyn in the desert, the miracle of god's lavishment upon his best chosen children. Finally Israel is inscribed, for Jews, as the home we can return to whenever we want, no matter what we've done. If this sounds infantile, that is part of the problem. For many U.S. Jews, Israel is fantasy. And the job of so much of mainstream Jewish institutions is to drum up support for this fantasy. "Birthright," the free trip for young Jews to visit Israel (while Palestinians born in Jerusalem, Haifa, etc., are refused entry); treks for North American students through Poland and the camps, ending in Israel, land of "hope and redemption"; the glorious shift to color at the close of *Schindler's List* as "Schindler's Jews" (those he saved) gather in Israel[64]—as if canceling out or at least concluding the Holocaust.

In New York in 2001, three out of four mayoral candidates donated money for bulletproof vests for settlers in the Occupied Territories, and swore Jerusalem would never be divided! New York politicians grovel like this not because most New York Jews identify with the settler movement, but because support for Israel is equated with support for Jews. Since the right-wing Orthodox communities are highly organized and donate significantly to election campaigns, candidates line up with the obligatory visit to Israel, including the prematurely named Yad Vashem. They do this even though most U.S. Jews, like most other people in the United States, are more concerned about health care, housing, schools, jobs, safety: basic human needs. Of course, actual incidents as well as claims of anti-semitism are used to lock Jews into a sense of existential isolation and thus strengthen support for "Jewish Defense" organizations[65] and for Israel.

ANTI-SEMITISM AND DIASPORISM

Shortly after September 11, 2001, I spent a month bouncing schizily between writing an essay placing anti-semitism in a contemporary context,[66] and writing a review of Kathleen Blee's *Inside Organized Racism: Women in the Hate Movement.*[67]

On one hand, post 9/11 Jews in the United States, at least those who are white, economically comfortable, straight and male, are definitely insiders—though history teaches us that this could shift at any moment.

On the other hand, journalist Daniel Pearl's throat was cut "partly" because he was a Jew.[68] Journalist Naomi Klein notes, "every time I log on to activist news sites like Indymedia.org, which practice 'open publishing,' I'm confronted with a string of Jewish conspiracy theories about 9/11 and excerpts from the *Protocols of the Elders of Zion,*"[69] the tired old forgery from tsarist Russia that purported to represent the Zionist plot to take over the world.[70] Though there are also scores of attacks on the *Protocols*, its revival, and the perceived need for discrediting it, are unnerving. I write this in fall 2006. Each year as the days of awe approach—the high holidays when Jews are most visible, most gathered—I always feel an element of risk. This year it's hard not to feel especially on edge. While anti-semitism is never the fault of Jews, the brutality of the Israeli occupation and destruction in Lebanon has got to pump up Jew-hating in a world that rarely distinguishes between Jews and Israelis; where Jewish and Israeli opposition to the occupation—while it is plentiful—is too seldom reported.

Hard not to notice that anti-semitism seems to be on the rise: Britain to Serbia to Montreal to Florida, where the same Katherine Harris who—as Florida's Secretary of State in 2000—refused a recount of that state's votes, has declared that voting for non-Christians amounted to legislating sin.[71] Two years ago Mel Gibson's *The Passion of the Christ* stirred the pot, coinciding as it did with the Bush presidency locked into a right-wing Christian agenda.[72] More recently, Gibson spewed drunk but clear Jew-hating onto a Jewish cop.[73]

In France, Jew-hating tangles with anti-Israeli sentiment, and attacks have gone beyond graffiti and desecration. In February 2006, Ilan Halimi, a twenty-three-year-old Jew, was tortured and killed. In France there is debate as to whether this was essentially a robbery–kidnapping bolstered by fantasies of Jewish wealth or was essentially a hate crime.[74] Among the more than ten suspects arrested, some

> told police that they chose to kidnap Jews because "all Jews are rich," and that they put cigarettes out on the victim's face because "he was Jewish and we don't like Jews."
>
> Most of the gang members were Muslim, of North African Arab and black African origins, but others involved were not, including the superintendent of the building where Halimi was held. . . . [According to Halimi's mother,] "It was an open secret in the neighborhood that a Jew was being held and tortured, and nobody called the police anonymously, not one person. . . . The elevator was blocked for 10 days and people were guarding the door to the apartment, and nobody called the police. It was not that all those neighbors were anti-Semitic. It's more that they simply did not care."
>
> Yet Halimi's mother is careful to say she has nothing against Muslims.
>
> "I grew up with Muslims in Casablanca, in Morocco," she says. "I never had any problems, never. The problem is with France. I

think the country has become sick from a lack of feelings, a lack of emotion."[75]

Even in places not traditionally anti-semitic—Saudi Arabia and other Arab nations, Japan, Indonesia and other parts of Asia—traditional European anti-semitic tropes appear: blood libel, the *Protocols* again. In the United States, sectors of the left are blaming Jews for Israeli brutality while sectors of the right blame Jewish money, Jewish homosexuality, and Jewish immorality for everything else. Add in the pro-Zionist Christian Right—the ones who love Jews because the second coming requires our presence—it's hard to know whom to fear most.

On yet another hand, Cecilie Surasky, Communications Director of Jewish Voice for Peace, reported from the 2004 World Social Forum in India:

> I attend most of the workshops I can find on the Israel–Palestine issue. What I do not hear (or see) is anything I would consider anti-semitic. In a global conference of 100,000 people, one expects to hear an enormous range of political perspectives, including the occasional extreme or intolerant remark. Given that I am prepared for the worst, I am shocked that the overwhelming majority of what is said in workshops critical of U.S. and Israeli policies in the territories is milder than the articles and essays one can read in Israeli newspapers on any given day.[76]

Recently I've gotten a slew of e-mails saying, for example, "HAIL [*sic*] HITLER"and "you disgusting jew cunt why don't you kill yourself?" I assume these emails are coming from the non-Jewish right. But the right-wing Jews are out there as well. The Masada 2000 website lists some 7,000 "self-hating" Jews (=critical of Israeli government) including me, my lover, many of my friends and comrades. For a moment I wonder, should it concern me that my picture is posted? I don't feel threatened but am I a fool? When I stand in vigil or protest against the Israeli occupation, I expect that my leaflets will be knocked out of my hands by some large man in a *kipa* shrieking in my face that I'm a whore.

Look at the attacks on academics Ward Churchill and Rashid Khalidi. I myself have been told of two instances in which I was excluded for consideration for positions in Jewish studies because of my politics on Israel/Palestine. At the center of the U.S. Jewish world, folks have risen to the occasion so beautifully on queer rights, on choice, health care, immigrant rights, labor, civil liberties, and even on opposing anti-Arab racism. Yet on this one issue, Israel/Palestine, it's still acceptable at the Jewish center to forget that Palestinians are people too.

We've been hearing a lot about anti-semitism on campus. An ADL survey found on college campuses in the United States *less* anti-semitism and *more* opposition to Israeli policies than among any other segment of the population. "While more than three out of five faculty members (62%) and a majority of undergraduates (51%) have an unfavorable impression of the current Israeli government, only 3% of students and 5% of faculty fall into the most anti-Semitic category."[77] That's a distinction we need to broadcast. The other activity we hear a lot about on campus is the surveillance being exercised, often by students, over professors who are critical of Israeli policies. To teach knowing you might be furnishing material towards your own economic demise is difficult.

So when I ask what is it like for Jews in the United States now, the answer is, for the moment, relatively speaking, "benign." It's not as if I think only Auschwitz counts. But look at anti-semitism in the United States in a context of physical assaults, racial profiling, FBI harassment, workplace discrimination, indefinite detention, and expulsion to face torture or death. In this context it's obvious: the distance between the majority of U.S. Jews and people of color is, at this historical moment, increasing, exaggerated. Simultaneously, the boundary between (Euro)Jews and whites has blurred. Arabs and Muslims, cast as a different sort of "minority from hell," make Jews look like harbingers of calm and civility. Have Jews ever seemed so American, so normal, so, well, (Judeo)Christian—with a slight variation in headgear? You could almost say in your most cynical voice, "Arab-hating is good for the Jews."

I read over Katherine Blee's discussion of Aryan Nation, the Ku Klux Klan, Christian Identity and Racist Skinhead movements,[78] all of which share a convoluted worldview with conspiratorial anti-semitism at the center, including three key elements: Jews have distorted modern history (one aspect of which is Holocaust-as-hoax); Jews seek world control through a one-world government (that sicko U.N.); and Jews manipulate racial strife. According to Blee, the central role played by anti-semitism is odd, "at a time when anti-semitism in the mainstream culture is at an all-time low." To Blee, this centrality provides one more example of how peculiar and isolated these hate groups are. Blee acknowledges the strength of Christian-centrism in the mainstream culture, but she finds that women entering the hate movements have to be taught to hate Jews. They lack specific images or complaints, a vagueness she attributes to the small number of Jews in the United States and the level of assimilation and invisibility in which these Jews live. Equally interesting, and not at all comforting, Blee documents that this *lack* of Jew-hating characterized many who were drawn to Nazism in Germany in the 1930s. (In England, on the contrary, anti-semitism was rampant, visceral, and quite specific.)

Islamic conspiratorial thinking similarly distorts, scapegoats Zionists/ Israel/Jews for the depredations of Western imperialism, and for the oppression of the East by the West. Yet given the actual role of the Israeli state in oppressing Palestinians, the broad and endless support diaspora Jewry seems to lavish on Israel, and the apparent lack of any Jewish agenda except with regard to Israel, this conspiratorial anti-semitism can get confused with reasonable rage at the Israeli oppressors.[79]

While I am working on the Blee review and the anti-semitism essay, I dream I am trying to explain to a former comrade with whom I once worked very closely on Israel/Palestine, why I no longer feel compassion for Jews whose fear is so strong that they cannot assess it accurately, cannot or will not see what is happening to the Palestinians. In the dream I am crying: I have lost something precious, my sense of Jewish solidarity.

But when I'm awake, though I feel grief, I describe it differently. For years I've been working to make audible the divisions in "the" Jewish community. The solidarity I continue to feel is with other radical Jews who work against the occupation, with the Israeli resistance, and with the aspirations of the Palestinians for self-determination and peace. It's true that I find myself impatient with those Jews who insist (out of ignorance more than anything else) that former Israeli Prime Minister Barak was so generous, or that the Palestinians "answered peace with violence," when, in the years since the Oslo Accords (1993) Palestinian lives have gotten so much harder. Israel has doubled the population of its settlements in the Occupied Territories, continued to inflict collective punishments, killing and wounding civilians, blowing up homes, destroying orchards, confiscating land, assassinating at will, and, perhaps most devastating, building Jewish-only bypass roads along with what has been dubbed the "Apartheid Wall," carving up Palestinian territory into disconnected fragments. While I too fear for my Israeli friends' safety, in the light of increasingly harsh conditions for Palestinians, I feel impatient with the sensitivity of U.S. Jews, their demands for reassurance that strike me as narcissistic or, at best, clueless. What will make Israelis safe? More settlements? One hundred more home demolitions?

There is a struggle for morality in the Jewish community. But combating racism against Arabs at home and abroad, or solving the quagmire of Israel/Palestine must not wait for the Jewish community to find its morality or its courage either. Jews in diaspora, and especially Jews in the United States, need to understand that, ultimately, as dear as Israel may be to any of us—or not—it is not our surrogate identity kit, but a nation with its own destiny and the most powerful military in the region, heavily funded by U.S. tax dollars. Attention to the immensity of this aid, and to Israeli violations of human rights, will no doubt fuel both anti-semitism and Jewish fear. Working in Jewish or Jewish-friendly contexts, we can help each other untangle anti-semitism from honest critique from an under-standable response to oppression. At the same time, we can help each other keep our eyes on the prize, ending racism and all bigotry; making sure our Jewish communities reflect our racial and cultural diversity; and bringing economic and social justice into a live awakening; working with others to create the world we want to live in.

Sam Freedman's *Jew vs. Jew* argues compellingly that Jews are approaching something like a reformation, where fundamentalists will split off from modern Orthodox, who then, along with Conservative, Reform, and Reconstructionist will compose one strand of Judaism, com-parable to Protestants. Freedman seems unaware of such trends as Jewish renewal, Jewish feminism, or Jewish secularism, but I think his notion of increased separation and conflict between the fundamentalists and the rest of denominational Jewry is accurate—whether a full-blown reforma-tion or continued drifting apart; whether the fault line will be Israel or women rabbis or gay marriage or . . .

I do not relish this vision of increased separation and alienation among Jews. We are a small community and I'd rather struggle than split. But this kind of conflict is, I believe, preferable to allowing fundamentalist or other right-wing voices to represent the Jewish people.

The point is, Jews, like everyone else, make political choices. Whatever privilege the moment grants us, we, people of the book, people of history, should understand the danger of racism. With whose interests will we identify and stake our future? Many Jews engage in justice-seeking work, some as visible Jews, many more invisible *as Jews*, doing their political work as progressives, as women, as workers, as queers, as whites, as people of color. . . . Meanwhile Jewish political conservatives are highly visible, claim-ing the Jewish voice. In this way, some of us relinquish to the Jewish center and right wing the claim to represent the Jewish community. Secular Jews abandon Jewish culture to Orthodox Jews, as if they are the "real Jews" and we are not. We neglect powerful traditions of Jewish radicalism, a potential source of instruction, inspiration, and courage.

A JEWISH TRADITION: RADICAL JUSTICE-SEEKING

To be a Jew in the twentieth century
Is to be offered a gift. If you refuse,
Wishing to be invisible, you choose
Death of the spirit, the stone insanity.
Accepting, take full life. . . . Full agonies:
Your evening deep in labyrinthine blood
Of those who resist, fail, and resist; and God
Reduced to a hostage among hostages.

The gift is torment. Not alone the still
Torture, isolation; or torture of the flesh.
That may come also. But the accepting wish,
The whole and fertile spirit as guarantee
For every human freedom, suffering to be free,
Daring to live for the impossible.

—Muriel Rukeyser[80]

Will we choose death of the spirit, and forfeit the gift of our Jewishness?

In the fight against slavery, when the Jewish population in this country was minuscule, among John Brown's small band were three Jews—August Bondi, Theodore Wiener, and Jacob Benjamin. According to Bondi,

> When we followed Captain Brown up the hill . . . I behind Brown and behind us Weiner—we walked with bent backs, almost crawling, so that last year's tall dead grass would at least shield us from the ruffian marksmen. But the bullets kept on whistling. Weiner was 57 years old and weighed 250 pounds and was puffing like a steamboat, crawling behind me. I called to him, "*Nu, was meinen Sie jetzt?*" (Well, what do you think of this now?). He answered [in Yiddish, then switching to Hebrew], "*Was soll ich meinen? Sof odom moves*" (What should I think? Man's life ends in death.).[81]

Could this story be more Jewish, with its bilingual punch line?

In "My Mother, Leah, and George Sand," Vera Williams' character Leah epitomizes the instinctive Diasporist:

> —Is she acquainted with George Sand? Would your daughter, and Rotsky's daughter, and a history teacher to boot not know a

213

George Sand? A woman who was so much in the forefront of her time even Bella needs to run to catch up with her. Though Rotsky, and I myself for that matter, would not have agreed with Sand on the Paris Commune.

—Leah! Still the Paris Commune. Forget the Paris Commune.

—Forget the Paris Commune. This would be like forget you're a human being.[82]

In a book by the Boyarin brothers aptly titled *Powers of Diaspora,* I come upon the words of Marek Edelman, for whom Brad and Meg named their son. Marek Edelman was co-commander of the Warsaw Ghetto Uprising, a Bundist and an anti-Zionist. He survived, remained in Poland, and became a doctor and a leader in Solidarity. About the Uprising, Edelman says:

> This was a revolt? The whole point was not to let them slaughter you when your turn came. The whole point was to choose your method of dying. All of humanity had already agreed that dying with a weapon in the hand is more beautiful than without a weapon. *So we surrendered to that consensus.*[83] (Emphasis in original.)

"This was a revolt?" When I first read Marek's words I laughed. Across the ocean, his whole life in Poland and he sounds like the Bronx (or, rather, the Bronx sounds like him.) Then, like ice water, it hits me. Despair. Big fat choice, your method of dying. How do I explain my pride in the resistance, as though knowing about it purges something shameful?

The Boyarins comment: "The notion that dying with a weapon is more beautiful and honorable than dying without one is a surrender of Jewish difference to a 'universal,' masculinist consensus."[84] What good anti-sexism allies the Boyarins are; but I disagree. Fighting with one's last breath might not be masculinist; maybe it's just human.

Spring 1980, Passover was close. I was living in Santa Fe, and I went looking for matzoh. After a while, between the blank stares and the churches, I started reading everything in the Santa Fe library about the Holocaust. I had worked as a Rape Crisis Counselor, so I knew Resistance 101: People always resist as they can, how they can. So I looked for and found: *They Fought Back. On Both Sides of the Wall. The Warsaw Ghetto* (where Marek Edelman and other young Jews held out against the Nazis longer than Poland did). I collected the stories of women who resisted, and a couple of years

later, when I read these stories to 500 (mostly) Jewish lesbians in Boston and San Francisco, they shrieked with need
and joy. As if they themselves had fought back.[85]

Today Israeli Jews face a different dilemma: How to not fight. The numbers of soldiers refusing to serve in the Occupied Territories was 1,664
at last count, not including AWOLs and other less visible means of resistance. High school students have begun their own campaign of refusal;
as of March 2005, more than 300 students are refusing induction. The
numbers keep going up. Soldiers and students have served time in prison
for refusing to serve in the Occupied Territories precisely because it's not
self-defense.[86]

History, story, argument are the life blood of Diasporism: an unfinished continually transforming project. Polish immigrant Ernestine Rose
became an ardent abolitionist. Rabbi David Einhorn's anti-slavery position got him drummed out of his Baltimore congregation. In the urban
struggles of working people to organize labor unions, in the fight to stop
lynching, to save the Scottsboro "boys", in the civil rights movement, with
all the contradictions and trouble spots, Jews played a significant role.
Rabbi Marshall Meyer stood in Argentina with the mothers of the disappeared; JFREJ was founded in 1990 in Marshall's living room.

In South Africa, Joe Slovo, Ruth First, Albie Sachs, Nadine Gordimer,
Abie Nathan, and Helen Suzman are only among the most famous of the
many Jews who joined the fight to bring down apartheid. Though a careful
analysis reveals how most South African Jews benefited from a hierarchy
which both privileged and separated them (thus sparing the Jewish community the mixed blessing of assimilation), nevertheless, among whites
who joined the African National Congress and other anti-apartheid movements, "Jews constituted a staggering proportion."[87] A touching piece of
linguistic evidence appears in the memoir of Gillian Slovo, one of the
First-Slovo three daughters. First's parents were founding members of
the South African Communist Party. In 1960, after the Sharpeville massacre, the ANC called protests nationwide and the government declared
an emergency, ultimately arresting some twenty thousand political activists
all over the country. Slovo writes,

> My grandfather was one of the people whose fingers were busy
> dialing. Friends of his, asleep in bed, picked up their receivers
> to hear his voice speaking a language that came from deep in his
> childhood. *'ze zuchen,'* he said. They are looking.[88]

Slovo takes for granted but it bears mentioning: Yiddish must also have come from deep in the childhood of those he was phoning.

Peter Beinart argues against the idea that "communist-inspired participation in the ANC reflected a kind of Jewish tradition and Jewish identity when the people who embodied that supposed tradition scorned Judaism: like most old-line communists, they were atheists."[89] Yet religion, as I have argued throughout this book, is only one of the Jewish traditions.

Mark Naison, in his distinguished study *Communists in Harlem during the Depression*, offers the following intriguing remark:

> Though their Jewish ancestry may have endowed them with cultural reflexes that dictated a strong emotional response to black oppression, and though as individuals they may have been aware of this, the assimilationist atmosphere in the Party, as well as their own political ambitions, probably discouraged them from calling attention to it in any systematic way."[90]

This concept of *cultural reflex* seems worth exploring. From another perspective, Paul Gilroy, seeking connections between black and Jewish thinkers, urges caution "because the significance of Jewishness for figures like Lukàcs, Adorno, Benjamin, Kafka . . . is an obscure and hotly debated question which haunts the great radical movements of the twentieth century."[91] Gilroy might well cite Franz Kafka's 1914 diary entry: "What have I in common with Jews? I have scarcely anything in common with myself."[92]

Yet this is exactly the tradition claimed by Isaac Deutscher: the tradition of the non-Jewish Jew, as Deutscher explained to the World Jewish Congress in 1958:

> The Jewish heretic who transcends Jewry belongs to a Jewish tradition. . . . Spinoza, Heine, Marx, Rosa Luxemburg, Trotsky, and Freud . . . all went beyond the boundaries of Jewry. They all found Jewry too narrow, too archaic, and too constricting. . . . Yet I think that in some ways they were very Jewish indeed. . . . as Jews they dwelt on the borderlines of various civilizations, religions, and national cultures.[93]

Raised Orthodox, steeped in the tradition he rebelled against, Deutscher could grasp the "Jewishness" of his own rebellion. Typical "non-Jewish Jews" today, lacking Deutscher's knowledge of Jewish tradition, often fail to see ourselves as acting within this tradition. We have even permitted the Jewish right to claim the term *Jewish radical*. Diasporists need to reclaim it.

We have Diasporist models right here in the present.

SHIRA KATZ

Shira Katz is a public school teacher in her early thirties, dual-citizened U.S.-Israeli. I call her up to ask about anti-semitism and the Middle East peace movement. She was living in Jerusalem in the mid-nineties when, in the face of "the unbelievable settler violence happening in Hebron," she helped found the Hebron Solidarity Committee. Their group of Jewish Israelis, U.S. Jews living in Israel, and Palestinian citizens of Israel paid solidarity visits to Hebron families "who had pogroms visited on them. We helped Palestinian residents across from a settlement build a fence—then we were beat up by settlers. When people were killed by the military, we'd attend funerals and we'd visit people in their homes."

I ask if she encountered anti-semitism, either there or in solidarity work she's been involved with here since the more recent Intifada.

"You have to understand Palestinian anti-semitism in the context of the occupation. The occupation is the biggest factor in the lives of Palestinians. The people I work with, they're internationalists and Marxists. They distinguish between being Jewish and supporting a certain political ideology. But we participated in some events where people were chanting who knows what—I have the blissful ignorance of not understanding Arabic. At one meeting, some Hamas people wouldn't look at us because we were women, and I'd think 'our grandparents are rolling in their graves right now!' But there was such a lack of action and awareness even among leftist Jewish Israelis that we felt like someone needed to stand up and take risks. And we actually felt like our going to Hebron was going to break some anti-semitic stereotypes."

"Did you feel afraid?"

"My dad's a Holocaust survivor, so Jewish fear is part of who I am. I have to shut down to it; to act in spite of it. Only once a rock was thrown at a taxi we were in. But really our fear of violence from settlers or from Hamasniks was equal. And doing this work, it's like a dance: having the fear and having the convictions. If I had let my fear control me or stop me from acting—look what I would have lost: connections with Palestinians; a deep sense of working for what's right and—this may sound corny—seeing what's true. Moving through the fear has enriched my life."

Or listen to Nurit Peled-Elhanan, the mother of thirteen-year-old Smadar, who was killed by a suicide bomber in Jerusalem in September 1998. Nurit said:

When my little girl was killed, a reporter asked me how I was willing to accept condolences from the other side. I replied without hesitation that I refused it: When representatives of Netanyahu's government came to offer their condolences I took my leave and would not sit with them. For me, the other side, the enemy, is not the Palestinian people. For me the struggle is not between Palestinians and Israelis, nor between Jews and Arabs. The fight is between those who seek peace and those who seek war. My people are those who seek peace. My sisters are the bereaved mothers, Israeli and Palestinian, who live in Israel and in Gaza and in the refugee camps. My brothers are the fathers who try to defend their children from the cruel occupation, and are, as I was, unsuccessful in doing so.

September 11 called forth the heroism of ordinary people, Jews among them. Abe Zelmanowitz worked at the World Trade Center. Instead of escaping, Abe chose to stay with his friend who was in a wheelchair and couldn't get down the stairs. On October 7, 2001, the day the United States began waging war on Afghanistan, at an anti-war rally in New York City, Abe Zelmanowitz's sister Rita Lasar spoke against her brother's death being used to justify war. Phyllis and Orlando Rodriguez, parents of Gregory Rodriguez, who worked at the World Trade Center and died there, wrote a letter against the war, which was read at the October 7 demonstration by Phyllis's father Reuben Schaffer (without whose name we would have missed the bicultural Gregory's Jewishness). At that same October rally, I read a statement from the Israeli Women in Black, which expressed their determination to stand up for Palestinian rights. Afterwards a Lebanese woman I know only casually hugged me.

"Your words made me feel strong," she said.

In Brooklyn, when a vigil was called to support Arab Americans, Jews showed up in large numbers, with signs proclaiming *Jewish Voices Against Anti-Arab Racism*. Singing *Peace, Salaam, Shalom, Peace Salaam Shalom,* the entire procession marched along Atlantic Avenue to the Brooklyn promenade, where the view of lower Manhattan marked the absence of the twin towers. Curls of smoke were still rising.

These stories are not meant to let us off the hook, but to help us situate ourselves in what is rightfully one of the unfolding Jewish traditions, the tradition of fighting for justice.

TO CHANGE THE WAY RACISM IS FOUGHT:
SHIFTING THE CENTER

The work of ending racism demands not only that Jews shift the paradigm of whiteness and Ashkenazism; not only that we abandon whatever comfort or protection we might imagine resides in defining ourselves as victims.

Larger than that: we have to shift the center of Jewish culture and history.[94] So that the European sojourn is seen as one sojourn of many. So that whatever value we ascribe to Ashkenazim is exactly the same as what we ascribe to Mizrahim; and—here is the big leap—exactly the same as what we ascribe to Palestinians. Make racism marginal, on its way to extinction.

Jewish culture should be opening its arms wide. So that a Jewish event focused on Ashkenazi culture is named proudly—like the Toronto festival of new Yiddish culture *Ashkenaz!*—but not presented or imagined as inclusively Jewish. So that resources to celebrate and transmit Mizrahi, Sephardi, and other Jewish cultures are accessible, and defined and controlled by the scholars and community activists who know their cultures, not by the Yitzhak-come-latelys who spot a new fashion.

Minimally we want to savor the richness of our extended communities, and we want our Jewish sisters and brothers of all colors to feel welcome all over the Jewish world. Jews of color may continue to be a minority, but you don't have to be the majority to feel at home. As a lesbian I rarely expect to be in the majority, but I can spot in an instant where I am welcome—which has everything to do with how queerness and straightness are acknowledged. It doesn't mean everyone is seeking my suddenly representative lesbian opinion or assuming I am wild about Ellen DeGeneres.[95]

But larger still. We want Jews of all colors to feel at home, but not as Jewish exceptions to the rules of racism. Exceptionalism provides space into which Jews of color can be welcomed as Jews, while racism continues undaunted. Whenever someone says, "You're not like the others," look out. We reject exceptionalism as pitifully unsatisfying. Nothing is good enough that does not end racism, or that ends racism only by denaturalizing the bond of race and class so that exploitation by class—or gender—still prevails.

─────── I have just come from a conference in Washington, D.C., where I spoke on a panel with two young women, neither

219

of whom wanted to go first, and since I am older and more experienced, I agreed to begin. I talked, somewhat scatteredly, about the way women's culture is not created in a vacuum, about class and profit and the need to think in units of solution larger than the individual, the family, or the tribe.

The second woman on the panel—I'll call her Anne—white, tall, thin, and blond—begins by announcing her father's six-figure income and how she won't take money from him, because "it's wrong." She names Elizabeth Cady Stanton as the founder of the abolitionist movement, as though no African Americans worked for their own liberation. She concludes by praising the women's museum in Washington because the building looks like Tara in *Gone with the Wind*. By the time she finishes speaking, the temperature of the room has escalated, a fact of which she seems entirely unaware.

The third speaker, Katie, is a filmmaker who has just completed a project about color in the black community. Katie is African American, light-skinned enough to pass as white, she tells us. Even when she explains her background, people say, "You don't look black." She tells us that her sister is darker, doesn't look white; that her own feelings are different because of how people treat her sister.

What sticks with me later is not Anne—a fairly common white narcissism, after all—but Katie, who "doesn't look black." In truth, Katie looks like a light-skinned black, and those who fail to notice this must so presume whiteness that anything else has to smack them in the face. What I keep circling back to, though, is how Katie, the filmmaker, reacts to white people's response to her darker-skinned sister. If Anne is narcissistic, Katie is the opposite, joining her sister to herself.

Do we have a name for Katie's reaction—beyond altruism, which sounds to my (Jewish?) ears like self-sacrifice and self-denial; or empathy, which suggests an effort to respond to another's experience? What Katie implied sounded effortless—not without cost, but beyond will. In a deep sense, her sister *is* her self.

Thinking about poet Toi Derricotte's *The Black Notebooks*, which chronicles the experiences of a light-skinned African American who often passes, so that white people say in her hearing things they would never say if they recognized who she is.[96] Derricotte writes about crossing the color line inside her own family, her marriage, even though everyone involved is "black." But however others see her, she is totally clear on who she is.

Or Jane Lazarre's *Beyond the Whiteness of Whiteness*,[97] a white Jew married to an African American man, she comes to understand whiteness (if not Jewishness), and to identify with the struggles of blackness through her love for her husband and their sons.

Or the challenging and contradictory analyses of racism in Brazil, where different races exist inside the same nuclear family, in children from the same parents; where many Brazilians deny that racism exists, while explaining the domination of elite positions by Euro-Brazilians with "there are more of them" (the ratio is 55 percent Euros to 45 percent Afros).[98] Still, in 2003, Brazil voted for massive affirmative action for the universities.[99]

Or Grace Paley's outrageously wise story, "Zagrowsky Tells." Zagrowsky, a retired pharmacist, has been an ordinary racist his whole life—not dangerous but definitely hurtful. But now he's got a black/Jewish grandson, whom he adores, and it changes him. "You have an opinion. I have an opinion," Zagrowsky tells one of the women who picketed his pharmacy years ago. "Life don't have no opinion."[100]

Identity as it is ordinarily conceived: as if we were each completely distinct individuals separated one from the other by the boundary of, exactly, skin.

DIASPORISM AND THE COLORS OF JEWS

What has Diasporism to do with the colors of Jews?

Diasporism begins but does not end with Jewish diversity and boundary crossing. Diasporism demands that we mix it up in ways we don't even know yet. Diasporism places at the center our memory of strangeness, and our desire (not duty, *desire*) to welcome strangers. Diasporism means, given the multicultural nature of the Jewish community, inside "the" Jewish community we should expect to experience the simultaneity of home and strangeness. If we are at an event that claims to be for the whole Jewish community, at any given moment *something* must feel unfamiliar to *someone;* it just shouldn't always be the same people. Creating an inclusive tradition means letting go of some familiarity, welcoming some dissonance. The first time I listened to Iraqi Jewish music, oud and violin, it didn't feel like my music. So? The first time anyone listens to anything, it probably doesn't feel like theirs.

Diasporism seeks and embraces difference. As racism is a widening maw, so is its opposite, a heart beating more and more powerfully open. How then should I exclude my sister's cousin, my brother's children, my aunt's lover, my lover's friend? Diasporism means we seek fruitful interaction with our neighbors and coworkers whose paths cross ours.

I said earlier in this book: love across the lines of race is intolerable to racists; it is also profoundly disturbing to xenophobes. I said, the political version of love, the opposite of xenophobia, is solidarity. Diasporists value solidarity not as a necessary evil; not solely because, as we confront the most powerful machines of war and capital the world has ever known, we understand that solidarity is our only power. Diasporists choose solidarity as the highest expression of humanity. It's about, for example, Rachel Corrie from the state of Washington, placing her body, her life against the Caterpillar bulldozing one more Palestinian home.[101] As I write, in the United States millions are in the streets supporting immigrant rights; people who are not themselves targeted at this moment marching along side those who are immediately at risk. We seek allies and we seek to *be* allies.

Diasporism cherishes love across the borders—and let's face it, every reaching out beyond one's own body is a border crossing. If we can stick up for each other across the borders of race, we have defeated racism's most powerful weapon. Thus Diasporism welcomes intermarriage, embraces mixed-race, mixed-culture babies. Diasporism is anti-assimilation, not anti-change. We want to raise *truly* bi- and multicultural children, knowledgeable, proud, and connected. Our vehicle is not the bloodline but culture, history, memory. Diasporists recognize our identity as simultaneously rock, forged under centuries of pressure, and water, infinitely flexible. Diasporism requires those who know and value past and existing tradition, and those who create new ones.

Diasporists resonate to the remark I heard years ago from theologian Judith Plaskow, in response to someone's discomfort with new prayers reformed to eliminate male god language.

"Those aren't the prayers I grew up with," the woman said, "I don't feel comfortable with them."

"We're not the generation that gets to feel comfortable," Plaskow responded. "We're the generation that gets to create a tradition so the next generation grows up in it, and for them it will be the authentic tradition, and they will feel comfortable."[102]

Some might shudder at Rabbi Lynn Gottlieb's blowing the "freedom horn" on *Pesakh,*[103] or welcoming rosaries into the shul. Others might burst into joyful laughter, as some did when I told her story at a JFREJ Hanukkah party; or feel their eyes well up, as I did when Lynn told it to me. Diasporists don't want to dilute Judaism into a shallow anything-is-Jewish-tradition-because-I-say-it-is,[104] but we welcome principled argument about the particulars. *Flexibility is a spiritual issue. Hospitality is the first principle.*

As Diasporists committed to working across our differences, we conceive of Jewish education not only for Jews, but also to educate non-Jews about us. Similarly, we are committed to learning about the cultures of others with depth and respect. Diasporists might eye suspiciously the bizarre popularity of klezmer in Germany, a fad that has much in common with romanticization in the United States of Native American cultures.[105] First wipe them out, then try on their culture, like your dead enemy's skin. Diasporists ask: who is making money from whose culture? Are others learning to appreciate, preserve, protect the culture, or are they simply expiating a vague unarticulated guilt?

Diasporism is an exercise with two hands. We insist on both. On one hand, we celebrate our stance as outsiders; on the other, we can never forget what it means to have—or need—a passport. We support refuge for all who need it, stand in solidarity with immigrants, documented and undocumented; and we stand with workers' right to organize. Diasporism is non-nationalist; but we recognize the role of nationalism and national integrity in the process of liberation. We challenge the rigid borders of the imperial nations, and say people (people, not NAFTA) should be free to cross where they will. We resonate with the postcolonial voices in England who defend themselves by invoking history: *We are here,* they say, *because you were there.* In the mega-global-capitalist states we might update it. *We are here because you are everywhere.*

In the United States, Diasporists are still struggling to grasp all that globalization, September 11, the increasing power of the American Empire and of the Christian right means for refugees and immigrants, for human rights and civil liberties, for those who wish they could stay home, who wish they had a home, who are trying to make a new home. That is, Diasporism is shaped by the historical moment, and will and should change.

Shortly after George W. Bush was sort-of elected president, I dreamed I was married to him. In the dream I am horrified. I ask myself, "How did I let it come to this?"

How did we let it come to this?

As this book goes to press, I talk with my older friends, people who lived through the Great Depression, the McCarthy period. This is worse, they say. A harsh present regularly superceded by an even harsher present. You think things can't get worse but they do.

Recently reported in the Jewish press: mainstream Jewish organizations are concerned about young Jews who seek to express their Jewish values by working to ameliorate human suffering, but fail to focus only on Jewish suffering.

> The good news is, then, that Jewish education works. A generation of young Jews around the world have internalized the message that "being Jewish" means fixing the world in its totality, without regard to race, religion or nationality.
>
> The bad news for the Jewish state and people is that this generation of American Jews have taken from their education that acting Jewish means doing justice without regard to nationality or peoplehood. [106]

I would argue instead that the bad news is not news: insularity of the mainstream organizations. The good news is precisely the young Jews' definition of Jewish values. *Welcome the stranger.* Clearly in Jewish communities, as in the larger society, we need changes in leadership, changes that will come only through boldly including the excluded and relentlessly centering the marginalized. In short, we need democracy.

For the past several years, when I walk a picket line, or speak out against racism, or oppose the Israeli Occupation, frequently some other Jew yells at me: *Why do you only care about blacks?* or, *Why do you only care about Arabs?* or, *Don't you care about Jews?* As though these are mutually exclusive. As though you can't care about both; all.

The wrong answer—though it's true: *I don't ONLY care about blacks or Arabs.*

The right answer—though it's ungrammatical: *We are them. They are us.*

Finally, a story within a story and both are about solidarity. Years ago, during one of the African American/Jewish media-orchestrated flare-ups—this one was an anti-semitic diatribe by Khalid Muhammed at Keane College in New Jersey—as usual the press was phoning up men for inflammatory comments. Things around the Jews for Racial and Economic Justice office were hectic and raw. My friend Kathleen Saadat, a leading African

American human rights activist in the state of Oregon, called to see how I was doing, and left a message on my machine. When I called back, I got her machine. Kathleen always leaves a poem or a song on her machine, and this time, her voice announced, "From *Tales of the Hasidim.*"

So that's the first point: a leader in the African American community picked that moment to draw publicly on Jewish wisdom.

And the second point is the tale itself.

> Someone goes to the rebbe to find out, how do you know when night has ended? And the rebbe says, you can tell night has ended when you can see that the person standing next to you is your sister or brother.[107]

May night end. May we see.

NOTES

1. *The Tribe of Dina: A Jewish Women's Anthology*, eds., Melanie Kaye/
Kantrowitz and Irena Klepfisz (Boston: Beacon Press, 1989; 1st pub., *Sinister
Wisdom*, 1986).

2. I first coined the term in 1996 in a talk I gave at a conference in Toronto,
published as "Diasporism, Feminism, and Coalition," in *Jewish Women's Voices*,
Swartz and Wolfe, eds. (Toronto: Second Story Press, 1998). I have since discovered Philip Roth's brilliant satire *Operation Shylock*. Roth's diasporism solves
the problem of anti-semitism by forcing the Jews to leave Israel and return to
Europe. As should be apparent, this is not my meaning. See Adam Shatz's trajectory from a traditional Zionist home to an opponent of Zionism: "In Praise of
Diasporism, or, Three Cheers for Irving Berlin," *The Nation*, web only, 4/9/04
(www.thenation.com/doc/20040426/shatz).

3. Whatever one's stance on nationalism, I think most people in the United
States are ignorant about what Zionism has meant and continues to mean to
the Palestinian people. See Edward Said, "Zionism from the Standpoint ," in
Bayoumi and Rubin, eds., *The Edward Said Reader* (New York: Vintage, 2000),
114–68.

4. Shohat, "Reflections of an Arab Jew," in Khazzoom, ed., *Flying Camel*, 120.
Khazzoom, 234, explains, "*Al Neharoth Babel* is a traditional Jewish prayer that
says, "By the rivers of Babylon, we sat and wept, when we remembered Zion."

5. Gloria Anzaldúa, *Borderlands/Las Fronteras* (San Francisco: Aunt Lute,
1987). Gloria, a Texas Chicana, used to half-joke that she was part Jewish—
half-joke because of the vast mixing of Jew, Spanish, and indigenous people
all over the Americas.

6. See interviews with Ivri-NASAWI leadership in chapter 5.

7. See Daniel Boyarin, "Masada or Yavneh?" in Boyarin and Boyarin, eds.,
Jews and Other Differences (Minneapolis: University of Minnesota Press, 1997),
305–30.

1. ARE JEWS WHITE?

1. Cornel West, *Keeping Faith Alive*, 19.

2. Margaret Talbot, "Getting Credit for Being White."

3. According to United for a Fair Economy's 2004 report, "The State of
the Dream: Enduring Disparities in Black and White," by Dedrick Muhammad,
Attieno Davis, Meizhu Lui, and Betsy Leondar-Wright. "Progress has been made

in narrowing the [white/black] divide in per capita income, poverty, homeownership, education, life expectancy and median wealth, but so slowly that the gaps would take decades or even centuries to close at the current rate." Cf. the Community Service Society's study "based on data from the federal Bureau of Labor Statistics and focus[ed] on the so-called employment-population ratio—the fraction of the working-age population with a paid job—in addition to the more familiar unemployment rate, the percentage of the labor force actively looking for work."

4. Patricia Williams, *The Rooster's Egg*, 29.

5. Kathleen Blee, *Inside Organized Racism*.

6. Theodore W. Allen, *The Invention of the White Race*, vol. II; Michael Omi and Howard Winant, *Racial Formation;* David R. Roediger, *The Wages of Whiteness*. Others include Matthew Frye Jacobson, *Whiteness of a Different Color;* Noel Ignatiev, *How the Irish Became White*.

7. Robert Terry, *For Whites Only* (Detroit Industrial Missions, 1970), cited in Amanda Miriam Chaya Siegel, "Vital Distinctions: Ashkenazi Jews and Whiteness in the Contemporary United States," unpub. paper, Hampshire College, 1998, 4.

8. Peter McLaren, "Decentering Culture," in Wyner, ed., *Current Perspectives on the Culture of Schools*, 244.

9. Ruth Frankenberg, *White Women/Race Matters*, 1.

10. Peggy McIntosh, "Unpacking the Invisible Knapsack," in *Peace and Freedom* (July/August, 1989): 10–12.

11. Toni Morrison, *Playing in the Dark*, 47.

12. Katya Gibel Azoulay, *Black, Jewish, and Interracial*, 93.

13. Gibel Azoulay, "Jewishness after Mount Sinai," *Bridges* 9, no. 1 (2001): 33.

14. Omi and Winant, *Racial Formation*, 53–54.

15. Katya Gibel Azoulay (a.k.a. Mevorach), interview, 8/12/03.

16. See Elinor Langer's compelling analysis, *A Hundred Little Hitlers*.

17. United Press International, "Biracial Baby Remains Interred in All-white Cemetery," Thomasville, Ga., March 28, 1998.

18. The book, for many years available only by mail order, in survivalist stores, or at gun shows from the likes of Oklahoma City bomber Timothy McVeigh, has sold between a quarter of a million and 300,000 copies according to its publishers, an astonishing feat of underground distribution. *The Turner Diaries: A Novel* (Hillsboro, WV: National Vanguard Books, 1995; 1st pub., 1980); on the Web, at http://www.skrewdriver.net/turner23.html.

19. Gibel Azoulay: "There are people here in Iowa . . . as far as they're concerned, a Jew is not a white person. It has nothing to do with what you look like: Jews aren't white. Like an oxymoron." Interview, 8/12/03.

Similarly, when I lived in Maine a Jewish woman—call her Sally—dark-skinned Ashkenazi—told me several times about moving to Maine and hearing about a black woman who'd moved to her town. Sally was excited to meet another "other" until she figured out that she herself was the "black woman." That Sally told this story repeatedly suggests another level of inquiry? What in this story pleased her so much?

20. Gibel Azoulay, interview.

21. Ruth Behar, *Adio Kerida* (Goodbye Dear Love), 2002. See www.ruthbehar .com or contact Women Make Movies. Behar is also a celebrated anthropologist at the University of Michigan.

22. Karen Brodkin, *How Jews Became White Folks;* similarly, Stephen Steinberg, *The Ethnic Myth,* cites such concrete Jewish advantages as urbanity and a high percentage of skilled laborers with experience in manufacturing and commerce.

23. Nancy Ordover, conversation, December 1994. For an excellent discussion, see Omi and Winant, *Racial Formation.*

24. Daniel Itzkovitz, "Secret Temples," in Boyarin and Boyarin, *Jews and Other Differences,* 176–77.

25. Of course everyone is darker or lighter according to context.

26. Sander Gilman, *The Jew's Body,* 174, cites Houston Stewart Chamberlain and Robert Knox for the Jew-as-black-hybrid trope. Theorists about whiteness have mostly ignored Jews, tacitly subsuming Jews into whiteness; e.g., Frankenberg, *White Women/Race Matters.* Frankenberg offers useful insight on whiteness as an unmarked racial category, but misses opportunities to note the significance of *Jewish* as a category, although she and a disproportionate number of the white antiracist activists she interviewed are Jews. Theorists about Jews seem to agree only on some kind of in-between status for Jews: thus Brodkin writes of "racial middleness," a not-quite-white status. Race mongrels are a common white supremacist theme, cf. *The Turner Diaries.*

27. We could add Red Hot Mama singer Sophie Tucker, vs. 1950s television's Molly Goldberg, the eternal-fount-of-chicken-soup. On Jack the Ripper as a Jew, see Gilman, *The Jew's Body.* Woody Allen contains the dichotomy in himself: his nerdy neurotic screen persona vs. his classic dirty-old-man "seduction" of his teenage stepdaughter. Marjorie Morningstar, in the Herman Wouk novel, is probably fiction's first Jewish American Princess, bourgeois to her core, whereas one flagrant characteristic of the woman- and-Jew-hating Jewish American Princess stereotype is her very un-Lewinskyish refusal to sexually service men (as in the sick joke, *make her prove she's not a JAP: make her swallow*).

28. Itzkovitz, "Secret Temples," 180 ff.

29. Gilman, *The Jew's Body,* 174.

30. Published in 1938 to commemorate an exhibition of degenerate music in Düsseldorf. George Mosse, *Toward the Final Solution,* 34.

31. Mary Lowenthal Felstiner, *To Paint Her Life,* 13–18.

32. Purity of blood; that is, untainted by Jewish blood.

33. In Simon et al., eds., *Jews of the Middle East,* passim.

34. Victor Perera, *The Cross and the Pear Tree,* 63.

35. Racial categorizing in the U.S. South sometimes stretched as far as 1/32nd; see discussion, above, about Susie Phipps's attempt to legally turn herself white.

36. George Mosse, *Toward the Final Solution,* xxix.

37. Ibid., xii–xiii, cites: "for example, the Frankfurt schoolmaster Johann Jacob Schudt, writing in 1714, asserted that through conversion to Christianity

Jews lost their peculiar odor, which had been imposed upon them as God's punishment." Johann Jacob Schudt, *Jüdische Merkwürdigkeiten*, I (Frankfurt-am-Main, 1715), 344.

38. Ibid., 28–29.

39. Ibid. The internal quotation Mosse cites from Gobineau, *L'Essai sur l'inégalité des races humaines* (Paris, 1967), 84.

40. Ibid., 14.

41. Gilman, *The Jew's Body*, 172.

42. Itzkovitz, "Secret Temples," 198.

43. Mosse, 29: the Jewish nose seems "to enter popular consciousness . . . as a result of the many broadsides and cartoons in 1753 and 1754 that were published around the attempt to emancipate the Jews in England. The "Jew Bill," as this measure for emancipation in 1753 was popularly called, pushed the Jew into the center of attention. . . . Before that time, Jews in England had been portrayed realistically; but now, to give one example, caricaturists who knew perfectly well what the Jewish banker Samson Gideon really looked like gave him a nose he did not possess in real life. . . ."

44. Gilman, *The Jew's Body*, 173.

45. Mosse, *Toward the Final Solution*, 92 ff. The survey was intended to dispel the myth of a pure German or pure Jewish race.

46. Ibid., 99.

47. Paul Gilroy, *The Black Atlantic*, 213.

48. Nancy Ordover, *American Eugenics*, 41.

49. Ibid., 9.

50. Ibid., 42.

51. Ibid., 41–42.

52. Puerto Ricans, with commonwealth status, continued to come to the mainland.

53. Manhattan Valley, Columbus Avenue between 100th and 110th Streets, was a heavy drug neighborhood.

54. CCCS (Centre for Contemporary Cultural Studies) Collective, *The Empire Strikes Back*, 134; Edward Said, *Orientalism;* both cited in Claire Alexander, "(Dis)Entangling the 'Asian Gang'," in Barnor Hesse, ed., *Un/settled Multiculturalisms*, 137.

55. Ibid., 137, cites Kobena Mercer and Isaac Julien, "Black Masculinity," in Chapman and Rutherford, eds., *Male Order*, 108. Similarly, gay filmmaker Richard Fung, *Looking for My Penis*. Trinidadian-Canadian of Asian origin, Fung describes how (East) Asian men in the West are eroticized but denied agency.

56. It is hard to grasp what makes it socially acceptable to mock Indian accents and culture. David Letterman, for example, seems practically unable to stop himself from making jokes about taxi drivers with turbans.

57. Graenum Berger, *Black Jews in America*, 114.

58. Cf. the "colonial sandwich" created in Africa by British colonial policy, "with Europeans at the top, Asians in the middle, and Africans at the bottom . . ." Avtar Brah, *Cartographies of Diaspora*, 3, 31.

59. Roger Sanjek, "Intermarriage and the Future of Races," in Gregory and Sanjek, eds., *Race*, 113. Sanjek's analysis points to a likely future of blurring of race into ethnicity and absorption of ethnics but with a continued exclusion and isolation of people of African descent.

60. See Edward Said, *Orientalism.*

61. These statistics are everywhere, but the most impressive and depressing array is appearing under the rubric of the Critical Resistance movement, organizing to challenge increasing emphasis on imprisonment as a social solution. See http://www.criticalresistance.org.

62. Table 2A: Employment status of the civilian population by race, sex, and age (last modified date, February 3, 2006); U.S. Bureau of Labor Statistics. Postal Square Building, 2 Massachusetts Ave., NE, Washington, DC 20212-0001; http://www.bls.gov/news.release/empsit.t02.htm.

The "Black Ulysses" stereotype dating from the 1920s from Howard Odum's "Black Ulysses" folklore trilogy depicts black Southern men as inherently (genetically?) out of step with the present, thus incapable of agency, much less of organizing. A recent book by William P. Jones, *The Tribe of Black Ulysses: African American Workers in the Jim Crow South,* draws on history of the southern lumber industry to refute the stereotype. Need it be noted how Black Ulysses resembles the colonized "Oriental" and the Sephardim, especially the women (see Bahloul, below): timeless and passive all.

63. Alexander, "(Dis)Entangling the 'Asian Gang'," 129.

64. See, for example, Dana Takagi, "Post-Civil Rights Politics," in Gregory and Sanjek, eds., *Race*. Also Peter Kwong, *The New Chinatown.*

65. No one was *Asian* either before they came to the United States, where a diversity and history of alliances and antagonisms at least as broad as Europe's got collapsed into a monotype.

66. Daniel and Jonathan Boyarin, *Powers of Diaspora*, 91.

67. Joëlle Bahloul, "Gender, Colonialism," in Levitt and Peskowitz, *Judaism Since Gender*, 82–85.

68. Saraswati Sunindyo, e-mail communication, 2/20/99.

69. For insight into the radical politics and leadership of Chinese in the Asian diaspora (as well as for a fabulous read), see Indonesian writer Pramoedya Ananta Toer's *Buru Quartet.*

70. For example, Michael Lerner, "Jews Are Not White," *Village Voice* 38:33–34.

71. Howard Brotz, ed., *Negro and Social Political Thoughts-1850–1920* (New York: Basic Books, 1966), 241–42, quoted in Berger (1978), 4.

72. McCoy, interview.

73. Karen Brodkin Sacks, "How Did Jews Become White Folks?" in Gregory and Sanjek, *Race*, 87.

74. First expressed by Moses Mendelssohn (1729–86), the central figure in the German Jewish *Haskalah* (Enlightenment), as the ideal of Jewish assimilation.

75. See Sarah Stein, *Making Jews Modern*. Stein argues, among other things, the permeable boundary between Jewish religious and secular culture in both the Russian and Ottoman Empires.

76. At least partly familiar; Sephardic and Ashkenazic practices often use different cantillation (chanting the prayers), and there are also variations between Reform, Conservative, Orthodox, and Reconstructionist.

77. Two noted exceptions: in Ethiopia, where rabbinic teachings were not followed; and a religious sect called Karaism, begun as a reform movement in eighth-century Iraq, a sort of Calvinist Judaism, vaguely Zionist, calling for direct reading of Torah and less meddling by the rabbis. Movable Hebrew type was introduced by the expelled Sephardim to the Islamic world. "Soon a voluminous rabbinic responsa flowed from the presses of Salonika and Istanbul." Jane S. Gerber, "History of The Jews in the Middle East and North Africa," in Simon et al., eds., *Jews of the Middle East*, 14.

78. One is, however, hard put to be a Jew without Jewish community. Even in religious practice, the unit of prayer is not the individual but the minyan, at least ten adult Jews (the Jewish quorum)—in Orthodox Judaism, still ten men, but all other practice of Judaism today includes women, thanks to struggle by religiously observant Jewish feminists. See E. M. Broner, *Mornings and Mourning: A Kaddish Journal* for a moving and sometimes hilarious account of Broner's insistence on saying *Kaddish* (the prayer for the dead) for her father in her neighborhood—Orthodox—shul.

79. There is painful irony in the fact that Yiddish, the beloved *mameloshn* of Jewish socialists, is now a living language only for the ultra-Orthodox Hasidim. See chapter 6 for a mention of the Bund, and suggestions for further reading.

80. This insight shimmers in the remarks of several of the nine artists in "Sister: Mizrahi Women Artists in Israel," in Shula Keshet and Sigal Eshed, eds., *Bridges* 9, no.1 (2001): 49–58. See also Ella Shohat, "Sephardim in Israel," *Social Text* 19/20 (Fall 1988): 1–35.

81. Manjiri Damle, "Bene Israel hail DNA result," *Times of India* (July 24, 2003). The Web is chock full of information about the Cohanim DNA; see http://www.khazaria.com/genetics/abstracts-cohen-levite.html.

82. See Aisha Berger's poem, "Nose is a country . . . I am the second generation," in Kaye/Kantrowitz and Klepfisz, eds., *Tribe of Dina*, 134–38. One of Berger's many illuminating images: "this unruly semitic landmass on my face." The era of Jewish nose jobs is not over—witness the heartbreak of Jennifer Gray, post-*Dirty Dancing*—though Barbra Streisand broke the spell that mirrored Jewish noses as inherently ugly.

83. Ella Shohat, "Reflections of an Arab Jew," in Khazzoom, *Camel*, 119.

84. Christians usually see this as a generous feature of their religion—after all, anyone can become one, forgetting that not all of us wish to.

85. From http://usinfo.state.gov/products/pubs/muslimlife/demograp.htm.

2. BLACK/JEWISH IMAGINARY AND REAL

1. See Katz-Fishman and Scott, "The Increasing Significance of Class," in Franklin et al., eds., *African Americans and Jews*, 313–14: "Between 1910 and 1970 6.5 million Blacks migrated from countryside to city; 5 million did so after 1940.

. . . the cruel irony for Black workers was just as they were making their way into the manufacturing jobs in the industrial heartland . . . ," those jobs were beginning to disappear.

2. James Baldwin, "Negroes Are Anti-Semitic Because," in *Black Anti-Semitism and Jewish Racism*, 3–12.

3. I allude to *The Secret Relationship*, the not-so-secret relationship that blames Jews for the slave trade (rather than engaging Jews in discussions of responsibility along with the many peoples who participated in the enslavement of Africans).

4. Marshall Stevenson, Jr., "African Americans and Jews," in Franklin et al., eds., *African Americans and Jews*, grants the possibility that a sense of common oppression might have motivated Jews to work against racism, but notes, "given the racially polarized and anti-semitic climate of Detroit in the 1930s and early 1940s, these leftists very likely saw racism and anti-semitism as products of the same flawed and corrupt capitalist system," 242.

5. JFREJ activist Rachel Mattson describes the importance for her of this solidarity work: "[the winter] JFREJ spent every Sunday afternoon on the picket line in front of the Silver Palace with the Chinese Staff and Workers Association—which culminated in a victory, something I'd never experienced in my years of protesting." From "Overheard in the Trenches," in *Mensches in the Trenches* (program celebrating JFREJ's tenth anniversary, December 10, 2000), 14.

6. Hill, "Black-Jewish Conflict," in Franklin et al., eds., *African Americans and Jews*, 276.

7. Margarita Lopez, quoted in Earl Caldwell, "When a House Can't Be Your Home," *New York Daily News*, June 1, 1983, 4; cited in Hill, "Black-Jewish Conflict," in Franklin et al., eds., *African Americans and Jews*, 277.

8. Ibid., 278.

9. Ibid., 264.

10. See Stevenson's fascinating narrative about this premature affirmative action struggle, complete with charges (by Walter Reuther and his ilk) that "there's no one qualified," "Organized Labor," in Franklin et al., eds., *African Americans and Jews*, 251 ff.

11. Women of color colleagues at elite academic institutions report that their white students frequently expect pampering and caretaking. This expectation is usually unconscious and automatic.

12. "Though the plaintiff named was a different person with the same surname, a black man named Oliver Brown"; Nussbaum Cohen, Jewish Telegraph Agency, 1/14/2000, discussing the then-new book by Rabbi Marc Schneier, *Shared Dreams: Martin Luther King, Jr. and the Jewish Community*.

13. Marshall Stevenson, Jr., "The Politics of Households and Homes," paper presented at the Ninth Annual Conference on Black-Jewish Relations," Dillard University, New Orleans, Louisiana (April 14–15, 1998). See also Schultz, *Going South*.

14. Nussbaum Cohen, "Shades of Gray," *Jewish Week*, June 28, 2000.

15. "and has never been forgiven for by people every one of whom had heard *shvartse* at least once in her or his life without protest." Kaye/Kantrowitz, "Some

Pieces of Jewish Left," *My Jewish Face*, 208. (*Shvartse*, Yiddish for *black*, when used as a noun, is widely understood as pejorative; see Yavilah McCoy, below.)

16. Jackson has publicly and repeatedly demonstrated growth and change. One wishes one could say the same for Minister Farrakhan who, as I write, has issued a Nation of Islam press release 2/26/06 claiming, "It's the wicked Jews, the false Jews that are promoting lesbianism, homosexuality" and blaming that darned "Synagogue of Satan" for pumping out evil. See NOI website http://www.noi.org. Jew-demonizing rhetoric in the African American community has not vanished but it no longer occupies the space it claimed in the 1990s.

17. On the contrary, research conducted in 1986 among 189 African American Protestants indicated a tendency toward favorable attitudes about Jews, explained by a shared connection with the Jewish Bible. (This same analysis argues that Leonard Dinnerstein's explanation of anti-semitism as a function of Christian ideology is better suited to explain European anti-semitism.) V. P. Franklin, "The Portrayal of Jews in *The Autobiography of Malcolm X*," in Franklin et al., eds. (1998), 301–302.

18. The theory underpinning this is, of course, Fanon, *The Wretched of the Earth.*

19. As in chapter 1.

20. Gibel Azoulay, "Jewishness after Mount Sinai," *Bridges* 9, no. 1 (2001): 32.

21. Bernard J. Wolfson, "African American Jews: Dispelling Myths," in Chireau and Deutsch, eds., *Black Zion*, 38. According to Michael Gelbwasser, "Organization for black Jews claims 200,000 in U.S.," *Boston Jewish Advocate* (April 10, 1998): 38, estimates range from 100,000–250,000.

22. Navonah (a pseudonym at her request and choice), interview, 1/18/05.

23. African American who converted to Judaism; see *Lovesong.*

24. The estimate is Barry Kosmin's, who directed a study for the Council of Jewish Federation's National Jewish Population in 1990, as reported in Wolfson, "African American Jews: Dispelling Myths," in Chireau and Deutsch, eds., *Black Zion*, 38–39.

25. Carolivia Herron, "Peacesong," in *Bridges* 9, no. 1 (2001): 9–14.

26. Gibel Azoulay, "Jewishness after Mount Sinai," *Bridges* 9, no. 1 (2001): 43: "In 1963, the New York Times published a report on a doctoral project conducted in 1960 by Charles Smith (Teachers College at Columbia University) which noted that in interracial marriages in New York between whites and Blacks most of the white spouses were Jewish. . . ."

27. Graenum Berger, *Black Jews in America*, 126, cites Louis A. Berman, *Jews and Intermarriage.*

28. Ibid., 125, cites Calvin C. Hernton, *Sex and Racism in America* (Garden City: Doubleday, 1965).

29. Gibel Azoulay, "Jewishness after Mount Sinai," *Bridges* 9, no. 1 (2001): 43.

30. Gibel Azoulay, *Black, Jewish, and Interracial*, 27.

31. Hettie Jones, *How I Became Hettie Jones*, and her daughter, Lisa Jones, "Mama's White," in *Bulletproof Diva*. Also Rebecca Walker, *Black, White, and Jewish.*

32. Albert J. Raboteau, "Exodus, Ethiopia," in Hutchison and Lehmann, eds., *Many Are Chosen*, 192.

33. Howard M. Brotz, *The Black Jews of Harlem*, 10.

34. Rabbi S. B. Levy, President of the Israelite Board of Rabbis, at website http://www.blackjews.org/american_communities.htm outlines three kinds of Israelite synagogues, which he names *Rabbinic* (traditional); *Karaites* ("very similar to that sect of Israelites in ancient times who rejected equating the Talmud [oral lore] with the Torah [the five books of Moses from Genesis to Deuteronomy]"; and *Messianic* (believes Jesus is the Messiah.

35. Brotz, *The Black Jews of Harlem*, 27 and passim.

36. In Queens, Harlem, Chicago, Philadelphia, and two in Brooklyn; at website http://www.blackjews.org/american_communities.htm. I also know of congregations in Atlanta, St. Louis, and the Bronx.

37. Tobin et al., *In Every Tongue*, 67 ff. Their summary, 80, of Jewish life in Africa is invaluable.

38. See interview with Rabbi Capers Funnye, chapter 5.

39. Tobin et al., *In Every Tongue*, 103, cites the longevity and consistency of practice of several congregations of Hebrew Israelites "who are in every respect, deeply observant Jews, who practice no other religion. And yet, their legitimacy —the Jewishness of their blood and therefore their ability to bear Jewish children—is placed under a cloud of doubt by some Jews."

40. From *New York Times* (July 2, 1976), quoted in Berger, *Black Jews in America*, 25–26.

41. E. Franklin Frazier, *The Negro in the United States* (New York: Macmillan, 1949), 87, quoted in Brotz, *The Black Jews of Harlem*, 1.

42. Gilroy, *The Black Atlantic*, 207. Also, Raboteau, "Exodus, Ethiopia," in Hutchison and Lehmann, eds, *Many Are Chosen*, 176 ff.

43. See E. David Cronon, *Black Moses*. Gilroy, *The Black Atlantic*, 207, following Raboteau, cites the importance of the Exodus story for the slaves, and notes, "The heroic figure of Moses proved especially resonant for slaves and their descendants."

44. Berger, *Black Jews in America*, 77 ff. Ford served as a rabbi (though "there is no record of his either being converted to Judaism or having been formally ordained"), and taught Hebrew and Judaism to Wentworth A. Matthews, who served as rabbi for the Commandment Keepers (the "Black Jews of Harlem") until Matthews's death in 1973. One story has it, when Ford's Harlem congregation "was hauled into court for failure to pay its rent, he spoke Yiddish to Judge Jacob Panken, a prominent Jewish socialist and active in many Jewish secular organizations, and argued his case into acquittal." From *New York Amsterdam News* (Dec. 23, 1925), quoted in Berger, 77.

Garvey strongly identified with fascist leadership, and has often been associated with anti-semitism. Paul Gilroy, *Against Race*, 232, remarks, "Garvey himself compared his organization's activities to those of Hitler and Mussolini." Gilroy quotes Garvey, from J. A. Rogers, *The World's Great Men of Color* (J. A. Rogers, c. 1947), 420.

We were the first fascists. We had disciplined men, women and children in training for the liberation of Africa. The black masses saw that in this extreme nationalism lay their only hope and readily supported it. Mussolini copied fascism from me but the Negro reactionaries sabotaged it.

45. Hollis R. Lynch, *Edward Wilmot Blyden, 1832–1912: Pan Negro Patriot* (Oxford and New York: Oxford University Press, 1967), 54, quoted in Gilroy, *The Black Atlantic*, 208.

46. Edward Wilmot Blyden, *The Jewish Question* (Liverpool: Lionel Hart, 1989), 7, quoted in ibid., 209.

47. Herron, "Peacesong," *Bridges* 9, no. 1 (2001): 10.

48. Brotz, *The Black Jews of Harlem*, 47.

49. Ibid., 47.

50. Berger, *Black Jews in America*, 22.

51. Maxwell Whiteman, "Introductory Essay," *The Kidnapped and the Ransomed* (Philadelphia: Jewish Publication Society, 1970), 21–24, quoted in ibid., 4.

52. Whiteman, in ibid., 15; see also the story of Uncle Billy, 22–23. Beejhy Barhany tells another primal burial story about the Yemenites arriving in Israel. A baby died and the question was where could the baby be buried? "The Ashkenazim said the Yemenite aren't Ashkenazi, you cannot bury the baby here. And the Sephardim said, we don't know. Eventually the Sephardic was the one who agreed to bury the child, and Yemenite Jews are now considered as Sephardic." Barhany, interview.

53. Hasia Diner, *In the Almost Promised Land*. At least one Yiddish periodical evaded tsarist censorship by focusing on "the tempestuous relations between blacks and whites in the United States" instead of on ethnic minorities in Imperial Russia, presumably counting on their readers' ability to make the connections. Stein, *Making Jews Modern*, 90.

54. According to Diner, *In the Almost Promised Land*, 30, some 77 percent of those who read the Yiddish press apparently also could read English.

55. Ibid., 69.

56. Fredric Jameson, "History and Class Consciousness as an Unfinished Project," *Rethinking Marxism* 1, no. 1 (Spring 1988): 70, quoted in Gilroy, *The Black Atlantic*, 206.

57. In the early 1970s, I wrote a doctoral dissertation on women in the tragedies of Shakespeare and his successors, examining why men choose to write about women. I argued that men in an increasingly chaotic period feel powerless, and so are drawn to explore the condition of powerlessness. The parallel with Jews exploring the experience of African Americans is provocative. The full argument can be found in Melanie Kaye, *"The Sword Philippan."*

58. Diner, *In the Almost Promised Land*, xii, xv.

59. Ibid., 99.

60. Kishinev was the site of a particularly devastating pogrom. Diner, ibid., reports a difference in coverage. The Yiddish papers dwelt on gory details; the English language papers were more discreet.

61. Ibid., 55.

62. Ibid., 79.

63. Ibid., 100.

64. Ibid., 202.

65. A. Philip Randolph, African American socialist, was a journalist who became the brilliant organizer—and president—of the Brotherhood of Sleeping Car Porters. Sidney Hillman, Jewish socialist, was a leader of the Amalgamated Clothing Workers of America. The Harlem Labor Committee, "founded in 1935, was a federation of all black trade unionists in New York City." Ibid., 210, 211.

66. Diner, ibid., cites these events as determining the starting point of her analysis.

67. See Rod Bush, *Black Nationalism*.

68. Conversation 1993 with the late Gary Rubin, stalwart progressive with the American Jewish Committee.

69. Rachel Pomerance, "Jewish-Black Ties Loosen."

70. The driver was part of the Lubavitcher rebbe's (leader's) entourage, a fact that exacerbated tensions, as the Lubavitch community was widely seen by Crown Heights blacks as enjoying special privileges, including the right to a weekly motorcade.

71. Giuliani's yarmulke fetish was satirized in a *New Yorker* cartoon that showed a woman in a store telling the clerk, "I want to buy a yarmulke like Ruby Giuliani's."

72. Unfortunately, nothing—as far as I know—for the teenage girls.

73. Stevenson, "Cincinnati Is Not New York," unpublished paper quoted in Friedman, *What Went Wrong?* 351.

74. Davis was elected with substantial Jewish support in 1943. See Gerald Horne, "Black, White, and Red," in Brettschneider, ed., *The Narrow Bridge*, 123–35.

75. Jonathan Kaufman, *Broken Alliance*. As Debra Schultz, *Going South*, 27, note 33, points out, these figures are often cited though Kaufman doesn't identify his source.

76. See my discussion of Jewish nonsaliency in the civil rights movement, Melanie Kaye/Kantrowitz, "Stayed on Freedom," in Brettschneider, ed., *The Narrow Bridge*, 105–22.

77. Goodman was killed along with James Chaney and Michael Schwerner; often cited as movement martyrs, though Schwerner's wife Rita, activist in her own right, was quick to tell the press, "You wouldn't be here interviewing me if my husband was Black." Schultz, *Going South*, 66. I have heard Rita Schwerner on several occasions point out that Chaney's death would not have received the media attention if not for white (Jewish) Schwerner and Goodman.

78. The first sentence is Saperstein quoted by Pomerance, "Jewish-Black Ties Loosen"; the following half sentence is Pomerance commenting on Saperstein.

79. Gilroy, *The Black Atlantic*, 213.

80. Baldwin, "Negroes Are Anti-Semitic," in *Black Anti-Semitism*, 11.

81. Gilroy, *The Black Atlantic*, 207.

82. This synagogue "claimed an organic relationship to the Jews of Ethiopia, the *Beta Yisroel.*" Chireau and Deutsch, "Introduction," in *Black Zion*, 7.

83. See Gibel Azoulay, "Jewishness after Mount Sinai," *Bridges* 9, no.1 (2001): 37.

84. At least since Clarence Thomas, as Angela Davis has articulated, "racial or cultural essentialism has been a high risk assumption; "Rope," in Anna Deavere Smith, *Fires in the Mirror*, 27–32.

85. Horne, "Black, White, and Red," in Brettschneider, *The Narrow Bridge*, 123.

86. Cynthia Enloe, *Bananas, Beaches, and Bases.*

87. Sunindyo, "Feminism and Militarism in Indonesia," lecture, Hamilton College, January, 1996.

88. You have to wonder where Malcolm was heading, intriguingly turning away from narrow nationalism.

89. Lerner and West, *Jews & African Americans.*

90. Paul Berman, *African Americans and Jews.*

91. See Yavilah McCoy's narrative about her college experience in chapter 5.

92. Jewish student life on campus is commonly supported through a network of Hillels, which are to Jews as Newman Clubs are to Catholics. Naturally the politics of the Jewish student activities are controlled by the funding sources, typically though not always centrist-to-right.

93. Simple apathy and narcissism don't register or warrant attention. Cf. "As one observer, on the eve of the Simpson verdict, put it: 'When O.J. gets off, the whites will riot the way we whites do: leave the cities, go to Idaho or Oregon or Arizona, vote for Gingrich . . . and punish the blacks by closing the day-care programs and cutting off their Medicaid.'" Quoted in Frank Rich, "The L.A. Shock Treatment," *The New York Times* (October 4, 1995), cited in William Julius Wilson, *When Work Disappears*, xx.

94. Some campuses I visited in this way include Antioch, Oberlin, SUNY-New Paltz, Columbia University, Brooklyn College, University of Wisconsin-Madison, University of Washington-Seattle, and University of California-Santa Cruz.

95. For example, with Kathleen Saadat at Hamilton College and at University of California-Santa Cruz; with the late Patricia Ruffin at Brooklyn College, with Linda Burnham at Antioch; with Patricia Williams at Columbia.

96. Example: A conference at Dillard University in New Orleans in April, 1998, took a stab at answering the question. Dillard's president, Michael Lomax, appointed as organizers for the Dillard's National Center for African American-Jewish Relations Ninth annual conference feminists Beverly Guy-Sheftall and Miriam Peskowitz. Keynote speakers were myself and African American legal scholar Kimberlè Crenshaw, with a closing reading by writer Rebecca Walker. The tone of the conference was holistic—not "Ladies Auxiliary" but "A Dialogue on Race from Women's Perspective." Instead of focusing on recycled examples of antagonism, new terrain was explored; for example, the talk by Marshall Stevenson on housekeepers cited above.

97. Or—in the case of the American Jewish Committee—after significant internal struggle, kept silent.

98. I had the surprise pleasure of learning the identity of the brave San Francisco State Professor at the Western Jewish Studies Association Third Annual Conference (University of Arizona, Tucson, April 6–8, 1997), where I presented an earlier version of this section, praising the mystery woman's courage, and Professor Lyles, a sister speaker on the panel on "Contested Identities," identified herself as the actor.

99. Indeed, it's tempting to suggest gender as a possible partial explanation for the ILGWU—a Jewish Socialist largely women's union—making it a priority to organize African American women workers. See Diner, *In the Almost Promised Land*, 199 ff.

100. The issue of gay rights, especially gay marriage, splits a generally more progressive coalition (the Kerry campaign), with liberal and moderate Jews lining up in support, while many otherwise liberal Christians—people of color and white—see gay marriage as contrary to god's will.

101. Alain Finkielkraut, *The Imaginary Jew.*

102. I think that lesbians and those bisexuals who truly identify with and stake their claim with queers often see these interconnections most clearly because our movement and communities, while far from fully racially integrated, still are more inclusive and multiracial than most other places.

103. It's interesting to realize that the considerable Jewish support for protest against the police murder of Amadou Diallo in 1999 was characterized solely in terms of black–Jewish alliance, although Diallo was Muslim and an immigrant. *Black* has certainly not disappeared as a salient category, but Muslim and immigrant are, at this time, hyper-salient.

104. New Jersey poet laureate Amiri Baraka responded

> Who knew the WORLD Trade Center was gonna get bombed
> Who told 4,000 Israeli workers at the Twin Towers
> To stay home that day
> Why did Sharon stay away?

Other versions claimed Jews rather than Israelis were warned; in an anti-semitic world, Israelis and Jews are interchangeable. The public Jewish response was predictable: in the name of Jews, people tried to force Baraka out of the poet laureate office, which could not be done; tried to force him to resign, which he refused; and finally tried to defund the position and so cancel the office of New Jersey poet laureate: this is what happened.

3. WHO IS THIS STRANGER?

1. From Tobin et al., *In Every Tongue*, 68; Avi Beker, ed., *Jewish Communities of the World* (Minneapolis: Lerner Publications Company, Institute of the World Jewish Congess, 1998). In 2005 according to one set of statistics, Jews were .227 percent of the world's people. Of these, 5.9 million, the largest community, lived in the United States. The second largest, 5.02 million, lived in Israel. Jewish populations included, in descending order of numbers: Russia, 717,101; France,

606,561; Argentina, 395, 379; Canada, 393,660; United Kingdom, 302,207; Ukraine, 142,276; Germany, 107,160; Brazil, 95,125; Australia, 90,406; South Africa, 88,688; Belarus, 72,103; Hungary, 60,041; Mexico, 53,101; Belgium, 51,821; Spain, 48,409; Netherlands, 32,814; Moldova, 31,187; Uruguay, 30743; Italy, 30,213; Venezuela, 25,375; Poland, 24,999; Chile, 20,900; Iran, 20,405; Ethiopia, 20,000 . . . I am cutting off arbitrarily at Jewish populations less than 20,000. All these statistics are from http://www.jewishvirtuallibrary.org/jsource/Judaism/jewpophtml dated 2005.

2. I refer readers to the extremely useful volume by Tobin et al., *In Every Tongue.* Here I will only suggest the broad range of Jewish identity, and the impact of this information on how Jews in the United States envision the Jewish future.

3. Gordon, interview.

4. "We say 'estimated' not just because of the traditional Jewish reluctance to count its people, but also because of the impossible task of reaching out to so many unaffiliated Jews in the Diaspora." http://www.jewishvirtuallibrary.org/jsource/Judaism/jewpop.html.

5. Hebrew Israelites are sometimes called the "Black Hebrews"; see website http://members.aol.com/Blackjews/bjew1.html. The latter suggests for additional reading Brotz, *The Black Jews of Harlem;* Ella J. Hughley, *The Truth About Hebrew-Israelites;* Yosef Ben Jochannan, *We the Black Jews Vol. I and II;* and Rudolph R. Windsor and El Hagahn, *From Babylon to Timbuktu: A History of the Ancient Black Races Including the Black Hebrews.* (Windsor Golden Series (1988).

6. See Gordon's interview, "Jews Were All People of Color," in chapter 5.

7. Rabbi Angela Warnick Buchdahl, unpublished sermon, Rodeph Shalom, New York City.

8. Hilary Than, from "Marriage and Conversion," in *Counting,* reprinted in *Bridges* 9, no.1 (2001): 20.

9. *Sephardim* commonly "refers to Jews whose ancestors fled or were expelled from Iberia [around] 1492 who maintained a distinct Hispanic culture, whereas North African Jews (known as *Maghribim* or *Mizrahim,* some of whom were originally Sephardim) were Arabized in culture and language. Campos, "Between 'Beloved Ottomania,' 5.

10. Scheindlin, "Merchants and Intellectuals," in Biale, ed., *Cultures of the Jews,* 318.

11. Generalizations are elusive: Iran and Afghanistan seem to defy the experience of the rest of the region, and there are periods of movement in various regions from relative freedom to increased ghettoization and isolation.

12. Sheindlin, "Merchants and Intellectuals," in Biale, ed., *Cultures of the Jews,* 318.

13. Scheindlin, "Merchants and Intellectuals," in Biale, ed., *Cultures of the Jews,* 317, argues against using "Judeo-Arabic" for the language, which he says was just Arabic written in Hebrew characters. He restricts the term *Judeo-Arabic* for the culture.

14. Ella Shohat, "Arab Jew," in Khazzoom, ed., *Camel,* 120.

15. In Bayoumi and Rubin, eds.; *The Edward Said Reader.*

16. Orly Halpern, "Iraqi-Israeli Jews Plan to Visit Their 'Roots'," *Jerusalem Post*, December 27, 2005.

17. Yemenite woman's song, from Israel, in Ashton and Umansky, eds., *Four Centuries*, 186–87.

18. Alcalay, *After Jews and Arabs*, 290, note 11, cites Shlomo Swirski, *Education in Israel: Schooling for Inequality* (Tel Aviv: Breirot, 1990).

19. Ibid., 40, cites Swirski; also, 290, note 7, Ya'akov Nahon *The Nahon Report* (Jerusalem: Institute of Applied Social Research, 1988).

20. Alcalay, "Intellectual Life," in Simon, et al., eds., *Jews in the Middle East*. According to Ephraim Isaac, "Yemenite Jews, or 'Temani' in Hebrew, are great religious scholars, the only Jewish people in the world who read the Hebrew bible aloud accompanied by the recitation of the Aramaic Targum, according to the ancient synagogue custom described in the Talmud." Ephraim Isaac, "Judaism and Islam in Yemen," quoted in Tobin et al., *In Every Tongue*, 76, 214, note 20.

21. Shohat, "Arab Jew," in Khazzoom, ed., *Camel*, 118.

22. For audiotapes on the crypto-Jews made for National Public Radio, contact Nan Rubin, Project Director, "The Hidden Jews of New Mexico Radio Project," NanRubin@aol.com.

23. Perera, *The Cross and the Pear Tree*, 41.

24. Ibid., 63.

25. See Gerber, *The Jews of Spain*.

26. Perera, *The Cross and the Pear Tree*, 55.

27. Winters in the concentration camps of Eastern Europe were especially devastating to Jews from Mediterranean climates.

28. See Behar's "Poem XI," in chapter 6, the section called "Home."

29. Ben-Ur, "Where Diasporas Met," (Diss.), 241.

30. Isaac de Pinto, *Apologie pour la nation juive ou Réflexions critiques sur le premier chapitre du VII Tome des Oeuvres de Monsieur de Voltaire au sujet des Juifs* (Amsterdam, 1762), 16, quoted in Yosef Kaplan, "Bom Judesmo," in Biale, ed., *Cultures of the Jews*, 649–50.

31. Simon, "Europe in the Middle East," in Simon et al., eds., *Jews in the Middle East*, 21.

32. On Sephardi in the former Ottoman Empire, see interview with Haya Shalom in Kaye/Kantrowitz and Klepfisz, eds., *The Tribe of Dina*, 214–226. Shalom, a fourth- or fifth-generation Jerusalemite and a political radical, was raised in a traditional Ladino-speaking family to identify as *samakhet*—pure Sephardim. She describes Ashkenazi racism against Sephardi, *samakhet* racism against Arab Jews; and the complexities of passing and assimilation in Israel. See, also, Ella Shohat's analysis of Israeli Eurocentrism, *Israeli Cinema*, and in the anthology she coedited with Robert Stam, *Unthinking Eurocentrism*.

33. Zvi Zohar, "Religion: Rabbinic Tradition," in Simon et al., eds., *Jews in the Middle East*. Zohar argues compellingly that Sephardic elasticity mirrors Islamic society, as opposed to the religious fragmentation of the Christian West.

34. Philip Skippon, "An Account of a Journey Made Thro' Part of the Low Countries, Germany, Italy, and France (1663), in *A Collection of Voyages and Travels*, vol. 6 (London, 1732), 406; quoted in Kaplan, Yosef. "Bom Judesmo," in Biale, ed. *Cultures of the Jews*, 639.

35. Simon, "Europe in the Middle East," in Simon, et al., eds., *Jews in the Middle East*, 24.

36. Gerber, "History of the Jews," in Simon et al., *Jews of the Middle East*, 14.

37. "Blood libel" is the charge that Jews require non-Jewish blood to make matzoh. The Damascus Blood Libel of 1840 began in Syria with the disappearance of an Italian friar and his Muslim servant. Jews were charged with kidnapping and murder, and many were arrested, tortured, and sentenced to death. American Jews, few and scattered, had never before responded collectively, but they joined in action from several cities to pressure the president of the United States to intervene with the head of the Ottoman Empire. The pressure from the United States, England, and France worked, and those arrested were released. Source, American Jewish Historical Society, http://www.us-israel.org/jsource/anti-semitism/reaction.html.

38. Simon, "Europe in the Middle East," in Simon, et al., eds., *Jews in the Middle East*, 24; Laskier and Simon, "Economic Life," in Ibid., 38. See also Stein, *Making Jews Modern*, 13, discussion of the Alliance, whereby "French Jewry . . . offered itself as a model."

39. Ilana Halevi, *A History of the Jews*, trans., A. M. Berrett (London and Atlantic Highlands (New Zealand: Zed Books, 1987), 208–209, quoted in Alcalay (1993), 37.

40. Alcalay, interview.

41. Ben-Ur, "Where Diasporas Met," (Diss.) 55–56.

42. Ibid., 56, cites Joseph M. Papo, *Sephardim in Twentieth Century America*, 43, quoted without attribution.

43. Tobin et al., *In Every Tongue*, 94.

44. Ibid., 95; they cite Michael Pollack, "The Jews of Kaifeng," *Sino-Judaic Institute*, http://www.sino-judaic.org/jewsofkaifeng.html.

45. Ibid., 95–96.

46. Ibid., 89 ff. They cite some of the political explosiveness around the issue of aliyah, 93–94.

47. Ibid., 89–90.

48. Ibid., 90. http://www.jewishvirtuallibrary.org/jsource/Judaism/jewpop .html.

49. Orpa Slapak, ed., *The Jews of India: A Story of Three Communities* (Jerusalem: Israel Museum, 1995). Also Nathan Katz's *Who Are the Jews of India?* (Berkeley: University of California, 2000), discusses racial division and complexity in each of the three communities (minus B'nai Menashe). I am drawing on Tobin et al., *In Every Tongue* and on the website http://www.english.emory.edu/Bahri/Jews .html.

50. Tobin et al., *In Every Tongue*, 92 ff.

51. Gordon, interview.

52. Tobin et al., *In Every Tongue*, 78.

53. See Ibid., 215–16, notes 33 and 34.

54. Flora Samuel, "The Bene Israel Cradle Ceremony," *Bridges* 7, no.1, (1997): 43–44.

55. http://www.jewishvirtuallibrary.org/jsource/Judaism/jewpop.html.

56. Before the large-scale immigration of Russian Jews, the proportion was estimated at more than 60 percent Sephardim/Mizrahim and the rest Ashkenazim. Where do the Jews of Southern Africa, India, Asia get counted? In any case, the influx of Russian Jews has shifted proportions once again.

57. "and when I told the woman—a survivor, a fighter in the Warsaw Ghetto Uprising—about the Holocaust conference in Maine, and how many of the people there had known *nothing*, she said, *They still know nothing*." Kaye/Kantrowitz, "Kaddish," in Beck, *Nice Jewish Girls*, 107–11.

58. In the United States, as in Germany, pressure to assimilate to the dominant vernacular was intense.

59. Salo W. Baron, "Ghetto and Emancipation," *Menorah Journal* 14 (June 1928): 515–26, cited in Chireau and Deutsch, eds. *Black Zion*, 5.

60. See the film *Image Before My Eyes* by Aviva Kempner; also available as a book (photographic essay) by Lucjan Dobroszycki, for a startling and brilliant portrait of the range and variety of Ashkenazi life before the war. Also see Klepfisz, "Secular Jewish Identity," in Kaye/Kantrowitz and Klepfisz, eds., *The Tribe of Dina;* and "*di mames, dos loshn*," *Bridges* 4, no.1 (1994). Klezmer music (Ashkenazi jazz/blues) is in revival with groups such as Brave Old World, the Klezmatics, and Mikveh, contemporary awesome talents such as Michael Alpert, Alicia Svigals, Lorin Sklamberg, Frank London, Adrienne Cooper, and archivist Henry Sapoznik.

61. Gottlieb, interview.

62. Mendes-Flohr and Reinharz, eds., *The Jew in the Modern World*. The 1995 edition offers only a few tokenistic tidbits outside of the West.

63. "Estimated Number of Jews Killed by the Nazis," Leon Poliakov and Josef Wulf, eds., *Das Dritte Reich und die Juden: Dokumente und Aufsaetze* (Berlin: Arani-Verlag, GmbH, 1955), 229, cited in ibid., 520.

64. See Rachel Wahba, "Benign Ignorance," in Khazzoom, ed., *Camel*, 57.

65. Kyla Wazana Tompkins, "Home is Where You Make It," in Khazzoom, ed., *Camel*, 137.

66. Simon, "Europe in the Middle East," in Simon, et al., eds., *Jews in the Middle East*, 27.

67. Down from between 4½ –7 million Jews in the world in 70 C.E., under the Roman Empire. "The Demography of Modern Jewish History," Uriah Zevi Engelman, "Sources of Jewish Statistics," in *The Jews: Their History, Culture, and Religion*, ed., L. Finkelstein (Philadelphia: JPS, 1966), vol. 2, 1517–19, cited in Mendes-Flohr and Reinharz, eds., *The Jew in the Modern World*, 525.

68. The publication cited is *Moment* magazine, whose depiction of Tunisians exactly "orientalizes" them, in the language of Edward Said.

69. "News & Views from Ivri-NASAWI," week of January 15, 2000.

70. Tobin et al., *In Every Tongue*, otherwise excellent, used this unfortunate terminology, naming as *diverse* all Jews of color, so that the center remains with Euro/Jews.

71. Shoshana Simons, "Reflections Sparked by *In Gerangl*," in *Jews for Racial and Economic Justice Bulletin* 11 (April 1994).

72. I learned the term from Irena Klepfisz, and she, I, and Bernice Mennis used it as the title of a handbook on resisting anti-semitism in the anthology we coedited; Kaye/Kantrowitz and Klepfisz, eds., *The Tribe of Dina*, 334–46.

73. Edward Alcosser, in his talk titled "Outside *Yidishkayt:* Sephardic Progressive Thought," at *In Gerangl:* Teach-In on Progressive Jewish History, organized by Jews for Racial and Economic Justice (Cooper Union, New York City, December 1993).

74. See Wahba, "Benign Ignorance," 55, for a touching admission, "I joke about having become 'allergic' to Yiddish"—because of relentless Ashkenazi presumptions; e.g., Shohat, "Sephardim in Israel," in *Social Text* 19/20 (Fall 1988): 8: "'Those who do not speak Yiddish,' Golda Meir once said, 'are not Jews.'"

75. Kaplan, "Bom Judesmo," in Biale, ed., *Cultures of the Jews*, 640.

76. Alcalay, *After Jews and Arabs*, 49.

77. Ibid., 10. Alcalay cites Sami Mikhael's novel *Refuge* (Philadelphia, New York, Jerusalem: Jewish Publication Society, 1988), translated by Edward Grossman into English eleven years after it first appeared in Hebrew.

78. Ibid., 50, 234, 235; Also Stillman, *Jews of Arab Lands*, 150–51.

79. Ben-Ur, "Where Diasporas Met," (Diss.) 5, 24, 264.

80. Joanne Lehrer, our blessed intern at that time, and I conducted the amazing and frustrating linguistic search.

81. Ironically, the snazzy rhyme, *Menches in the Trenches*, is Yiddishly incorrect: Mentshn is the plural of mentsh.

82. Thanks to Emily Levy, who supplied us with *con peña;* we reached Ms. Levy through her daughter, writer Gloria Kirchheimer.

83. AJS, December 21–23, 2003, Boston, session 6.5. I am grateful to the participants for sharing handouts, syllabi, and copies of their talks.

84. Marina Rustow, talk at AJS, December 21–23, 2003.

85. Alcalay, in an interview, cites Maimonides, the greatest Jewish philosopher of the Middle Ages, who came from Spain and spent years in Egypt. Alcalay asks: So was he European or Arab—or both?

86. Shohat, "Arab Jew," in Khazzoom, ed., *Camel*, 121.

87. Knafo Setton, "Jew/Arab/Woman," in Kahn et al., eds., *Jewish Women from Muslim Societies Speak*, 19.

88. Wahba, "Benign Ignorance," in Khazzoom, ed., *Camel.*

89. See Yelena Khanga, *Soul to Soul.*

90. Gibel Azoulay, "Jewishness after Mount Sinai," *Bridges* 9, no.1 (2001): 32.

91. Knafo Setton, "The Life and Times," in Khazzoom, ed., *Camel*, 5.

92. Ibid., 8.

93. Scheindlin, "Merchants and Intellectuals," in Biale, ed., *Cultures of the Jews*, 327.

94. Biale, ed., *Cultures of the Jews*, xx.

95. Gilroy, *The Black Atlantic*, 7.

96. Schnee, interview.

97. *The National Jewish Population Survey 2000–2001*, bankrolled by the United Jewish Committees, was not released until 2003. Its findings have been widely criticized. I am indebted for information on the *Jewish Community Study of New York 2002* (conducted by researchers paid by the United Jewish Appeal-Federation of New York) to Daniel Lang/Levitsky's presentation at the Jews for Racial and Economic Justice retreat in September 2003.

98. Tobin et al., *In Every Tongue*, 19 ff.

99. E-mail communication from Gary Tobin, March 11, 2004.

100. Tobin et al., *In Every Tongue*, 21–22 ff.

101. Ibid., 51.

102. Cf. Sanjek, "Intermarriage and the Future, in Gregory and Sanjek, eds., *Race*, 103–30.

103. Tom Segev, *1949: The First Israelis* (Jerusalem: Domino Press, 1984) (Hebrew), cited in Shohat "Sephardim in Israel," in *Social Text* 19/20 (Fall 1988): 17.

104. At the Jews of Color Speak Out (10/20/03), see chapter 5 below.

105. Toni Eisendorf, "An Ethiopian Gilgul," *Bridges* 9, no. 1 (2001): 25.

106. Salamon, "In Search of Self," in Tessman and Bar On, eds., *Jewish Locations*, 81.

107. Gibel Azoulay, interview.

108. Salamon "In Search of Self," in Tessman and Bar On, eds., *Jewish Locations*, 81. I'm reminded of a bold act by the Eisenhower presidency, of integrating the blood plasma banks which had been segregated into black and white and into Christian and Jew. (One wonders where the Jewish blood went). Conversation, Blanche Wiesen Cook, October 2004.

109. Hisham Aidi, "Hip Hoppers and Black Panthers in the Holy Land," http://www.africana.com/index.htm (9/23/02).

4. PRAYING WITH OUR LEGS

1. For example, Jane Ramsey of JCUA spent some time with JFREJ in its early days; JFREJers Cindy Greenberg and Esther Kaplan led JFREJ's antiracism workshop for JCA.

2. The Jewish Social Justice Network was fostered by Marlene Provizer, Executive Director of Jewish Fund for Justice—also one of the founders of Jews for Racial and Economic Justice—and guided by Cindy Greenberg, former staff and current board member of JFREJ. In addition to the groups whose leaders I interviewed, other JSJN member organizations I've mentioned in this section include Progressive Jewish Alliance (Los Angeles; http://www.pjalliance.org) and Jews United for Justice (Washington, D.C.).

3. Ramsey, interview.

4. The increase in anti-semitism is mostly seen outside the United States, often in some relation to Israel/Palestine, and thus presents itself as an international issue. Given the ever-increasing influence of the Christian Right, we can expect to see more garden-variety anti-semitism here at home.

5. This text is the fourth and final point in JFREJ's Policy on International Issues, adopted on 11/28/02 after much struggle.

> 1. JFREJ reaffirms its mission to fight racial and economic injustice in New York City.
>
> 2. Our public activist, advocacy and educational programming will remain focused on this mission. Still, JFREJ values the growth of the Jewish left broadly speaking, as well as the diverse activist commitments of our members, and we encourage the exchange of ideas and information among them—on issues that fall inside and outside of this mission.
>
> 3. We believe in collaborating with organizations with whom we have common cause. We abhor the "litmus test" syndrome that prevails in the organized Jewish community, and do not choose our allies based on their having cleared a set of political hurdles irrelevant to the issues on which we are making common cause. See website, www.jfrej.org.

6. Ramsey, interview.

7. Rosenthal, interview.

8. Ramsey, interview. Jewish Council on Urban Affairs can be reached at 618 S. Michigan Avenue, Chicago, IL 60605; Phone: 312 663 0960; E-mail jcuamail@jcua.org; website, www.jcua.org.

9. Reminiscent of some of the most inspiring activities of the Communist Party in its heyday, see Mark Naison, "Communists in the Lead," in Lawson and Naison, eds., *The Tenant Movement in New York City*.

10. Jewish Federation of Philanthropies collects and distributes funds city by city.

11. Tobin et al., *In Every Tongue*. Interview with Rabbi Funnye follows in Chapter 5.

12. Holtzman, interview. Jews United for Justice can be reached at 7232 Chamberlain, St. Louis, MO, 63130; Phone: (314) 560-2994; website, http://www.jujstl.org/.

13. New Jewish Agenda was a progressive multi-issue Jewish organization that spanned the 1980s and folded in 1992. The language "a Jewish presence, etc." comes from NJA.

14. *Rebitsn*, the rabbi's wife, a position of some formal authority.

15. See interview with Rabbi Susan Talve in chapter 5.

16. Rosenthal, interview. Jewish Community Action can be reached at 2375 University Ave. W., Suite 150, St. Paul, MN 55114-1633; Phone: (651) 632-2184; website www.jewishcommunityaction.org/.

17. "Labor on the Bima" was initiated by the National Interfaith Committee for Worker Justice as "Labor in the Pulpits, Interfaith Resources for Services

about Worker Justice. For more information, visit http://www.labor-religion .org/laborinpulpit.htm. The *bima* is the Jewish pulpit. The 2003 focus was on the Immigrant Workers Freedom Ride.

18. Braine and Kaplan, interview.

JFREJ can be reached at 135 West 29th St., suite 600, New York, NY 10001; Phone (212) 647 8966; E-mail jfrej@igc.org; website: www.jfrej.org.

19. Coached and directed by Jenny Romaine, theater's gift to progressive Jewry.

20. Edison Schools, Inc., the huge corporation that sought to privatize public schools all over the nation, was soundly defeated in New York City. JFREJ was part of a strong and active coalition that worked to defeat Edison.

21. American Jewish Committee stalwart progressives included the late Gary Rubin, Marlene Provizer, and Marilyn Braveman; Ken Stern of AJC worked with JFREJ on the Radical Right Teach-In.

22. The Jewish Multiracial Network was created by and for two distinct groups of Jews: Jews of color, and Euro-Jews raising Jewish children of color. A program of the Jewish Retreat Center at Camp Isabella Freedman, it can be reached at www.multiracialjewishnet.org/resources.html.

23. These events are all specifically JFREJ, but each of these groups focuses on the holidays at times, as a way of building support for campaigns, evoking Jewish values and building progressive Jewish community. In New York, Summer 2004, JFREJ, in addition to organizing a Jewish contingent in the huge march protesting the Republic National Convention, organized a *Shande* (shame) Awards Ceremony to protest the Republican Jewish Coalition's party at the Plaza Hotel.

24. Again with the exception of the JFREJ radio show, which as a media event does not have to translate into political action.

25. Braine, interview.

5. JUDAISM IS THE COLOR OF THIS ROOM

1. See below for information on the Jews of Color Speak Out. Robin Washington is founder of the African American Jewish Alliance.

2. The Bikkurim residencies for both BINA and Ayecha are an exception." Bikkurim is a joint project of JESNA (Jewish Education Service of North America), UJC (United Jewish Communities), and the Kaminer family. JESNA's goal is to make engaging, inspiring, high quality Jewish education available to every Jew in North America." See bikkurim.org/index.htm and www.jesna.org /j/main.asp.

3. McCoy, interview.

4. Barhany, interview.

5. Funnye, interview.

6. Barhany, interview.

7. Elgrably, interview.

8. Elgrably, interview.

9. McCoy, interview.

10. McCoy, interview. Ayecha can be reached through its website www.ayecha.org or at 111 Eighth Avenue, 11th fl., New York, NY 10011-5201; Phone, 800.929.3242; 212. 284.6627; fax 212.284.6951.

11. New York's Symphony Space: Joshua Nelson and the Kosher Gospel Singers; Danny Maseng, composer of contemporary Jewish liturgical music; Voices of Shalom an African American-Jewish Jazz ensemble; Alula and the Beta Israel of North America Ethiopian Dance Troupe; Yoel Ben-Simhon & The Sultana Ensemble, whose distinctive sound preserves Judeo-Arab and Middle Eastern music, creating a bridge between Eastern and Western music traditions. December 2005.

12. Elgrably and Maio, interview. To contact the Levantine Center, go to www.levantineculturecenter.org.

13. www.masada2000.org/list-A.html, a list of several thousand supposed self-haters because critical of Israel: Jordan and Joyce are both on the list, as am I.

14. *Israeli Black Panthers* was shown in the African Diaspora Film Festival and the New York University Arab Film Festival, but not in the Sephardic Film Festival.

15. American Israeli Political Action Committee, right wing powerful lobby. In early 2006, a debate raged over the relative power of AIPAC in determining U.S. foreign policy.

16. http://www.bethshalombz.org. Funnye, interview.

"Beth Shalom is an affiliate congregation of the International Israelite Board of Rabbis Inc. and fully embraces the ideals of Resolution 801A, passed by the Board in 1981, which affirms the brotherhood of all people who worship the G-D of Abraham, Isaac and Jacob without regard to tradition, or terminology (for example: Black Jews' Hebrews, Israelites, Jews, etc.) However, when among us, visitors are obliged to respect the customs and traditions followed by members." From the Beth Shalom website section titled "History." Beth Shalom can be reached at 6601 S. Kedzie Ave, Chicago, IL 60629, tel. 773 476 2924; email bshalombz@sbcglobal.net; website, www.bethshalombz.org.

17. The open practice of Rabbi Funye's congregation is not unique but it is rare.

18. *Kashrut* is the practice of keeping kosher.

19. Tobin et al., *In Every Voice*, 86–87, mentions the work of Rabbi Funnye and Beth Shalom in helping to strengthen the Nigerian Jewish community. They add: "Because no formal census has been taken in the region it is unknown how many native Jews reside in Nigeria . . . estimates of possibly as many as 30,000 Ibos practicing some form of Judaism. Further research is necessary."

20. E-mail, Funnye, 1/20/2006.

21. Barhany, interview.
BINA-CF can be reached at 111 Eighth Ave., 11th Flr., New York, NY 10011-5201; Phone 212-284-6942 website: www.binacf.org email info@binacf.org or Beejhy@binacf.org.

22. Lynn Gottlieb, interview.

Nahalat Shalom can be reached at PO Box 40723, Albuquerque NM 87196-0723 Phone: (505) 343-8227 website www.NahalatShalom.org.

23. There is a long-standing tradition of *conversos* who retain connection with the church but also relate culturally to the Sephardic community. See Yosef Kaplan, "Bom Judesmo," in Biale, ed., *Cultures of the Jews*, 642; for example, "after the establishment by former conversos of the Sephardic community in London in the early days of the Restoration (1660), a minority of the Portuguese Catholics of Jewish origin who had found their way to London chose to live on the margins of the new community without converting to Judaism. Despite their strong ethnic and cultural ties with the Portuguese Jews, they remained Catholic." I imagine one might also say, "despite strong religious ties to Catholicism, they remained ethnically and culturally Jewish."

24. A Christian sect in northern New Mexico; people flagellate themselves at Easter. Its practices are highly secretive.

25. Check out www.InterfaithInventions.org.

26. Gordon, interview.

Professor Gordon and the Center can be reached at gordonl@temple.edu, Institute for the Study of Race and Social Thought, Anderson Hall, 1114 West Berks Street, Philadelphia, PA 19122-6090

27. Tobin et al., *In Every Tongue*.

28. See Ibid., 94 ff.

29. See Ibid., 167 ff.

30. Talve, interview. The Central Reform Synagogue can be reached through its website www.centralreform.org or by mial at CRC, 5020 Waterman, St. Louis, MO 63108.

31. Workshop facilitators at the off-site retreat were Yavilah McCoy, Linda Holtzman (of Jews United for Justice, see interview above), and myself.

32. "A new anti-bias initiative being launched in St. Louis will utilize the power of popular rock music to engage teens in the work of breaking down bias and prejudice in their communities. *Tear Down the Walls*, a unique new two-phase community teen initiative, is being presented by Jewish Rocker Rick Recht and the Anti-Defamation League (ADL)" Professional Free Press Release News Wire. For more information about Tear Down the Walls, call St. Louis Live Agency at 314-991-0909, or contact www.rickrecht.com.

33. Princeton University Scholar Ephraim Isaac, mentioned several times.

34. At the Jewish Community Center of the Upper West Side; cosponsored by Jews for Racial and Economic Justice, Swirl Inc., Kulanu, the Jewish Multiracial Network, and Congregation Beth Simchat Torah (the gay/lesbian synagogue). Inspired by the overwhelming response, Yavilah McCoy and Ayecha created an Afrocentric Hanukkah celebration (2003), again held at the JCC, with co-sponsorship by Ayecha, JCC, JFREJ, SWIRL/a mixed community, the American Sephardic Federation, Kulanu, and the North American Conference on Ethiopian Jewry. Another Ethiopian Hanukkah celebration took place in 2004, with co-sponsors galore.

35. The energy at this event reminded me of the Boston opening reading from *Nice Jewish Girls: A Lesbian Anthology* in Boston in 1982, a community which had often been dismissed as marginal and tiny manifesting itself as huge and enthusiastic.

36. Debra Nussbaum, "Finding Their Voice."

37. By Jewish law, Angela was not Jewish until her conversion, since her mother is not Jewish; one of the contemporary breakdowns in the Jewish world is Reform Judaism's acceptance of children of either Jewish parent as Jews, while Conservative and Orthodox still follow matrilineality.

38. A largely Dominican neighborhood in upper Manhattan.

39. Quoted in Nussbaum, "Finding Their Voice."

40. In New York City, Makor, 35 W. 67th St., 212-601-1000, has announced a Jews of Color network and a "vibrant Latino Jewish arts and cultural community with its first FERIA ARTISTICA (Artists' Fair)—a week of film, music, theater and art by Latino Jews.

41. See Maio's interview, above.

42. Soc.Culture.Jewish Newsgroups, FAQs, URL: www.scjfaq.org/faq/21-01-08.html.

6. TOWARD A NEW DIASPORISM

1. Roi Ottley, *New World A-Coming* (Boston: Houghton-Mifflin, 1943), 141–42, quoted in G. Berger, *Black Jews in America*, 17. Stein, *Making Jews Modern*, 104, quotes from *Der Bezem*, no. 72 (1906), a once-Zionist periodical, this satire of territorial Zionism:

> London. A telegram has been received from Mr. [Israel] Zangwill stating that the minister of the ocean has agreed to give the Jews a charter for the land that was created [by the parting of the Red Sea] when the Jews left Egypt.
>
> Egypt. 24 hours ago, [Manya] Vilbushevitsh studied the ocean territory and reached the conclusion that it is the first spot in history where Jews laid a free foot. . . .
>
> Ramses. [Protests denounce the granting of] the "historical ground" [identified in] Vilbushevitsh's announcement.

2. Sarah Stein, *Making Jews Modern*, 46. "Putative" because religious constructions of Zionism appear as early as Karaism, in 8th-century Iraq. It seems that Zionism is not recognized as such until its European version is founded in 1897.

3. Includes such luminaries as Judah Magnes, Martin Buber, Hannah Arendt, Albert Einstein, and others. Neimark, "What We've Always Known," in Kushner and Solomon, eds., *Wrestling with Zion*, 15–36. The century of dissent spans 1891–1982.

4. Deutscher (first published in 1954), in ibid., 30.

5. Michelle Campos, "Between 'Beloved Ottomania,'" 9–10, cites the editor of *Meserit in Izmir* (note 55) and *El Liberal* (14 May 1909) (note 56).

6. Ibid., 2.

7. Ibid., 6. "The new Zionist immigrants . . . numbered several thousand of Palestine's approximately 50,000–70,000 Jews."

8. Ibid., 2, 6. cf. Ottomanist Albert Antébi, "I desire to make the conquest of Zion economically and not politically."

9. Ibid., 3. Campos cites memoirs of Yosef Eliyahu Chelouche, Ya'akov Yeshoshu'a, Elie Eliachar, and Avraham Elmaliach. See also chapter 3, voices of Jacqueline Kahanoff, Ella Shohat, and Ya'aquob Yehoshua (Ya'akov Yeshoshu'a).

10. Ibid., 14. Also, see Rashid Khalidi, *Palestinian Identity.*

11. Ibid., 15.

12. Ibid., 15–16, note 104, cites Elmaliach, "Oral History Project, 23 February 1964. Ruppin [Arthur Ruppin, head of the World Zionist Organization's Palestine Office in Jaffa] and other functionaries also considered calls for Hebrew labor dangerous and certain to elicit 'dire consequences.'"

13. Ibid., 5.

14. Ibid.

15. Ibid.

16. Abigail Jacobson, "Sephardi Jewish Community," *Sephardic Heritage Update*, 19.

17. Ibid.

18. Ibid., 5. The newspaper was *ha-Po'el ha-tza'ir*, c.1908.

19. Ella Shohat, "Sephardim in Israel," 10.

20. British Foreign Secretary Arthur James Lord Balfour's letter (11/2/17) to Lord Rothschild giving his approval to the concept of a Jewish "national home" in Palestine. Beginning in 1922 a series of White Papers reneged on the agreement.

21. Ibid., 16. From the perspective of Palestinian Jews, as well as Palestinian Arabs, the incursion of Ashkenazim into partitioned Palestine must have felt like a European invasion.

22. I recommend the endlessly fascinating anthology edited by David Biale, *The Cultures of the Jews*, first published in 2002. What I am talking about here is the diffusion of this information into the mainstream Jewish community, Jewish education, as well as into multicultural and postcolonial theory.

23. *Haviva Ottomania* means Beloved Ottoman Homeland.

24. *Doikayt* is Yiddish for here-ness, the Bundist principle that stresses Jews' right to be wherever we are; the JFREJ statement on Israel/Palestine cited here asserts *doikayt* as its governing principle.

25. Boyarin and Boyarin, *Powers of Diaspora*, offers a gendered critique, challenging eloquently the negative view of diaspora.

26. See preface about Philip Roth's coinage of diasporism in *Operation Shylock.*

27. Avtar Brah, *Cartographies of Diaspora*, 192. Brah writes from her location as a woman born in the Panjab who grew up in Uganda.

28. Aurora Levins Morales, "Dancing on Bridges," in *Bridges* 2, no. 1 (1991): 43.

29. Ruth Behar, "Poem XI," from a bilingual sequence *Forty Nameless Poems/ Cuarenta Poemas Sin Nombre*, in *Bridges* (1997): 49. The sequence is dedicated to the Cuban poet Dulce Maria Loynaz. Behar, a Sephardic Jew born in Cuba, grew

up in the U.S. Of her sequence she writes, "These poems, which also exist in my own Spanish translations, are the work of a woman who speaks with a forked tongue, a woman whose English is haunted by Spanish." The keys refer to a Sephardic folklore, that the Jews expelled from Iberia took with them the keys to their houses, to signify a promise to return.

30. Kyla Wazana Tompkins, "Home Is Where You Make It," in Khazzoom, ed., *Camel*, 140.

31. S. Sayyid, "Beyond Westphalia," in Hesse, *Uns/ettled Multiculturalisms*, 38.

32. Ibid., 38.

33. Ibid., 41–42.

34. For more information on the Bund, see Tobias, *The Jewish Bund in Russia;* Jacobs, *On Socialists and "the Jewish Question";* Klepfisz, "*Di mames, dos loshn,*" *Bridges* 4, no. 1 (1994) and Klepfisz, "Secular Jewish Identity," in Kaye/Kantrowitz and Klepfisz, eds., *The Tribe of Dina.*

35. Campos, "Between 'Beloved Ottomania.'"

36. See preface, note 3.

37. Brah, *Cartographies of Diaspora*, 16, 180.

38. Barnette and Lander, "To Our Son," in Kushner and Solomon, eds., *Wrestling With Zion*, 293–94. The Right of Return is guaranteed to any *halachic* Jew, meaning anyone with a Jewish mother or who has undergone as Orthodox conversion

39. I am indebted to recent discussions of the African, Chinese, and South Asian diasporas. My thinking has been challenged by the work of S. Sayyid, Paul Gilroy, and Avtar Brah. See also Barkan and Shelton, eds., *Borders, Exiles, Diasporas.*

40. Cf. Brah, *Cartographies of Diaspora*, 226.

41. bell hooks, *Feminist Theory: From Margin to Center.*

42. Boyarin and Boyarin, *Powers of Diaspora*, 9.

43. Thank you, Steven Spielberg. Spielberg funded an immense oral history project to capture the experience of survivors before they died.

44. Elgrably, interview.

45. "I lived in the first century of world wars," "Poem," in Kaufman et al., eds., *The Collected Poems of Muriel Rukeyser,* 430.

46. Roosevelt depended on Southern Democrats. Remember, the U.S. army was still segregated.

47. Similarly, in the film *Dances with Wolves*, the moral and narrative center is the white man.

48. This act of sabotage is documented in the exquisite song "*Shtil, di nacht,*" about Vitke Kempner, the young woman who, along with Itsik Matskevitsch, blew up the train. See the late Ruth Rubin's compilation of Yiddish folk songs, *Voices of a People*, 450–51, 460, note 50.

49. *The Partisans of Vilna.*

50. I am grateful to psychologist Toby Miroff for this concept of export and import.

51. Rela Mazali, "Someone Makes a Killing off War: Militarization and Occupation in Israel-Palestine," presented at JUNITY Conference (Chicago, May 2001), http://www.junity.org/conference/rela.html.

52. Mitchell Plitnick, from the Jewish Peace News/Jewish Voice for Peace 2/8/04.

53. Israel Democracy Institute (2005 Israeli Democracy Index). For more information, see http://www.idi.org.il/english/catalog.asp?pdid=480&did=50.

54. Shohat, "Sephardim in Israel," *Social Text* 19/20 (Fall 1988): 30–31.

55. The image of a racially bifurcated society was seized upon in the 1970s by Sephardi radicals—inspired in part by African American radicals—to organize the Black Panthers (also, as Shohat points out, a play on *shwartze-chaies* [*sic*], Yiddish for black beasts, one of the many charming names Ashkenazi gave their Sephardi brother and sister Jews). "They often used the term *dfukim veshehorim* (screwed and black) to express the ethnic/class positioning of Sephardim." Ibid., 30.

56. See Seidman, "Lawless Attachments," in Boyarin and Boyarin, *Jews and Other Differences*, 279–305.

57. Segev, *The Seventh Million*, 104.

58. Grodzinsky, *In the Shadow*, 117, 119.

59. Ibid., 171.

60. Ibid., 225–26.

61. Ibid., 199.

62. Ibid., 226.

63. Democratic like Athens—worked for male Athenian citizens, but not for women, slaves, or noncitizens. Or like the pre-black and women's suffrage U.S., democracy for white men.

64. Irena Klepfisz drew the connection between Birthright and *Schindler's List* at the May 2001 JUNITY conference in Chicago, on a panel comprising Irena, Cherie Brown, and myself.

65. Jewish Defense organizations are those who define a major part of their mission as guarding against anti-semitism: the Anti-Defamation League (ADL); American Jewish Committee, American Jewish Congress, Simon Wiesenthal Center, etc.

66. Published in *Sojourner* (March 2002).

67. Blee, *Inside Organized Racism*. Kaye/Kantrowitz, "The Banality of Evil," *Women's Review of Books* (March 2002).

68. In Pakistan, in 2002.

69. Naomi Klein, "Sharon, Le Pen, and Anti-Semitism," in Kushner and Solomon, eds., *Wrestling with Zion*, 266.

70. The *Protocols* were widely distributed all over the globe, including by Henry Ford, a major fan.

71. Of course Harris's assertion insulted all non-Christians, not only Jews.

72. See Kaplan's expose, *With God on Their Side*.

73. Gibson found some surprising defenders (He didn't mean it!), but one suspects this is not the end of Gibson and anti-semitism.

74. According to one reporter, the perpetrators "first demanded half a million dollars, which Halimi's family insisted it couldn't afford. They then amateurishly suggested the family 'get the money from your synagogue,' and even called a local rabbi to tell him, 'We have a Jew,' mistakenly believing this would galvanize him to raise money." Sarah Whalen, "'Barbarians': Ilan Halimi and Anti-Semitism," *Arab News,* March 11, 2006.

75. Brett Kline, "Ilan Halimi's Mother Speaks Out," from JTA, March 26, 2006, reprinted in *Sephardic Heritage Update* 206. Other similar kidnapping attempts of Jewish men have been reported. In March 2006, in the working-class suburb of Sarcelles, a rabbi's son was beaten by eight men. The next day another Jew was attacked, as reported by Craig S. Smith, "Jews in France Feel Sting . . ." *New York Times,* March 2, 2006, 12.

76. Cecilie Surasky, "World Social Forum," in *Reframing Anti-Semitism.*

77. *Anti-semitism in America,* ADL Highlights from May 2002 Report. http://www.adl.org/anti_semitism/2002/as_survey.pdf p. 37.

78. Blee, *Inside Organized Racism,* 86 ff.

79. See Philip Green's remarkable piece of sanity, "'Anti-Semitism,' Israel and the Left," in *The Nation* (May 3, 2003), reprinted in Kushner and Solomon, eds., *Wrestling With Zion,* 243–48.

80. Rukeyser, "Letter to the Front, 7," in Kaufman et al., eds., *Collected Poems,* 243.

81. Yankl Stillman, "August Bondi," *Jewish Currents* (March–April 2004): 29, drawing on Bondi's papers at the American Jewish Historical Society. Jules Chametzky also tells this story in his introduction to Chametzky et al., eds., *Jewish American Literature,* 9.

82. Vera Williams, "My Mother, Leah, and George Sand," in Kaye/Kantrowitz and Klepfisz, eds., *Tribe of Dina,* 82.

83. Quoted in Boyarin and Boyarin, *Powers of Diaspora,* 53; from L. Zertal, "The Sacrificed and the Sanctified: The Construction of a National Martyrology," *Zemanim* 12, no. 48 (Spring): 26–45. For information on Edelman, see Krall, *Shielding the Flame.*

84. Boyarin and Boyarin, *Powers of Diaspora,* 53.

85. The events were the first readings in 1982 from the first edition of the anthology edited by Evelyn Torton Beck, *Nice Jewish Girls: A Lesbian Anthology.*

86. Email communications from Rela Mazali, of New Profile (high school students) and Mitchell Plitnick of Jewish Voice for Peace (soldiers), 4/08/06.

87. Beinart, "Jews of South Africa," *Transition,* 66–67, points to the rate of "out-marriage" to non-Jews among American Jews (one out of two), while in South Africa it's more like one out of ten; he also notes the increased level of Jewish education and religious observance.

88. Slovo, *Every Secret Thing.*

89. Beinart, "Jews of South Africa," *Transition,* 76–78.

90. Naison, *Communists in Harlem*, in an appendix "Black-Jewish Relations in the Harlem Communist Party," 322; notes, 327. I am grateful to Dr. Nancy Ordover for drawing my attention to Naison's concept of *cultural reflex*. Similarly, Bauman notes "a religious/cultural thrust toward social consciousness," in a review of Schultz, *Going South*, and Webb, *Fight against Fear*, *American Historical Review* 107, no. 4 (Oct. 2002).

91. Gilroy, *Black Atlantic*, 206.

92. Kafka's quintessentially Jewish? Kafkaesque? aphorism is quoted by Chametzky, *Jewish American Literature*, 2.

93. Isaac Deutscher, "The Non-Jewish Jew," in *The Non-Jewish Jew*, 26–27. Cf. this line from Jonathan Safran Foer's dazzling tragicomic novel *Everything Is Illuminated*, 104: "I informed her that you are . . . not a Jew with a large-size letter J, but a jew, like Albert Einstein or Jerry Seinfeld."

94. For one example of the burgeoning Jewish musical multiculture, see Elena Oumano, "Get Down, Moses: Upstart Local Jewish Musicians Weave a Coat of Many Colors," in *Village Voice* (December 20, 2005).

95. For the record, I like Ellen DeGeneres okay.

96. Toi Derricotte, *Black Notebooks*.

97. Jane Lazarre, *Beyond the Whiteness*.

98. Winddance Twine, *Racial Democracy*.

99. Jon Jeter, "Affirmative Action Debate forces Brazil," *Washington Post*, June 16, 2003.

100. Paley, "Zagrowsky Tells," 353.

101. Rachel Corrie was working in the Palestinian Occupied Territories with the International Solidarity Movement, using her (American/white) body as protection for Palestinians. She was killed by a bulldozer on March 16, 2003. Three years later, a play created from her journal, which had played in England, was supposed to open at a progressive theater in New York, but the theater backed off, clearly under pressure. For good coverage, see Philip Weiss in the *Nation*. http://www.thenation.com/doc/20060403/weiss.

102. See Plaskow, *Standing Again at Sinai*.

103. The ram's horn is the Shofar, especially associated with the High Holy days of Rosh Hashanah and Yom Kippur.

104. This is Katya Ghibel Azoulay's point at the end of chapter 3, above.

105. Jonathan Boyarin makes this point in "Europe's Indian, American's Jew," in his brilliant *Storm from Paradise*.

106. Ariel Beery, "Breech in the Dam," Op-Ed, *Jerusalem Post*, September 4, 2006. http://www.jpost.com/servlet/Sattelite?apage=2&cid=1154525996440&pagename=JPost%2FJPArticle%2FShowFull.

107. As I write, I am encouraged to get a postcard from A Jewish Voice for Peace which tells a slightly longer version of this story.

BIBLIOGRAPHY

INTERVIEWS

Alcalay, Ammiel 12/30/03

Barhany, Beejhy (BINA) 11/23/04

Braine, Naomi and Esther Kaplan (JFREJ) 1/21/04

Elgrably, Jordan (Ivri-NASAWI) 1/25/04

Funnye, Capers (Beth Shalom B'nai Zaken Ethiopian Hebrew Congregation) 12/27/05

Gordon, Lewis (Center for Afro-Jewish Studies, Temple University) 10/2/05

Gibel Azoulay, Katya (a.k.a. Mevorach) 8/12/03

Gottlieb, Lynn (Nahalat Shalom) 12/9/03

Holtzman, Linda (JUJ) 11/24/03

Maio, Joyce (Ivri-NASAWI) 1/23/04

McCoy, Yavilah (Ayecha) 9/8/03 and 12/24/03

Navonah (pseudonym) 11/18/05

Ramsey, Jane (JCUA) 12/16/03 and 2/10/04

Rosenthal, Vic (JCA) 8/20/04

Schnee, Emily 4/6/04

Talve, Susan (Central Reform Congregation) 1/24/06

BOOKS, ARTICLES, AND FILMS

Alcalay, Ammiel. *After Jews and Arabs: Remaking Levantine Culture.* Minneapolis: University of Minneapolis Press, 1993.

———. "Intellectual Life." In Simon et al., *Jews of the Middle East,* 85–112.

Alexander, Claire. "(Dis)Entangling the 'Asian Gang': Ethnicity, Identity, Masculinity." In Hesse, ed., *Multiculturalisms,* 123–47.

Allen, Theodore W. *The Invention of the White Race, Volume Two: The Origin of Racial Oppression in Anglo-America.* New York: Verso, 1994.

Anzaldúa, Gloria. *Borderlands/Las Fronteras.* San Francisco: Aunt Lute, 1987.

Ashton, Dianne, and Ellen M. Umansky, eds. *Four Centuries of Jewish Women's Spirituality: A Sourcebook.* Boston: Beacon Press, 1992.

257

Bahloul, Joëlle. "Gender, Colonialism, and the Representation of Middle Eastern Jews." In Levitt and Peskowitz, eds., *Judaism since Gender*, 82–85.

Baldwin, James. "Negroes Are Anti-Semitic Because They're Anti-White." In *Black Anti-Semitism and Jewish Racism*. New York: Schocken Books, 1969, 3–12.

———. "On Being 'White' and Other Lies." *Essence* (April 1984).

Barkan, Elazar, and Marie-Denise Shelton, eds. *Borders, Exiles, Diasporas.* Stanford, Calif.: Stanford University Press, 1998.

Barnette, Meg, and Brad Lander. "To Our Son, Marek Alexander Barnette, on the Occasion of His Naming." In Kushner and Solomon, eds., *Wrestling with Zion*, 293–94.

Bauman, Mark K. Review of Schultz, *Going South* and Webb, *Fight against Fear. American Historical Review* 107, no. 4 (Oct. 2002).

Beck, Evelyn Torton, ed. *Nice Jewish Girls: A Lesbian Anthology.* 2nd ed. Boston: Beacon Press, 1989. 1st ed., Watertown, Mass.: Persephone Press, 1982.

Behar, Ruth. Film. *Adio Kerida.* 2002.

———. "Poem XI," from *Forty Nameless Poems/Cuarenta Poemas Sin Nombre*, in *Bridges* 7, no. 1 (1997): 45–49.

Beinart, Peter. "The Jews of South Africa." *Transition Issue* 71 (1997).

Ben-Ur, Aviva. "Where Diasporas Met: Sephardic and Ashkenazic Jews in the City of New York. A Study in Intra-Ethnic Relations, 1880–1950." Diss., Brandeis University, 1998.

Berger, Aisha. "Nose is a Country . . . I am the Second Generation." In Kaye/Kantrowitz and Klepfisz, eds., *Tribe of Dina*, 134–38.

Berger, Graenum. *Black Jews in America: A Documentary with Commentary.* New York: Commission on Synagogue Relations, Federation of Jewish Philanthropies of New York, 1978.

Berman, Paul, ed. *African Americans and Jews.* New York: Delacorte, 1994.

Biale, David, ed. *Cultures of the Jews: A New History.* New York: Schocken, 2002.

Blee, Kathleen. *Inside Organized Racism: Women in the Hate Movement.* Berkeley: University of California Press, 2001.

Boyarin, Daniel. "Masada or Yavneh? Gender and the Arts of Jewish Resistance." In Boyarin and Boyarin, eds., *Jews and Other Differences*, 305–30.

Boyarin, Jonathan. *Storm from Paradise: The Politics of Jewish Memory.* Minneapolis: University of Minnesota Press, 1992.

Boyarin, Jonathan, and Daniel Boyarin, eds., *Jews and Other Differences: The New Jewish Cultural Studies.* Minneapolis: University of Minnesota Press, 1997.

———. *Powers of Diaspora.* Minneapolis: University of Minnesota Press, 2002.

Brah, Avtar. *Cartographies of Diaspora: Contesting Identities.* New York: Routledge, 1996.

Brettschneider, Marla, ed. *The Narrow Bridge: Jewish Views on Multiculturalism.* New Brunswick, N.J.: Rutgers University Press, 1996.

Bridges: Sephardi and Mizrachi Women Write About Their Lives 7, no. 1 (1997).

Bridges: Writing and Art by Jewish Women of Color 9, no. 1 (2001).

Brodkin, Karen. *How Jews Became White Folks & What That Says about Race in America.* New Brunswick, N.J.: Rutgers University Press, 1998.

Brodkin Sacks, Karen. "How Did Jews Become White Folks." In Gregory and Sanjek, eds., *Race*, 78–102.

Broner, E. M. *Mornings and Mourning: A Kaddish Journal.* San Francisco, Calif.: HarperCollins, 1994.

Brotz, Howard M. *The Black Jews of Harlem: Negro Nationalism and the Dilemmas of Negro Leadership.* New York: Schocken, 1970.

Bulkin, Elly, Minnie Bruce Pratt, and Barbara Smith. *Yours in Struggle.* New York: Long Haul Press, 1984.

Bush, Rod. *We Are Not What We Seem: Black Nationalism and Class Struggle in the American Century.* New York: New York University Press, 1999.

Campos, Michelle U. "Between 'Beloved Ottomania' and 'The Land of Israel': The Struggle over Ottomanism and Zionism among Palestine's Sephardi Jews, 1908–13," *Sephardic Heritage Update*, special edition, reprinted from *The International Journal for Middle East Studies* 37 (2005).

Chametsky, Jules, John Felstiner, Hilene Flanzbaum, and Kathryn Hellerstein, eds. *Jewish American Literature.* New York: W. W. Norton, 2001.

Chireau, Yvonne, and Nathaniel Deutsch, eds. *Black Zion: African American Religious Encounters with Judaism.* New York: Oxford University Press, 2000.

Cronon, E. David. *Black Moses: The Story of Marcus Garvey and the Universal Negro Improvement Association.* Madison: University of Wisconsin Press, 1955.

Davis, Angela. "Rope," in Smith, *Fires in the Mirror.* New York: Anchor, 1993, 27–32.

Derricotte, Toi. *The Black Notebooks: An Interior Journey.* New York: W.W. Norton, 1997.

Deutscher, Isaac. *The Non-Jewish Jew and Other Essays.* London: Oxford University Press, 1968.

Diner, Hasia. *In the Almost Promised Land: American Jews and Blacks, 1915–1935.* Westport, Conn.: Greenwood Press, 1977.

Drake, St. Clair. "African Diaspora and Jewish Diaspora: Convergence and Divergence." In Washington, ed., *Jews in Black Perspectives*, 19–41.

Eisendorf, Toni. "An Ethiopian Gilgul Come to Life" (interview by Reena Bernards). In *Bridges* 9, no.1 (2001): 21–25.

Enloe, Cynthia. *Bananas, Beaches, and Bases.* Berkeley: University of California, 1990.

Fanon, Frantz. *The Wretched of the Earth.* New York: Grove, 1966.

Felstiner, Mary Lowenthal. *To Paint Her Life: Charlotte Salomon in the Nazi Era.* New York: HarperCollins, 1994.

Finkielkraut, Alain. *The Imaginary Jew.* Trans. Kevin O'Neill and David Suchoff. Lincoln: University of Nebraska Press, 1994.

Foer, Jonathan Safran. *Everything Is Illuminated.* New York: HarperCollins, 2003.

Frankenberg, Ruth. *White Women/Race Matters.* Minneapolis: University of Minnesota Press, 1993.

Franklin, V. P. "The Portrayal of Jews in *The Autobiography of Malcolm X.*" In Franklin et al., eds., *African Americans and Jews,* 293–308.

Franklin, V. P., Nancy L. Grant, Harold M. Kletnick, and Genna Rae McNeil. eds. *African Americans and Jews in the Twentieth Century.* Columbia: University of Missouri Press, 1998.

Freedman, Samuel G. *Jew vs. Jew: The Struggle for the Soul of American Jewry.* New York: Simon and Schuster, 2000.

Friedman, Murray. *What Went Wrong? The Creation and Collapse of the Black-Jewish Alliance.* New York: Free Press, 1995.

Fung, Richard. *Looking for My Penis: The Eroticized Asian in Gay Porn.* Washington: Bay Press, 1991.

Gerber, Jane S. "History of the Jews in the Middle East and North Africa from the Rise of Islam Until 1700." In Simon et al., *Jews of the Middle East,* 3–18.

———. *The Jews of Spain: A History of the Sephardic Experience.* New York: Free Press, 1992.

Gibel Azoulay, Katya. *Black, Jewish, and Interracial: It's Not the Color of Your Skin but the Race of Your Kin, and Other Myths of Identity.* Durham, N.C.: Duke University Press, 1996.

———. "Jewishness after Mount Sinai: Jews, Blacks and the (Multi)racial Category." *Bridges* 9, no.1 (2001): 31–45.

Gilman, Sander. *The Jew's Body.* New York: Routledge, 1991.

Gilroy, Paul. *Against Race: Imagining Political Culture beyond the Color Line.* Cambridge, Mass.: Harvard University, 2000.

———. *The Black Atlantic: Modernity and Double Consciousness.* Cambridge, Mass.: Harvard University Press, 1993.

Green, Philip. "'Anti-Semitism,' Israel and the Left." *The Nation* (May 3, 2003), reprinted in Kushner and Solomon, eds., *Wrestling with Zion,* 243–48.

Greenberg, Cheryl. "The Southern Jewish Community and the Struggle for Civil Rights." In Franklin et al., eds., *African Americans and Jews,* 123–64.

Gregory, Steven, and Roger Sanjek, eds. *Race.* New Brunswick, N.J.: Rutgers University Press, 1994.

Guinier, Lani. *Tyranny of the Majority.* New York: Free Press, 1994.

Grodzinsky, Yosef. *In the Shadow of the Holocaust: The Story of Jews in Displaced Persons Camps and their Forced Role in the Founding of Israel.* Monroe, Maine: Common Courage Press, 2004.

Halpern, Orly. "Iraqi-Israeli Jews Plan to Visit Their 'Roots.'" *Jerusalem Post* (12/27/05).

Haruach, Miri Hunter. "Born again Yemenite." In *Bridges* 9, no. 1 (2001): 84–89.

Herron, Carolivia. "Peacesong." In *Bridges* 9, no. 1 (2001): 9–14.

Hesse, Barnor, ed. *Un/settled Multiculturalisms: Diasporas, Entanglements, Transruptions.* New York: Zed Books, 2000.

Hill, Herbert. "Black-Jewish Conflict in the Labor Context: Race, Jobs, and Institutional Power." In Franklin et al., eds., *African Americans and Jews*, 264–92.

hooks, bell. *Feminist Theory: From Margin to Center.* Boston: South End Press, 1984.

Horne, Gerald. "Black, White, and Red: Jewish and African Americans in the Communist Party." In Brettschneider, ed., *Narrow Bridge*, 123–35.

Hutchison, William R., and Hartmut Lehmann, eds. *Many Are Chosen: Divine Election and Western Nationalism.* Minneapolis: Harvard Theological Studies 38/Fortress Press, 1994.

Ignatiev, Noel. *How the Irish Became White.* New York: Routledge, 1995.

Iny, Julie. "Ashkenazi Eyes." In Khazzoom, ed., *Camel*, 81–100.

Itzkovitz, Daniel. "Secret Temples." In Boyarin and Boyarin, eds., *Jews and Other Differences*, 176–202.

Jacobs, Jack. *On Socialists and "the Jewish Question" after Marx.* New York: New York University Press, 1982.

Jacobson, Abigail. "Sephardi Jewish Community in Pre-World War I Jerusalem: Debates in the Press." *Sephardic Heritage Update*, special edition; reprinted from *Jerusalem Quarterly File* (Fall 2001).

Jacobson, Matthew Frye. *Whiteness of a Different Color: European Immigrants and the Alchemy of Race.* Cambridge, Mass.: Harvard University Press, 1998.

Jeter, Jon. "Affirmative Action Debate Forces Brazil to Take Look in the Mirror." *Washington Post* (June 16, 2003).

Jones, Hettie. *How I Became Hettie Jones.* New York: Dutton, 1990.

Jones, Lisa. "Mama's White." In *Bulletproof Diva: Tales of Race, Sex, and Hair.* New York: Doubleday, 1994.

Jones, William P. *The Tribe of Black Ulysses.* Urbana: University of Illinois Press, 2005.

Kaplan, Esther. *With God on Their Side.* New York: New Press, 2004.

Kaplan, Yosef. "Bom Judesmo: The Western Sephardic Diaspora." In Biale, ed., *Cultures of the Jews*, 639–70.

Katz, Nathan. *Who Are the Jews of India?* Berkeley: University of California Press, 2000.

Katz-Fishman, Walda, and Jerome Scott. "The Increasing Significance of Class: Black-Jewish Conflict in the Post-Industrial Global Era." In Franklin et al., eds., *African Americans and Jews*, 309–45.

Kaufman, Jonathan. *Broken Alliance: The Turbulent Times between Blacks and Jews in America.* New York: Penguin, 1988.

Kaye, Melanie (a.k.a. Kaye/Kantrowitz). "The Sword Philippan: Woman as Hero in Stuart Tragedy." Diss., University of California-Berkeley, 1975.

Kaye/Kantrowitz, Melanie. "The Banality of Evil: review, Kathleen Blee, *Inside Organized Racism: Women in the Hate Movement.*" In *Women's Review of Books* (March 2002):4–5.

———. "Diasporism, Feminism, and Coalition." In Sarah Swartz and Margie Wolfe, eds., *Jewish Women's Voices: From Memory to Transformation.* Toronto: Second Story Press, 1998, 241–55.

———. *The Issue Is Power: Essays on Women, Jews, Violence, and Resistance.* San Francisco: Aunt Lute Books, 1992.

———. "Jews in the U.S.: The Rising Cost of Whiteness." In Becky Thompson and Sangeeta Tyagi, eds., *Names We Call Home: Autobiography on Racial Identity.* New York: Routledge, 1986, 121–37.

———. "Kaddish." In Beck, ed., *Nice Jewish Girls*, 107–11.

———. "Notes from the (Shifting) Middle: Some Ways of Looking at Jews." In Tessman and Bar On, eds., *Locations*, 115–29.

———. "Post 9/11: Assessing Anti-Semitism." In *Sojourner* (March 2002).

———. "The Price of Heroism: review, Gillian Slovo, *Red Dust* and *Every Secret Thing.*" In *Women's Review of Books* (July 2002), 30–31.

———. "Some Pieces of Jewish Left." In *My Jewish Face & Other Stories.* San Francisco: Aunt Lute, 1990, 179–211.

———. "Stayed on Freedom: Jew in the Civil Rights Movement—and After." In Brettschneider, ed., *Bridge*, 105–22.

Kaye/Kantrowitz, Melanie, and Irena Klepfisz, eds. *The Tribe of Dina: A Jewish Women's Anthology.* Boston: Beacon Press, 1989; 1st pub., *Sinister Wisdom* 29–30, 1986.

Keshet, Shula, and Sigal Eshed, eds. "Sister: Mizrahi Women Artists in Israel." In *Bridges* 9, no. 1 (2001): 49–58.

Khalidi, Rashid. *Palestinian Identity: The Construction of Modern National Consciousness.* New York: Columbia University Press, 1997.

Khanga, Yelena. *Soul to Soul.* New York: Basic Books, 1990.

Khazzoom, Loolwa. "Jewish Multiculturalism: Enhancing Our Awareness, Embracing Our Diversity." *Tikkun* (July–August 1997).

————, ed. *The Flying Camel: Essays on Identity by Women of North African and Middle Eastern Jewish Heritage*. New York: Seal Press/Avon, 2003.

Klein, Naomi. "Sharon, Le Pen, and Anti-Semitism." In Kushner and Solomon., eds., *Wrestling with Zion*, 266–68.

Klepfisz, Irena. "*Di mames, dos loshn* / The mothers, the language: Feminism, *Yidishkayt*, and the Politics of Memory." In *Bridges* 4, no. 1 (1994): 12–47.

————. "Secular Jewish Identity: *Yidishkayt* in America." In Kaye/Kantrowitz and Klepfisz, eds., *Tribe of Dina*, 32–50.

Kline, Brett. "Ilan Halimi's Mother Speaks Out." *JTA*, March 26, 2006. Reprinted in *Sephardic Heritage* Update 206.

Knafo Setton, Ruth. "Jew/Arab/Woman: Notes Toward an Identity." In Susan M. Kahn, Nancy F. Vineberg, and Sarah Silberstein Swartz, eds., *Jewish Women from Muslim Societies Speak*, 18–21. American Sephardi Federation and Hadassah International Research Institution on Women at Brandeis University, 2003.

————. "The Life and Times of Ruth of the Jungle," in Khazzoom, ed., *Camel*, 1–10.

Krall, Hanna. *Shielding the Flame: An Intimate Conversation With Dr. Marek Edelman, the Last Surviving Leader of the Warsaw Ghetto Uprising*. Trans. Joanna Stasinska and Lawrence Weschler. New York: Henry Holt, 1986.

Kushner, Tony, and Alisa Solomon, eds. *Wrestling with Zion: Progressive Jewish-American Responses to the Israeli-Palestinian Conflict*. New York: Grove Press, 2003.

Kwong, Peter. *The New Chinatown*, revised. New York: Hill and Wang, 1996.

Langer, Elinor. *A Hundred Little Hitlers: The Death of a Black Man, The Trial of a White Racist, and the Rise of the Neo-Nazi Movement in America*. New York: Metropolitan Books, 2003.

Laskier, Michael Menachem, and Reeva Spector Simon, "Economic Life." In Simon et al., eds., *Jews of the Middle East*, 29–48.

Lazarre, Jane. *Beyond the Whiteness of Whiteness*. Durham, N.C.: Duke University Press, 1996.

Lerner, Michael. "Jews Are Not White." *Village Voice* 38:33–34.

Lerner, Michael, and Cornel West. *Jews & Blacks: let the healing begin*. New York: Penguin/Plume, 1996.

Lester, Julius. *Lovesong: Becoming a Jew*. New York: Arcade, 1988.

Levins Morales, Aurora. "Dancing on Bridges." In *Bridges* 2, no.1 (1991): 42–43.

Levitt, Laura, and Miriam Peskowitz, eds. *Judaism since Gender*. New York: Routledge, 1997.

Levy, Lital. "How the Camel Found Its Wings." In Khazzoom, ed., *Camel*, 173–89.

Macdonald, Andrew (pseudonym). *The Turner Diaries: A Novel.* Hillsboro, W.V.: National Vanguard Books, 1995; 1st pub., 1980.

McBride, James. *The Color of Water.* New York: Riverhead, 1996.

McIntosh, Peggy. "Unpacking the Invisible Knapsack." In *Peace and Freedom* (July/August, 1989): 10–12.

McLaren, Peter. "Decentering Culture: Postmodernism, Resistance, and Critical Pedagogy." In Nancy B. Wyner, ed., *Current Perspectives on the Culture of Schools.* Boston: Brookline Books, 1991.

Mekonen, Avishai Yeganyahu, and Shari Rothfarb Mekonen. Film. *Judaism and Race.* In Progress.

Mendes-Flohr, Paul. "In Pursuit of Normalcy: Zionism's Ambivalence toward Israel's Election." In Hutchison and Lehmann, eds., *Many Are Chosen,* 203–24.

Mendes-Flohr, Paul R., and Jehuda Reinharz, eds. *The Jew in the Modern World: A Documentary History.* New York: Oxford University Press, 1980.

Mensches in the Trenches. Program celebrating 10 Years of Jews for Racial and Economic Justice, December 10, 2000.

Morrison, Toni. *Playing in the Dark: Whiteness and the Literary Imagination.* Cambridge, Mass.: Harvard University Press, 1992.

Mosse, George. *Toward the Final Solution: A History of European Racism.* New York: Fertig, 1985.

Muhammad, Dedrick, Attieno Davis, Meizhu Lui, and Betsy Leondar-Wright. "The State of the Dream: Enduring Disparities in Black and White" (United for a Fair Economy's 2004 report), January 15, 2004. Website www.FairEconomy.org

Naison, Mark. *Communists in Harlem during the Depression.* New York: Grove Press, 1985.

———. "Communists in the Lead: Early Depression Eviction Protests and Rent Strikes." In Ronald Lawson and Mark Naison, eds., *The Tenant Movement in New York City, 1904–1984.* New Brunswick, N.J.: Rutgers University Press, 1986.

Neimark, Marilyn Kleinberg. "What We've Always Known: A Century's Sample of Dissenting Voices." In Kushner and Solomon, eds., *Wrestling With Zion,* 15–36.

Ness, Immanuel. *Immigrants, Unions, and the New U.S. Labor Market.* Philadelphia, Temple University Press, 2005.

Nussbaum, Debra. "Finding Their Voice." *Jewish Week,* December 6, 2002.

Nussbaum Cohen, Debra. "Shades of Gray." *Jewish Week,* June 28, 2000.

Omi, Michael, and Howard Winant. *Racial Formation in the United States.* 2nd ed. New York: Routledge, 1994.

Ordover, Nancy. *American Eugenics: Race, Queer Anatomy, and the Science of Nationalism.* Minneapolis: University of Minnesota, 2003.

Oumano, Elena. "Get Down, Moses: Upstart Local Jewish Musicians Weave a Coat of Many Colors." *Village Voice,* December 20, 2005.

Paley, Grace. "Zagrowsky Tells." In *The Collected Stories.* New York: Farrar, Straus, and Giroux, 1994, 348–64.

Perera, Victor. *The Cross and the Pear Tree: A Sephardic Journey.* New York: Knopf, 1995.

Plaskow, Judith. *Standing Again at Sinai: Judaism from a Feminist Perspective.* San Francisco: Harper & Row, 1990.

Podair, Jerald E. *What Really Happened at Ocean Hill-Brownsville? The Strike That Changed New York: Blacks, Whites and The Ocean Hill-Brownsville Crisis.* New Haven, Conn.: Yale University Press, 2002.

Pomerance, Rachel. "Jewish–Black Ties Loosen over Years." *The Jewish Journal,* Jewish Telegraphic Agency, January 14, 2005.

Pramoedya Ananta Toer. *Buru Quartet* (vols. 1–4). Max Lane, trans. New York: Penguin, 1990–92.

Raboteau, Albert J. "Exodus, Ethiopia, and Racial Messianism: Texts and Contexts of African American Chosenness." In Hutchison et al., eds., *Many Are Chosen,* 175–95.

Roediger, David R. *The Wages of Whiteness: Race and the Making of the American Working Class.* New York: Verso, 1991.

Roth, Philip. *Operation Shylock.* New York: Vintage, 1994.

Rubin, Ruth. *Voices of a People: The Story of Yiddish Folksong.* Philadelphia: Jewish Publication Society of America, 1979.

Rukeyser, Muriel. *The Collected Poems of Muriel Rukeyser.* Janet E. Kaufman and Anne F. Herzog, eds., with Jan Heller Levi. Pittsburgh: University of Pittsburgh Press, 2005.

Said, Edward. *Orientalism.* New York: Pantheon Books, 1978.

———. "Zionism from the Standpoint of its Victims." In Moustafa Bayoumi and Andrew Rubin, eds., *The Edward Said Reader.* New York: Vintage, 2000, 114–68.

Salamon, Hagar. "In Search of Self and Other: A Few Remarks on Ethnicity, Race, and Ethiopian Jews." In Tessman and Bar On, eds., *Jewish Locations,* 75–88.

Samuel, Flora. "The Bene Israel Cradle Ceremony: An Indian Jewish Ritual for the Birth of a Girl." In *Bridges* 7, no. 1 (1997), 43–44.

Sanjek, Roger. "Intermarriage and the Future of Races in the United States." In Gregory and Sanjek, eds., *Race,* 103–30.

Sayyid, S. "Beyond Westphalia: Nations and Diasporas—The Case of the Muslim *Umma*." In Hesse, ed., *Multiculturalisms*, 34–50

Scheindlin, Raymond P. "Merchants and Intellectuals, Rabbis and Poets." In Biale, ed., *Cultures of the Jews*, 313–86.

Schultz, Debra L. *Going South: Jewish Women in the Civil Rights Movement.* New York: New York University Press, 2001.

The Secret Relationship between Blacks and Jews. Nation of Islam, 1991.

Seidman, Naomi. "Lawless Attachments, One-Night Stands: The Sexual Politics of the Hebrew-Yiddish Language War." In Boyarin and Boyarins, eds., *Jews and Other Differences*, 279–305.

Shalom, Chaya. Interview by Melanie Kaye/Kantrowitz and Irena Klepfisz. In Kaye/Kantrowitz and Klepfisz, eds., *Tribe of Dina*, 214–26.

Shohat, Ella. *Israeli Cinema: East/West and the Politics of Representation.* Austin: University of Texas, 1989.

———. "Reflections of an Arab Jew." In Khazzoom, ed., *Camel*, 115–21.

———. "Sephardim in Israel: Zionism from the Standpoint of Its Jewish Victims." *Social Text* 19/20, 7, no. 1–2 (Fall 1988): 1–36.

Shohat, Ella, and Robert Stam, eds. *Unthinking Eurocentrism.* New York: Routledge, 1994.

Simon, Reeva Spector. "Europe in the Middle East." In Simon et al., eds, *Jews of the Middle East*, 19–28.

Simon, Reeva Spector, Michael Menachem Laskier, and Sara Regeur, eds. *The Jews of the Middle East and North Africa in Modern Times.* New York: Columbia University Press, 2003.

Simons, Shoshana. "Reflections Sparked by *In Gerangl*, the December Teach-In on Progressive Jewish History." In the *Jews for Racial and Economic Justice Bulletin* 11 (April 1994).

Slapak, Orpa, ed. *The Jews of India: A Story of Three Communities.* Jerusalem: Israel Museum, 1995.

Slovo, Gillian. *Every Secret Thing: My Family, My Country.* Boston: Little, Brown, 1997.

Smith, Anna Deveare. *Fires in the Mirror.* New York: Anchor, 1993.

Smith, Craig S. "Jews in France Feel Sting as Anti-Semitism Surges among Children of Immigrants." *New York Times*, March 26, 2006: 12.

Stein, Sarah Abrevaya. *Making Jews Modern: The Yiddish and Ladino Press in the Russian and Ottoman Empires.* Bloomington: Indiana University Press, 2004.

Steinberg, Stephen. *The Ethnic Myth: Race, Ethnicity and Class in America*, 2nd ed. Boston: Beacon Press, 1989.

Stevenson, Marshall F., Jr. "African Americans and Jews in Organized Labor: A Case Study of Detroit, 1920–1950." In Franklin et al., eds., *African Americans and Jews*, 237–63.

———. "Cincinnati Is Not New York: Regional Differences in Black-Jewish Relations After World War II," unpublished paper quoted in Friedman, *What Went Wrong?* New York: Free Press, 1995.

———. "The Politics of Households and Homes: Jewish Housewives and Black Domestics in 20th Century America, 1915–1980." Paper presented at the Ninth Annual Conference on Black-Jewish Relations: "A Dialogue on Race From Women's Perspectives," Dillard University, New Orleans, Louisiana, April 14–15, 1998.

Stillman, Norman A. *Jews of Arab Lands in Modern Times.* Philadelphia: Jewish Publication Society, 1991.

Stillman, Yankl. "August Bondi and the Abolitionist Movement." *Jewish Currents* (March–April 2004): 28–30.

Surasky, Cecilie. "In Search of Anti-Semitism at the World Social Forum." In *Reframing Anti-Semitism: Alternative Jewish Perspectives.* Oakland, Calif.: Jewish Voice for Peace Publication, 2004.

Takagi, Dana Y. "Post-Civil Rights Politics and Asian-American Identity: Admissions and Higher Education." In Gregory and Sanjek, eds., *Race*, 229–42.

Talbot, Margaret. "Getting Credit for Being White." *New York Times Magazine.* Vol. 147, November 30, 1997.

Tessman, Lisa, and Bat-Ami Bar On, eds. *Jewish Locations: Traversing a Racialized Landscape.* Lanham, Md.: Rowman and Littlefield, 2001.

Than, Hilary. "Marriage and Conversion: A Poem Sequence." In *Counting: A Long Poem.* Washington, D.C.: The Word Works, 2000; reprinted in *Bridges* 9, no. 1 (2001): 15–20.

Tobias, Henry J. *The Jewish Bund in Russia from its Origins to 1905.* Stanford, Calif.: Stanford University Press, 1972.

Tobin, Diane, Gary A. Tobin, and Scott Rubin. *In Every Tongue: The Racial & Ethnic Diversity of the Jewish People.* San Francisco: Institute for Jewish and Community Research, 2005.

Tompkins, Kyla Wazana. "Home is Where You Make It." In Khazzoom, ed., *Camel*, 131–40.

Twine, France Winddance. *Racism in a Racial Democracy: The Maintenance of White Supremacy in Brazil.* New Brunswick, N.J.: Rutgers University Press, 2001.

Wahba, Rachel. "Benign Ignorance or Persistent Resistance?" In Khazzoom, ed., *Camel*, 47–65.

Waletsky, Josh. Film. *Image Before My Eyes.* 1980.

Waletsky, Josh, director, and Aviva Kempner. Film. *The Partisans of Vilna.* 1987.

Walker, Rebecca. *Black, White, and Jewish: Autobiography of a Shifting Self.* New York: Riverhead Books, 2001.

Washington, Joseph R., Jr., ed. *Jews in Black Perspectives: A Dialogue.* Rutherford: Fairleigh Dickinson University Press; London; Cranbury, N.J.: Associated University Presses, 1984.

West, Cornel. *Keeping Faith: Philosophy and Race in America.* London: Routledge, 1993.

Williams, Patricia. *Alchemy of Race and Rights.* Cambridge, Mass.: Harvard University, 1992.

———. *The Rooster's Egg: On the Persistence of Prejudice.* Cambridge, Mass.: Harvard University Press, 1995.

Williams, Vera. "My Mother, Leah, and George Sand." In Kaye/Kantrowitz and Klepfisz, eds., *Tribe of Dina,* 81–89.

Wilson, William Julius. *When Work Disappears.* New York: Vintage Books, 1997.

Wolfson, Bernard J. "African American Jews: Dispelling Myths, Bridging the Divide." In Chireau and Deutsch, eds., *Black Zion,* 33–54.

Zevadia, Belaynesh. Interview by Siona Benjamin. In *Bridges* 9, no. 1 (2001): 81–83.

Zohar, Zvi. "Religion: Rabbinic Tradition and the Response to Modernity." In Simon et al., eds., *Jews in the Middle East,* 65–84.

and, 28, 74, 80; Israel and, 196, 207, 208; Judeo-Christian designation and, 31; Latin, 2; Latinos and, 90, 101; leftist politics and, 108; Levantine Cultural Center, 154; mainstream or marginalized, 12; marriage and, 155; mixed marriages and, 9; mixed parentage and, 187; money and, 12; as mongrels, 15; multi-ethnic, 71; multiracial identity of, 2, 9, 40, 137, 191; Muslims and, 74, 76; *must 'arab*, 82–83; Near East, 90; non-Jews and, 165, 201; as not-black, 36; number in U.S., 70; opposing the Occupation, 155; Oriental, 79; other non-Christians and, 31; Palestinians and, 153; as people of color, 27, 37, 172–181; perceptions of, 10, 11; Persian (*see* Persians, Jews); politics and, 33, 64, 212; post-colonial, 85–86; power and, 12; progressive, 105, 130; race and, 11, 13, 14, 15, 26–29, 97, 100; racial diversity of, 70; racism and, 16, 34, 36, 37–38; Reconstruction-ist, 212; Reform (*see* Reform Jews); reformation and, 212; religion and, 13, 26–29; renewal, 189; right wing and, 209; Russian (*see* Russian Jews); Satan and, 13 (*see also* anti-semitism); scapegoats and, 24, 56; secular, 56, 196, 212; "self-hating," 151; skin color and, 2, 4, 15, 27; slavery and, 33; socially committed, 128; as stand-in for the West, 97; stereotypes about, 12, 15, 24, 25, 56; synagogue membership and, 196; tripartite racial classification, 24; Ugandan (*see* Uganda, Jews); unaffiliated, 119; in U.S. Christian culture, 31; as victims, 202; violence against, 9; as white, 1–32, 37, 41, 43, 96, 101, 158, 180; white Supremacists and, 24; Yiddish and, 96

Jews/Israelis, 65, 204
Jews by choice, 47, 70, 102, 165
Jews for Racial and Economic Justice (JFREJ) (New York), 19, 34, 106, 107, 128–134, 215, 223, 225; anti-Arab racism, 130, 132, 137; anti-racist work and, 132, 134; Arab Americans and, 131; Arab Jews and, 129, 132; Arabs, 132; Ashkenazim, 134; Ayecha and, 134; Beta Israel of North America, 134; *Beyond the Pale*, 133; Black Radical Congress, 130; Bukharian Jews from Uzbekistan and, 134; Chinese Staff and Workers Association, 129, 130; coalition work, 130; Conference on Jews and the Radical Right, 131; diversity in, 132; domestic workers and, 134; economic justice, 129; elderly Jews and, 129; identified Jews and, 130; immigrant rights and, 110, 136; Israel/Palestine issues and, 109; Ivri-NASAWI/Levantine Center, 133; Jews of color and, 129, 132, 133, 134; labor issues, 134; Ladino and, 93; Abner Louima, 129; mainstream Jewish communities and, 111; Middle East issues and, 129; mixed race Jews, 132, 134; Mizrahim, 132; multicultural identity and, 135; Muslims and, 131; Newt Gingrich protest and, 131; nursing home issue, 111; participation in protests of police killing of Amadou Diallo, 58; picket line, 129; police brutality and, 129; queers and, 129; racial justice, 129; Racial Justice Day, 129; racism, 110; as relatively homogenous, 130; Sephardim, 132; Silver Palace Restaurant and, 129; Teach-in on Radical Jewish History, 90–91; unaffiliated Jews and, 130; workshop on racism and homophobia, 129

Melanie Kaye/Kantrowitz is a feminist scholar, writer, and long-time activist whose books include *The Issue Is Power: Essays on Women, Jews, Violence, and Resistance; My Jewish Face & Other Stories;* and (co-edited) *The Tribe of Dina: A Jewish Women's Anthology.* Her essays, poetry, and fiction are widely anthologized, and she is a regular contributor to *Beyond the Pale,* a radio program of Jewish culture and politics. She is currently an adjunct professor in Comparative Literature at Queens College/CUNY and a teacher of writing for the Bard College Prison Initiative.

www.ingramcontent.com/pod-product-compliance
Ingram Content Group UK Ltd.
Pitfield, Milton Keynes, MK11 3LW, UK
UKHW030047060125
453220UK00005B/96